THE HOWS AND WHYS OF CORRECT ENGLISH GRAMMAR AND USAGE

—Which is correct: *me* or *I*, *he* or *him*, *she* or *her*, *we* or *us*, *they* or *them*?

—What is the difference between *lie* and *lay*; *principle* and *principal*; *hanged* and *hung*?

—Is *criteria* a singular or plural noun?

—How can you tell a *direct* from an *indirect* object?

—What exactly does an *adverb* do?

—What is the plural form of *wharf*?

You'll find immediate answers to these and other questions in

THE NEW AMERICAN DICTIONARY OF GOOD ENGLISH

NORMAN LEWIS has written a great many well-known and popular books on improving language skills, including *How to Read Better and Faster*, *30 Days to a More Powerful Vocabulary* (with Wilfred Funk), and *Instant Word Power* and *30 Days to Better English* (both available in Signet editions). He taught for many years at the City College of New York and at New York University. He is now Professor of English at Rio Hondo College, in Whittier, California.

THE NEW AMERICAN DICTIONARY OF GOOD ENGLISH

An A-Z Guide to Grammar and Correct Usage

by

Norman Lewis

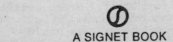

A SIGNET BOOK

NEW AMERICAN LIBRARY

A DIVISION OF PENGUIN BOOKS USA INC.

To my students and colleagues at Rio Hondo
College, especially Carolyn Russell, Don Jenkins,
Jean Kyle, Margie Lopez, Cynthia Reuben, and
Jo Watson. And with special thanks to Frances
M. Peterson, who so patiently and uncomplain-
ingly typed and retyped the manuscript of this
book.

SIGNET TRADEMARK REG. U.S. PAT. OFF. AND FOREIGN COUNTRIES
REGISTERED TRADEMARK—MARCA REGISTRADA
HECHO EN DRESDEN, TN, U.S.A.

SIGNET, SIGNET CLASSIC, MENTOR, ONYX, PLUME, MERIDIAN
and NAL BOOKS are published by New American Library,
a division of Penguin Books USA Inc.,
1633 Broadway, New York, New York 10019

First Printing, December, 1987

3   4   5   6   7   8   9   10

PRINTED IN THE UNITED STATES OF AMERICA

A Note from the Author
to the Reader

I have attempted, in this book, to provide the answers to any questions you may have about grammar or correct usage.

Questions like:

- the correct personal pronoun to use in a sentence—*me* or *I*?, *he* or *him*?, *she* or *her*?, *we* or *us*?, *they* or *them*?
- *lie* or *lay*?
- *hung* or *hanged*?
- *who* or *whom*?
- *affect* or *effect*?
- *principle* or *principal*?
- *continuous* or *continual*?

This book will tell you not only which of two possible words is better English, but also why. If a grammatical point is difficult or complicated, a clear and detailed explanation will be given and a short test will follow to assure that your understanding is complete.

If you need a quick review of grammatical terminology (*nouns, verbs, adjectives, adverbs, pronouns, prepositions, subjects, direct and indirect objects, subject and object complements,* etc.) you will find each term thoroughly discussed in its proper alphabetical position.

If you are not sure whether to hyphenate a compound word, or are in doubt about which of two common spellings is preferable, you will find an immediate answer in these pages.

If you are uncertain as to which one of two or more similar or related words properly expresses a concept you have in mind (*amiable* or *amicable*?, *assent* or *consent*?, *charlatan, quack,* or *impostor*?, *luxurious* or *luxuriant*?, *neglect* or *negligence*?, *numismatist* or *philatelist*?, *rebut* or *refute*?, etc.), you have only to turn to any one of the problem words to discover the clear-cut distinction.

Is *criteria* a singular or plural noun? How about *memo-*

randa, data, media, insignia? And what is the plural form of *wharf, cello, octopus, antenna, vertex, hippopotamus*? You will find at once not only the answer to such questions but also a list of words that present similar problems.

You can best understand the usefulness of this book by flipping through the pages and noting the wealth of valuable information contained in it. You may wish to use the book as a handy reference guide when a specific problem arises—or you may decide to browse through the pages, picking up useful hints on correct usage that will make your speech and writing correct, accurate, and more effective.

—NORMAN LEWIS
Whittier, California
June 1987

Structural Grammar

The grammatical terminology in this book is based on Structural Grammar, a simplified approach that became popular in the 1950s and that is now, together with Transformational Grammar, part of all linguistics courses taught on the college level. In those instances in which Structural Grammar differs from traditional grammar, the distinctions are clearly explained.

An important distinction that should be mentioned at the outset, however, is that the term *participle* in Structural Grammar refers only to the form of the verb called, in traditional grammar, the *past participle*, i.e., *taken, given, chosen*, etc. (See **participle**.)

In Structural Grammar only nouns, verbs, adjectives, and adverbs are called *parts of speech*. Pronouns, prepositions, conjunctions, and interjections are labeled *function words*. (See **parts of speech**.)

Pronunciation Symbols

Occasionally, in the pages that follow, a word is rewritten phonetically to indicate the correct pronunciation. For example:

abaci   AB'-ə-sī'
sarcophagi   sahr-KOF'-ə-jī'

You will note the use of the symbol ə, which indicates any quick vowel sound in an *unaccented* syllable. For example, TEN'-shən *(tension)*, LIN'də *(Linda)*, or kən-VINS' *(convince)*.

In the two examples above *(abaci, sarcophagi)*, the syllable that receives the primary accent is printed in capital letters followed by the accent mark (AB'; KOF'); the syllable that receives the secondary accent is printed in lowercase letters followed by the accent mark (sī'; jī').

Certain vowel sounds are respelled with these symbols:

Symbol	Example
Â, â	fare (FÂR)
	marital (MÂR'-ə-təl)
AH, ah	father (FAH'-thər)
Ī, ī	size (SĪZ)
Ō, ō	slow (SLŌ)
Ô, ô	fault (FÔLT)
OO, ōō	fruit (FRŌŌT)
OŎ, oŏ	book (BOŎK)
OU, ou	down (DOUN)

Certain consonant sounds are spelled or respelled as follows:

Symbol	Example
G, g	go (GŌ)
J, j	gradual (GRAJ'-ōō-əl)
S, s	reverence (REV'-ər-əns)
TH, th	thought (THÔT)
TH, th	mother (MUTH'-ər)
	this (*TH*IS)
ZH, zh	pleasure (PLEZH'-ər)

The pronunciation of any other symbols will be obvious.

A

a, an Before a consonant sound, *an* may be considered either affected or British. Usages such as *an hotel, an historic occasion, an hysterical outburst, an European city,* and *an unique book* are best avoided. *A* is preferable before a pronounced *h* (*humble, house,* etc.) or a vowel with a consonant sound (*usual, ewe, euphonious,* etc.)

a half, half a (an) See HALF A (AN), A HALF.

a lot, alot Always written as two words: *she enjoyed it a lot; she is a lot taller than her father.*

a lot of See LOT.

a number of See NUMBER.

abacus, *n.* For plural forms, see NOUN, 6P.

abet, aid, *v.* *Abet* is not an exact synonym of *aid.* You *abet* someone in an *improper* or *illegal* act only, and provide both help and encouragement.

abnormal, paranormal, *adj.* *Abnormal:* outside the usual, normal, or average range.

Paranormal: outside the range of what can be explained scientifically; usually descriptive of psychic phenomena.

abound, *v.* Followed by the preposition *with* when live creatures are involved: *abounds* with deer (*wild game,* etc.); otherwise by the preposition *in: abounds in natural resources.* See also ABUNDANCE, ABUNDANT.

about, around, round In the sense of *approximately,* **about** is preferable to *around: about* (not *around*) *ten miles away; about* (not *around*) *five dollars more.*

Around is the more precise word to use to mean *encircling: tall trees grew all around* (not *about*) *the house.*

The three words are interchangeable to signify *here and there: walked about* (*around* or *round*) *all day.*

In writing, avoid *'round*—there is no need for the apostrophe.

above Phrases like *the above paragraph* and *in reference to the above* are not acceptable in formal writing; such use of *above,* however, is common in legal documents. Preferable forms: *the paragraph above; in reference to the material above. All of the above* and

1

*none of the **above*** are now standard English.

abstain, *v.* This verb is followed by the preposition *from*. *Noun forms*: **abstention** (in reference to voting); **abstinence** (in reference to rich foods, alcohol, or other pleasures).

abstemious, ascetic, *adj.* The *abstemious* person either practices great moderation in eating and drinking or avoids any food or drink (usually alcoholic) that offers sensuous pleasure.

The *ascetic* person, through rigorous self-denial and self-discipline, shuns all physical and social pleasures, and attempts to lead a completely austere, monklike, existence.

abstention, abstinence See ABSTAIN.

abundance, *n.*; **abundant,** *adj.* The noun is followed by *of* (*abundance* of minerals), the adjective by *in* (*abundant* in minerals). See also ABOUND.

abut, *v.* May, but need not, be followed by a preposition: *the property **abuts** the highway*; or more commonly, *the property **abuts** on (upon* or *against) the highway*.

accelerate, *v.* See FACILITATE, EXPEDITE, ACCELERATE.

accelerator, exhilarator, *n.* The gas pedal of an automobile in an *accelerator*, not an *exhilarator*.

acceptance, acceptation, *n.* These words are *not* interchangeable. *Acceptation*, a term of infrequent occurrence, signifies *the generally understood and accepted meaning* (of a word or phrase).

acclaim, acclamation, *n.* As nouns, the words are interchangeable, both indicating loud praise, approval, or applause. *Acclaim* may be used as a *verb: the audience **acclaimed** her performance.*

To signify an enthusiastic voiced vote of approval, *acclamation* is the correct term: *elected by **acclamation**.*

acclimate, acclimatize, *v.* Both verbs mean *to adapt to a new or different environment.* To be strictly correct, however, you may wish to observe this distinction: one *acclimates* (or *acclimates* oneself, or becomes *acclimated*) to social or psychological environmental change; one *acclimatizes* (or *acclimatizes* oneself, or becomes *acclimatized*) to a change in weather conditions.

accompanied by, accompanied with A *person* is *accompanied by* another or others; *she was accompanied by her friends. A thing, condition,* or *quality* is *accompanied with* another or others: *it was accompanied with a note* (*anxiety, a drop in temperature,* etc.).

accompanist, accompanyist, *n.* The second word is rarely used.

accord, accordance, *n.* We are in *accord; he is in accord with my feelings* (i.e., in agreement).
In *accordance with your instructions* (*request,* etc.)— i.e., following.

accumulative, cumulative, *adj. Accumulative: tending to accumulate;* or (of persons) *enjoying the accumulation of possessions.*
Cumulative: increasing by continual additions—e.g., *cumulative interest.*

acoustics, *n.* See -ICS.

acquiesce, *v; acquiescence, n.* Preferably followed by the preposition *in,* rather than to: *acquiesce* in *their refusal; your acquiescence* in *their actions.*

acrobatics, *n.* See -ICS.

active voice See VERB, 9.

actor, actress, *n.* See NOUN, 2C.

actual fact See FACT, ACTUAL FACT, TRUE FACT.

A.D. *A.D.* precedes the date: *A.D.* 1401, not 1401 *A.D. B.C.,* on the other hand, follows the date: 300 *B.C.*

ad, advertisement, *n.* The shortened form is perfectly acceptable except, perhaps, in the most formal of writing.

adage, *n.* See OLD ADAGE.

adapt, adopt, *v.* You *adapt* (i.e., adjust) *to* a new situation, environment, etc.
You *adopt* (i.e., accept, take, etc.) children, attitudes, new ideas, etc.

addendum, *n.* Something added (to a book, paper, report, etc.) is an *addendum,* and is usually found following the main part of the text. The plural is *addenda*—added things, ideas, statements, etc. *The addenda* are (*not* is) in *the final pages of the book.* See also NOUN, 6Q.

addiction, addicted One has an *addiction* to or is *addicted* to (something).

ADJECTIVE

1. **Adjective pattern:**

YOU ARE VERY _____ or IT IS VERY _____.

A word that fits into the blank of this *adjective pattern* and makes sense, is an *adjective (adj.).* Thus:

YOU ARE VERY *poor* (*rich, beautiful, handsome,* etc.).
IT IS VERY *relevant* (*probable, concentrated,* etc.).

2. **Adjective inflections:** An adjective has three inflections (or forms): the *positive*, the *comparative*, and the *superlative*.

Positive	Comparative	Superlative
poor	poorer	poorest
rich	richer	richest
beautiful	more beautiful	most beautiful
probable	more probable	most probable

3. **Adjective position:** Adjectives precede nouns: *a poor* (adj.) *excuse* (n.); *the probable* (adj.) *cause* (n.).

Adjectives also follow linking verbs (see SENTENCE PATTERNS, 3, 3A) *He is poor* (adj.); *this dessert looks rich* (adj.).

4. **Adjective suffixes:** Some adjectives end in typical suffixes: *-ble* (possible), *-al* (comical), *-ant* (reluctant), *-ful* (useful), *-less* (powerless), etc.

---

adjoin, adjourn, *v.* There is no relationship in meaning between these words. *To adjoin* is *to be next to.* To **adjourn** is *to close (a meeting, session, conference, etc.) expecting to resume at a specified or unspecified later time.* In informal usage, *to adjourn* is also *to move as a group to another place to continue (a meeting, party, etc.): after dinner, the guests adjourned to the living room.*

administer, administrate, *v.* **Administer** is the preferable verb.

administrator, *n.* For feminine form, see NOUN, 2C.

administratrix, *n.* For plural, see NOUN, 6O.

admission, *n.* See ADMITTANCE, ADMISSION.

admit, admit to, admit of *Admit*, in the sense of *concede* or *acknowledge*, takes a direct object—you *admit* a mistake, not *to* a mistake. In the sense of *allow, permit,* or *provide the possibility of,* **admit** is followed by *of: a problem that admits of several solutions.*

admit, confess, *v.* You can either **admit** or **confess** a wrongdoing, sin, illegal act, etc., but **confess** is, of course, the stronger verb in such instances, perhaps, but not necessarily, implying an attempt to purge one's guilt. *Confess* may, but need not, be followed by *to: confess a crime; confess to a crime.*

Confess is also used without any reference to wrongdoing: *I must confess that I didn't like him the first time I met him.*

admit of See ADMIT, ADMIT TO, ADMIT OF.

admittance, admission, *n.* *Admittance* is either *actual physical entry into a place* or *the right to enter a place: no admittance beyond this point.*

Admission is *the right to enter and be a participant in,* or *to enjoy the privileges of: admission to a club (college, theater,* etc.).

Admission, less frequently, may also refer to physical entry or, more commonly, figurative entry, as in writing: *admission of the testimony to the record; admission of late filers to the list of candidates.* In the sense of *acknowledgment,* **admission,** not *admittance,* is used: *admission of error (wrongdoing,* etc.).

admit to See ADMIT, ADMIT TO, ADMIT OF.

adopt, *v.* See ADAPT, ADOPT.

adopted, adoptive Children are *adopted;* one who adopts a child is the *adoptive* parent.

adroit, *adj.* See DEXTEROUS, ADROIT, AMBIDEXTROUS.

adulterer, *n.* The feminine form is *adulteress,* not *adultress.*

advance, advancement, *n.* An *advance* is a *physical forward movement: advance of the army.*

Advancement is *figurative progress*—i.e., promotion to, or attainment of, a higher rank, as in a school, organization, etc.: *her advancement to the senior year of college; her advancement to an executive position in the company.*

advanced, advance, *adj.* *Advanced* describes that which or one who is further along, higher, or more complicated than other things or persons of the same kind: *advanced thinking; advanced degrees offered by a university;* **advanced algebra;** *quite advanced for her age;* etc.

Advance describes earlier time (*advance notice*) or forward position (*advance units of the army*).

adventurous, adventuresome, *adj.* Either adjective describes a person willing to take risks or engage in possibly hazardous or daring activities. For the activity itself, only *adventurous* is used: *adventurous journey.*

See also VENTUROUS, VENTURESOME.

ADVERB

1. An adverb usually answers one of three questions: *how?, when?,* or *where?*

   a. *Adverbs of manner* (how?): *rapidly, truthfully, splendidly,* etc.

b. **Adverbs of time** (when?): *often, never, always, rarely,* etc.

c. **Adverbs of place** (where?): *here, there, somewhere, nowhere,* etc.

2. Derivation of the adverb: Adverbs can be derived by adding *-ly* to an adjective: *rapid, rapidly; truthful, truthfully; occasional, occasionally;* etc. (*-Ly* is not necessarily an adverbial ending. If you add this suffix to a *noun,* you will derive an adjective: *friend, friendly; coward, cowardly; heaven, heavenly; leisure, leisurely;* etc.)

If an adjective ends in *-ic* (*fantastic, specific, heroic,* etc.), add *-ally* to derive the adverb (*fantastically, specifically, heroically,* etc.). *Exception: public, publicly.*

3. Most, but not all, adverbs can be shifted to different positions in a sentence. For example, in the following sentence the adverb *frequently* can occur wherever there is a caret (∧): ∧*The prisoners*∧*have*∧*been*∧*restricted*∧*to their cells.* Such shifts do not affect the meaning of the sentence. This movability is a characteristic that distinguishes adverbs from other parts of speech.

4. If a noun or noun phrase in a sentence tells *when, where,* or *how much,* such a noun or noun phrase is called, in Structural Grammar, an *adverbial.* For example, in the sentence *Hummingbirds eat a great deal every day, a great deal* tells *how much,* and *every day* tells *when;* the two noun phrases are called *adverbials.*

5. In traditional grammar, an adverb modifies a verb, adjective, or another adverb. In Structural Grammar, an adverb that modifies an adjective or other adverb is called a *qualifier.* See also QUALIFIER.

---

adverse, averse, *adj.* Things, circumstances, or conditions are *adverse* when they work against, or are hostile, opposed, or unfavorable to, one or one's welfare: *adverse effects on one's candidacy; received adverse criticism.* The derived noun *adversity,* signifies trouble, misfortune, hard times, etc.

A person is *averse to* engaging in, doing, or permitting an action—i.e., is reluctant, opposed, unwilling, etc.: *averse to joining us.* The derived noun *aversion* indicates strong distaste or dislike: *aversion to cheating on a test.*

advertisement, ad *n.* See AD, ADVERTISEMENT.

advice, advise *Advice* is the noun; *advise* is the verb:

*to give **advice**; to **advise** someone.*

advise, inform, *v.* To use **advise** as an exact synonym for **inform** is considered acceptable only in business or legal writing: *please inform* (not *advise*) *him that I will be late.*

advisedly, *adv.* See PURPOSELY, PURPOSEFULLY, ADVISEDLY.

adviser, advisor, *n.* Either spelling is correct; **adviser** is more commonly used.

aerate, airate, *v.* The sec-

ond spelling is not an accepted form.

aereal, airial, *n.* Only the first spelling is correct.

aeroplane, *n.* See AIRPLANE, AEROPLANE, AIROPLANE.

aesthete, esthete, *n.*; **aesthetic, esthetic,** *adj., n.* The first spelling of each word is correct; the second is a variant, but acceptable, form.

aesthetics, esthetics, *n.* The second form is a variant spelling.

See also -ICS.

AFFECT, EFFECT

With the exception noted in rule 3 below, the two words are pronounced identically (ə-FEKT'), so they pose a problem only in writing. The rules are simple if you can easily distinguish nouns from verbs. (If you cannot, see NOUN, 10.)

1. If the structure of the sentence requires a *noun*, use **effect**: *the effect* of the storm. (The single exception is noted in rule 3.)

2. If the sentence structure requires a *verb*, use **affect**: **affected** *her in many ways.* There is an important exception to this rule. If the verb clearly means *bring about, cause, accomplish, produce,* or *create,* use **effect**. The *verb* **effect** definitely expresses the production, creation, etc. of something that did not previously exist: *to **effect** a reduction of interest rates;* **effected** *a change in her behavior;* **effected** *his escape from prison by;* etc. In each of these instances, one of the verbs mentioned (*bring about, cause,* etc.) can be substituted for **effect** or **effected**.

3. **Affect**, pronounced AF'-ekt, is a *noun* only in psychological terminology, and indicates emotional response or feeling tone: *the psychiatrist noted that the patient showed no **affect** at any time during the interview.*

4. *The verb **affect** may also be synonymous with pretend, assume,* or *put on:* **affected** *a British accent.* With this

meaning, the derived noun is *affectation*; the derived adjective is *affected*: *an affectation of knowledge he does not possess; a very affected accent.*

A Test of affect, effect

1. What a glorious *(effect, affect)* the sunset has on the hills!
2. We have decided to *(effect, affect)* a reduction in the costs of doing business.
3. Your anger does not *(effect, affect)* me at all.
4. What *(effect, affect)* are you trying to achieve by keeping the lights so dim?
5. Her speech was intended to *(effect, affect)* a measure of sympathy from the jurors for the defendant.
6. The sound *(effects, affects)* in the motion picture were amazing.
7. Her speech did not *(effect, affect)* the outcome of the election.
8. The *(effects, affects)* of the famine were widespread.
9. He is an expert at *(effecting, affecting)* a tone of sincerity whenever he tells an outright lie.
10. The devastating *(effects, affects)* of the bombing were still visible.

KEY: 1. *effect* (n.); 2. *effect* (v.—bring about); 3. *affect* (v.); 4. *effect* (n.); 5. *effect* (v.—bring about); 6. *effects* (n. pl.); 7. *affect* (v.); 8. *effects* (n. pl.); 9. *affecting* (v.—pretending); 10. *effects* (n. pl.).

---

affection, infection, *n.* Both words refer to disease. *Affection* indicates an ailment or malfunctioning of a particular organ of the body: *affection of the liver (lymph glands, etc.)*

An *infection* is caused by invading bacteria, viruses, or other disease-producing organisms.

See also CONTAGIOUS, INFECTIOUS, COMMUNICABLE.

affluence, opulence, *n.* *Affluence* is not only wealth, in money and possessions, but wealth that continues to increase and that is combined with free and luxurious spending.

Opulence is greater in degree and includes ostentatious display.

aforementioned, aforesaid, *adj.* Used in legal terminology, awkward in nonlegal writing. Substitute *preceding, previous, previously mentioned*, etc.

afterward, afterwards, *adv.* See -WARD, -WARDS.

aged See ELDERLY, OLD, AGED.

agenda, *n.* This is the plural form of the noun *agendum* but, when used to mean *a list of items to be discussed at a meeting*, it is usually followed by the form of a verb that agrees with a singular noun: *the agenda is very long. Agendum*, strictly, is one item on such a list. See also NOUN, 6Q.

aggravate, irritate, *v.* In informal speech and writing, *aggravate* is acceptable as a synonym of *annoy* or *irritate.* In formal language, you *aggravate* a condition or situation by making it worse, more burdensome, etc.: *a heart condition may be aggravated by excessive physical effort.*

agnostic, atheist, *n.* An *agnostic* says that God may or may not exist, but claims that knowledge of such existence is unavailable to the human mind.

An *atheist* unequivocally rejects the possibility of the existence of a supernatural deity.

ago since; ago that Correct construction: *it was a week ago that* (not *since*) *they visited us.*

ahold, hold *Ahold*, as in *get ahold of yourself; take ahold of the other end;* etc., is not standard English. Use *hold* in these and similar constructions: *get hold of yourself, take hold of the other end.*

aid, abet, *v.* See ABET, AID.

aid, aide, *n.* A person or thing that helps is an *aid.* *Aide* is the term for an assistant in a professional capacity: *teacher's aide, nurse's aide,* etc.

aide-de-camp, *n.* For plural, see NOUN, 6U.

AIDS, *n.* See MEASLES.

ain't This handy negative verb, which can mean *am not, is not, are not, has not,* or *have not,* is popular only in substandard English. *Ain't* is used by educated speakers generally for humorous effect or for deliberate shock value.

airate, *v.* See AERATE, AIRATE.

aircraft, *n.* See CRAFT.

airial, *n.* See AERIAL, AIRIAL.

airplane, aeroplane, airoplane, *n.* *Airplane* is the standard American form; *aeroplane* is British; *airoplane* is a nonword.

albeit See ALTHOUGH, THOUGH, ALTHO, ALBEIT.

alga, *n.* For plural, see NOUN, 6M1.

alias, pseudonym, pen name, nom de plume, incognito All

these words are terms for *an assumed* or *fictitious name.*

An *alias*, though strictly *any fictitious name*, is generally used by a criminal.

A *pseudonym* is *an assumed name used by an author: Evan Hunter, writing under a pseudonym.*

Pen name or **nom de plume** (a French import literally translated as "name of pen") is the specific *pseudonym used by a writer: Ed McBain is a pen name* (or *nom de plume*) *of Evan Hunter.*

An *incognito* is *a name temporarily assumed by a famous person*, as when traveling or otherwise away from home territory, perhaps to avoid the petty annoyances that the famous have to endure from their admirers. *Incognito* is also an adverb: *she was traveling incognito.*

alibi, excuse, *n.* Legally, an *alibi* (from the Latin words for *elsewhere*) is *evidence or proof that an accused person was in some location other than the place where the crime was committed.* In informal speech or writing, *alibi* is an *excuse of any kind*; this usage is not acceptable in formal English.

alienist, *n.* See PSYCHIATRIST, PSYCHOANALYST, PSYCHOLOGIST, PSYCHOTHERAPIST, COUNSELOR, ALIENIST.

alighted, alit *Alighted* is the more commonly used past tense or participle of *alight, v.*; *alit* is often required in crossword puzzles.

align, aline, *v.* *Align* is the usual spelling, *aline* is a variant form.

alit See ALIGHTED, ALIT.

all, all of In formal writing, *of* is preferably omitted before a noun: *all the people, all the time,* etc.

all-around, all around See ALL-ROUND, ALL-AROUND, ALL ROUND, ALL AROUND.

all but one The subject all in such a construction is *plural: all but one have finished.*

all ... is, all ... are See SUBJECT, VERB AGREEMENT, 9.

all of See ALL, ALL OF.

all ready See ALREADY, ALL READY.

all right, alright *Alright* is a misspelling, not to be used in formal writing.

all-round, all-around, all round, all around As a modifier of a noun and denoting *comprehensive, total,* etc., *all-round* is preferable to *all-around: all-round excellent training.* Note the hyphen.

When *around* or *round* is used as a preposition, there is no hyphen, and either of the two words may be used following *all: all around* (or *round*) *the mulberry bush, walked all around* (or *round*) *the house.*

See also ABOUT, AROUND, ROUND.

all together See ALTOGETHER, ALL TOGETHER.

allegory, *n.* See FABLE, ALLEGORY.

allude, *v.* See REFER, ALLUDE.

almost, most, 'most The use of *most* or *'most* for *almost* (as in *most everyone came on time*) is considered nonstandard in speech and writing. Using the apostrophe in writing (*'most*) to show that the word means *almost* does not make the usage more acceptable.

alongside, alongside of The former is more commonly used, but both forms are correct as prepositions: *alongside* (or *alongside of*) *the dock.*

already, all ready *Already* is an adverb: *we have already spoken.*

All ready, as two words, is used in constructions like *are we all ready?*—i.e., are all of us ready?

alright See ALL RIGHT, AL-RIGHT.

altar, alter The words are pronounced identically, but *altar* is a noun (*the altar*), *alter* is a verb (*to alter*). See also CASTRATE, GELD, ALTER, FIX, CAPONIZE, EMASCULATE, SPAY.

alternative, choice, *n.* Strictly, an *alternative* is a *choice* between only *two* things, actions, possibilities, etc., but the word is often used in standard English when more than two choices are involved.

although, though, altho, albeit *Although* and *though* are interchangeable as connectors for clauses: *though* is used to connect words (*small though strong*).

Altho is an informal spelling.

Albeit, somewhat literary in tone, is mainly found as a connector contrasting single words (*unethical albeit legal*) or meaning *even though* (*albeit legal, the action is unethical*).

altogether, all together *Altogether* is an *adverb*: *altogether too fast; there are seven pages altogether* (i.e., in total).

All together as two words, is used in constructions like *the seven pages are all together*—i.e., all the seven pages are together (i.e., in one place).

alumnus, alumna, *n.* A male graduate of an institution of learning is an *alumnus*; a female graduate is an *alumna*. The plural of *alumnus* is *alumni* (ə-LUM'-nī); the plural of *alumna* is *alumnae* (ə-LUM'-nee). When the plural indicates both sexes, use *alumni*: *Sally and George are alumni of UCLA.* See also NOUN, 2C; NOUN, 6M1.

amanuensis, *n.* For plural, see NOUN, 6N.

ambassadress, *n.* See NOUN, 2A.

ambidextrous, *adj.* See DEXTEROUS, ADROIT, AMBIDEXTROUS.

ambiguous, equivocal, equivocable, *adj.* A statement, sentence, etc. is *ambiguous* if the meaning is unclear or misleading, or lends itself to more than one interpretation: *the owner told the mechanic to move his car out of the way.* (Whose car? The owner's or the mechanic's?) In the illustrative sentence, *his* is *ambiguous.*

An *equivocal* (*equivocable* is a nonword) statement, answer, position, etc., is *intentionally* misleading or *deliberately* *ambiguous* or vague.

ambush, attack, *n.* An *ambush* is a surprise *attack* made from a hidden position.

amiable, amicable, *adj.* Generally, people are *amiable*; conditions, attitudes, relationships, etc. are *amicable.*

amid, amidst, *prep.* These prepositions are interchangeable; the latter is more literary.

amoeba, ameba, *n.* *Amoeba* is the preferred spelling, *ameba* a variant. For plural, see NOUN, 6M.

amok, *n.* See AMUCK, AMOK, BERSERK.

among, amongst See BETWEEN, AMONG.

amoral, nonmoral, unmoral, immoral, *adj.* *Amoral* indicates that no question of morality is involved; in this sense it is synonymous with *nonmoral* and *unmoral.* In reference to a person, the word describes one who has no awareness of what is *moral* or *immoral,* who cannot differentiate between right and wrong.

Immoral describes persons, activities, attitudes, etc. that violate accepted morality. The word may, but need not, suggest sexual looseness.

See also ASEXUAL, NONSEXUAL, SEXLESS.

amount of, number of *Amount of* is followed by a singular noun: *large amount of butter* (*milk,* etc.).

Number of is followed by a plural noun: *large number of residents.*

See also NUMBER.

amuck, amok, berserk *Amuck* is generally found in the pattern *run amuck. Amok* is a variant spelling of *amuck.* One usually *goes berserk* or *is berserk.*

an, a See A, AN.

anachronism, incongruity, *n.* *Anachronism* refers to *time, incongruity* to *place.* A thing belonging to a much earlier era, and rare or nonexistent today, is *anachronous* or *anachronistic*. Something described as current when it is long since past, or, on the other hand, is expected in the future, is also an *anachronism*. A person may be called an *anachronism* if she (or he) has attributes or attitudes associated with the distant past.

Things or people that do not logically fit together are *incongruous*. An eighty-year-old woman married to a man of thirty—this is an *incongruous* couple. Something out of place with its surroundings is an *incongruity*—a swim suit worn at a formal ceremony, or a palatial mansion in a slum or factory district, for example.

analgesic, anesthetic, *n.* An *analgesic* reduces or deadens pain.

A local *anesthetic* removes all sensation in one part of the body; a general *anesthetic* causes total unconsciousness.

analysis, *n.* For plural form, see NOUN 6N.

analyst, *n.* See PSYCHIATRIST, PSYCHOANALYST, PSYCHOLOGIST, PSYCHOTHERAPIST, COUNSELOR, ALIENIST.

analyze, *v.* See PARALYZE, ANALYZE, PSYCHOANALYZE.

anarchy, anarchism, *n. Anarchy* is the *fact* of total absence of political rule, government, law, etc.

Anarchism is the *theory* that all forms of political rule should be abolished.

ancestress, *n.* See NOUN 2C.

And, *conj.* There is no law, principle, or rule that forbids starting a sentence or even a paragraph with **And**, nor, for that matter, with *But*, despite any interdictions laid down, at one time, by high school English teachers.

and *(connecting two subjects)* See SUBJECT, VERB AGREEMENT, 3.

and etc. Since *etc.* is an abbreviation for a Latin phrase meaning *and others* or *and so forth*, the *and* is redundant. *Etc.* is enough; *and etc.* is too much. The complete phrase is *et cetera.*

anent Rarely used, except humorously. Often found in crossword puzzles, where it is defined as *about, concerning*, or *regarding.*

anesthetic, *n.* See ANALGESIC, ANESTHETIC.

anesthetist, anesthesiologist, *n.* An *anesthetist* is the person, usually a physician, who administers an anesthetic; an *anesthesiologist* is a medical specialist with extensive training and certification in the field of anesthesia. So the *anesthesiologist* who puts a patient under is acting, at that time, as an *anesthetist*—but not every *anesthetist* is an *anesthesiologist*.

angry, mad, *adj.* *Mad* has many meanings, of which the least commonly used today is *insane*. In colloquial speech or informal writing, *mad* is often used as a synonym of *angry*.

angry at, angry with, angry about You are *angry with* a person, but *angry at* or *angry about* what has happened, what that person has done or said, etc.

anodyne, *n.* See CLICHÉ, BROMIDE, ANODYNE, PLATITUDE.

ante-, anti-, prefix *Ante-* means *before*: *ante*room, *ante*date; *anti-* means *against*: *anti*trust, *anti*septic.

antenna, *n.* As one of the "feelers" attached to the head of an insect or other creature, the noun is pluralized *antennae* (an-TEN'-ee); as an aerial for electronic transmission, the plural is generally *antennas*. See also NOUN, 6M.

anthropophagus, *n.* For plural, see NOUN, 6P.

anti-, *prefix* See ANTE-, ANTI-.

anticipate, *v.* See EXPECT, ANTICIPATE.

anticlimatic, *adj.* See CLIMATIC, CLIMACTIC.

antique, antiquated, *adj.* *Antique*, in its primary and usual sense, refers to antiquity—i.e., ancient times. An *antique* (n.) is a valuable object of art or artifact that is over 100 years old.

Antiquated, usually a term of disparagement, describes something so old-fashioned as to be no longer of current use or value: *antiquated laws* (*attitudes*, etc.).

antisepsis, asepsis, *n.* *Antisepsis* is *the fact or act of destroying disease-causing germs*.

Asepsis is *the state of being sterile*—i.e., completely free of such germs.

antisocial, asocial, unsocial, unsociable, nonsocial, *adj.* Strictly, *antisocial* people act to the detriment of society—they are *psychopaths*. However, the term often refers to those who do not enjoy the company of others—who, in short, are *unsocial* or *unsociable*.

Asocial people, on the other hand, are indifferent to the needs of society or the welfare of others; they are totally self-centered. *Asocial*, also, is often used as a synonym of *unsocial* or *unsociable*.

Nonsocial indicates that social relationships or activities are not involved.

See also PSYCHOPATH, SOCIOPATH; UNSOCIABLE, UNSOCIAL.

antithesis, *n.* For plural form, see NOUN, 6N.

anxious, eager, *adj.* *Anxious* suggests *worry* or *fear*, so its use as a synonym of *eager* is frowned upon by some authorities.

ANYBODY

Written as a solid word to mean *any person*. In careful writing, this pronoun, like **anyone, someone, somebody, nobody, no one, everyone,** and **everybody,** is followed by *he* or *she, his* or *her, him* or *her* rather than *they, them,* or *their.*

Granted, it may sound stilted or pedantic, especially in conversation, to say, "Will **everybody** please take *his* seat." If you fear that the females will then remain standing, you must be more precise: "Will **everybody** please take *his* or *her* seat."

How about: "If you see **anybody** outside, invite *him* (*him* or *her*)? in"? Or: If **anyone** comes early, *he* (*he* or *she*?) will have to wait"?

We have a problem with these pronouns. They are singular in grammatical number: *no one is,* **somebody** *is,* etc. However, there is an implication of *a number of individuals* in each such pronoun, as also in **nobody** and **no one,** the latter word suggesting *not any of all the people.*

In formal speech and writing, the rules require that *he, him, his,* and *she, her* agree in number with the singular **anybody, anyone, someone,** etc. Informally or colloquially, use *they, them, their* if you feel more comfortable or less pedantic with these plural words.

An additional problem is that the use of *he, his,* or *him* following such singular pronouns may be deemed sexist, and *he or she, him or her, his or her* may sound awkward. Many authors follow **anyone** with *he (him, his)* and use the disclaimer that these are generic words referring to either or both sexes.

See also HE/SHE.

---

anymore, any more Write solid as an adverb, and only when the sentence is negative or interrogative: *can't work* **anymore***; are you using it* **anymore***!* Write as two words when *more* is a pronoun, or both words are determiners before a noun: *do you have any more?; do you* have **any more** *time!* In an affirmative construction (*it's easy to see him* **anymore**) *anymore* is nonstandard.

anyone, any one As a pronoun, written solid: *is* **anyone** *here!* Meaning *any single one,* written as two words: *if* **any one** *of the projects is*

ready, send it along. See also
ANYBODY.

anyone else's, anyone's else
See ELSE.

anyplace, any place Written
solid to mean *anywhere:
you're not going anyplace*, and
considered colloquial rather
than formal. Written as two
words when *place* is emphasized: *there isn't any place at
all for the books*. See also NO
PLACE; SOME PLACE, SOMEPLACE.

anything, any thing Written
solid unless *thing* is emphasized, which is rare.

any time, anytime Always
written as two words: *I'll go
any time you're ready; do
you have any time left?*

anyway, any way, anyways
Anyway is an adverb: *you
won't approve, but we're
doing it anyway*.
   Any way is a determiner plus
a noun: *we'll drive any way*
(i.e., in whatever way) *you*
suggest.
   Anyways is nonstandard as
a substitute for the adverb
anyway.

anywhere, anywheres See
-WHERE, -WHERES.

apogee, perigee, n. The
farthest point in the orbit of
the moon around the earth is
the *apogee*; the *nearest* point
is the *perigee*. Hence, figuratively, the *apogee* is the *highest*, the *perigee* the *lowest*,
point of anything (career, ac-

complishment, etc.) See also
ZENITH, NADIR.

apostrophe See CONTRAC-
TIONS; NOUN, 7; PRONOUN, 6.

apparatus, n. The plural is
either apparatus *(all the
apparatus are working)* or *ap-
paratuses*. Despite the direct
derivation of the word from
Latin, *apparati* is a nonword.
See also NOUN, 6P.

appendix, index, n. The
appendix of a book, docu-
ment, etc. is added or supple-
mentary material; the *index*
is an alphabetical list, with
identifying page numbers, of
the contents of a book, docu-
ment, etc. You have a choice
of plurals: *appendixes* or
appendices; indexes or *indi-
ces*. The first plural forms are
more popular. See also NOUN,
6O.

appraise, apprise, *To appraise* is *to estimate the worth
of; to apprise* (someone) is *to
let* (that person) *know, to give
information that concerns, or
may be of interest to* (him or
her). You *apprise* someone *of*
(information, facts, etc.).

appreciate, understand, *v.*
Among the several meanings
of *appreciate*, to *understand*
(that) or *be aware (of)* is fully
acceptable: *I appreciate that
you are an expert in* . . .

apprehend, comprehend, *v.*
In the sense of *grasping with
the mind*—i.e., understanding—the two verbs are syn-

onymous and interchange-able, though **comprehend** is more commonly used.

apprise See APPRAISE, APPRISE.

apt (to) See LIKELY (TO), LIABLE (TO), APT (TO), PRONE (TO).

arbiter, *n.* See ARBITRATOR, ARBITER.

arbitrary, dogmatic, *adj.* An *arbitrary* decision, statement, etc. is made by whim or without basis, reason, or discussion, and stems from actual or assumed power.

A *dogmatic* statement is made in such a manner that no contradiction or question will be accepted, as if religious dogma were being invoked. A *dogmatic* person speaks as if no one dare challenge the truth of his or her statement.

arbitrator, arbiter, *n.* An *arbitrator* is chosen by, or acceptable to, both sides in a dispute. The purpose of *arbitration* is to settle differences or to effect a compromise.

An *arbiter* is a judge who has the final word in matters of style, taste, etiquette, the arts, or other areas in which there may be divided opinion.

arcanum, *n.* For plural form, see NOUN, 6Q.

archetype, *n.* See PROTO-TYPE, ARCHETYPE.

arise, rise, *v.* The words are synonymous in the sense of

waking up and *getting up*, *standing up*, etc. In the sense of *going higher* or *ascending*, *rise* is the preferable term.

armful, *n.* For plural form, see -FUL, -FULS.

around, round See ABOUT, AROUND, ROUND.

arsonist, incendiary, pyromaniac, firebug, *n.* The *arsonist* deliberately sets fire to property (usually a building) for economic gain—e.g., the collection of insurance.

The *incendiary* torches another's property out of malice (a desire for revenge, etc.).

The *pyromaniac* sets fires out of an irresistible compulsion.

In law and in newspaper reports, a distinction is seldom made; *incendiarism* and *pyromania* are usually called *arson*.

In informal usage, a *firebug* refers to an *arsonist*, an *incendiary*, or a *pyromaniac*.

article, *n.* In traditional grammar, *the* is called a definite article, *a* or *an* an indefinite article. In Structural Grammar, *the, a,* and *an* are determiners. See DETERMINER.

as, *conj.* (*plus a personal pronoun*) See THAN, CONJ. (PLUS A PERSONAL PRONOUN)

as . . . as, so . . . as The strict rule that *as . . . as* is used in *affirmative* constructions only, and that *so . . . as* must be used in *negative* constructions, is so often violated, even in formal writing, that it has lost much of its earlier validity. *Not as big as a breadbox* is fully acceptable, though pedants may insist on *not so big as a breadbox*.

as follows Use *as follows*, not *as follow* even when a plural or a list of two or more is involved—i.e., *the instructions (names, items, words,* etc.) *are as follows:* . . .

as if . . . was, as if . . . were In careful usage, this conjunction requires *were*, not *was*, after a singular subject: *he looked as if he were tired; she acted as if she were confused;* etc. The same rule applies to *as though*. See also IF . . . WAS, IF . . . WERE; IF ONLY . . . WAS, IF ONLY . . . WERE; SUBJUNCTIVE; WISH . . . WAS, WERE.

AS/LIKE, AS IF/LIKE

When a clause (i.e., subject plus verb) follows, formal usage requires *as* or *as if* rather than *like*:

> It tastes good, *as* (not *like*) a cigarette should [despite the claim of a tobacco company many years ago].
> She acts *as* (not *like*) a person in distress usually does.
> He talks *as if* he were (*not like* he is) dissatisfied.

In comparisons, *like* is a preposition, and is followed by a noun or pronoun, not by a clause: *looks like me; talks like an authority; acts like a person in distress.*

as though See AS IF . . . WAS, AS IF . . . WERE.

AS WELL AS, prep.

1. The senator *as well as* her secretary *was* (not *were*) out of town.
2. She *as well as* her husband *is* (not *are*) waiting for you.

In sentence 1, the subject of the verb is *senator; secretary* is the object of the preposition. Similarly, in sentence 2, the subject is *she; husband* is the object of the preposition. In both instances, the singular subject requires the S-FORM of the verb.

The same rule applies when the prepositions *in addition to* and *together with* are substituted for *as well as*.

See also PRONOUN, 8B; SUBJECT, VERB AGREEMENT, 5.

---

ascetic, *adj.* See ABSTEMIOUS, ASCETIC.

asepsis, *n.* See ANTISEPSIS, ASEPSIS.

asexual, nonsexual, sexless, *adj.* Biologically, *asexual* refers to reproduction that does not result from the union of male and female cells; in non-technical use, the word is a synonym of *sexless*.

Nonsexual indicates that sex is not involved: *a nonsexual relationship*, etc.

Sexless may mean either *neuter* or *having no interest in, or desire for, sexual relations or relationships*.

asocial, *adj.* See ANTISOCIAL, ASOCIAL, UNSOCIAL, UNSOCIABLE, NONSOCIAL.

aspirant, *n.* See CONTESTANT, CANDIDATE, ASPIRANT.

aspiration, *n.* Referring to hope, desire, or a goal, this noun is generally used in the plural and is followed by the preposition *to, for,* or *toward*: *aspirations to (for or toward) greater wealth*.

aspire, *v.* Usually followed by the preposition *to (aspire to excellence, aspires to a higher office)*, sometimes by the preposition *toward (aspires toward happiness)*.

assassination, *n.* See HOMI-CIDE, MANSLAUGHTER, MURDER, ASSASSINATION.

assay, essay To *assay* (v.) is to gauge the worth or value of (things, property, etc.), or to *analyze* (something). Far less commonly, the verb may mean *to try* (to), and thus is a synonym of *essay (v.)*.

To *essay* (v.) is *to make a try at (essayed a new approach),* or to *attempt (essay to finish on time).*

An *essay* (n.) is either *a short piece of nonfiction* or *an attempt (an essay at learning Sanskrit).*

An *assay* (n.) is *a test or critical examination.* The use of this noun as a synonym of *attempt (n.)* has long been obsolete.

assent, consent The words are, in general, synonymous. However, *assent* stresses agreement, while *consent* emphasizes giving permission or saying "yes" to a request. Both words are used as either nouns or verbs, and are followed by the preposition *to*.

assume, presume, *v.* These verbs are closely synonymous in the sense of *taking for granted*, though each has a number of additional meanings not related to one another.

When you *assume* (that . . .), you accept the possibility of (facts, conditions, etc.) for the sake of argument or as a basis for action: *let us assume* that he is honest.

When you *presume* (that . . .), you accept (facts or conditions) as being reasonable. Often, *presume* implies a question, looking for an affirmative answer or one that will provide evidence of the truth of your supposition: *I presume you're married!* See also PRESUME.

assumed name See ALIAS, PSEUDONYM, PEN NAME, NOM DE PLUME, INCOGNITO.

assure, ensure, insure, *v.* *Assure* and *ensure* may be used interchangeably to mean *guarantee* or *make certain:* to *assure* (or *ensure*) *safe delivery.* When the object of the verb is a person, use *assure*: *I assure you that I will be on time.*

Insure refers to insurance policies: *insured the house against fire and theft.*

astonished, *adj., participle* Followed by *at* or *by*: *astonished at* (or *by*) *what she heard.*

astronaut, cosmonaut, *n.* We use the term *astronaut* ("sailor among the stars"); the Russians use a word that translates into *cosmonaut* ("sailor through the universe").

atheist, *n.* See AGNOSTIC, ATHEIST.

athletics is, athletics are See -ICS.

attack, *n.* See AMBUSH, ATTACK.

attorney at law, *n.* For plural, see NOUN, 6U.

attorney general, *n.* For plural, see NOUN, 6U.

audience, spectators, *n.* An *audience* listens; *spectators* watch. So those who attend a concert, lecture, movie, play, etc. constitute an *audience* even though, of course, they see as well as hear what is going on.

Spectators watch a sports contest, athletic event, perhaps a dance recital (though in this last instance, *audience* may also be used), since what is happening is something meant primarily to be seen rather than heard. *Audience* is a *singular* noun, even though it may be composed of many people: *the audience was thrilled.*

audiologist, *n.* See OTOLOGIST, OTOLARYNGOLOGIST, AUDIOLOGIST.

auditorium, stadium, *n.* An audience listens to (and watches) a concert, play, etc. in an *auditorium*; spectators watch a sports contest, etc. in a *stadium*. A *stadium* is generally an outdoor structure, an *auditorium* a large room or hall within a building. The plural form of *stadium* is either *stadia*, if you prefer to use Latin forms, or *stadiums*. The plural form of *auditorium* is *auditoriums* or *auditoria*. See also NOUN, 6Q.

auditory, *adj.* See AURAL, ORAL, AUDITORY, AURICULAR.

aught, ought, naught See ZERO, AUGHT, OUGHT, NAUGHT, NOUGHT.

augment, enhance, *v.* To *augment* is *to increase in* size or numbers; *to enhance* is *to improve in* value, worth, beauty, usefulness, *etc.*

augury, *n.* See OMEN, AUGURY.

aural, oral, auditory, auricular, *adj.* *Aural* refers to the ear or to hearing: *aural* problems; *acute* *aural* perception.

Oral refers to the mouth or to spoken communication: *oral* surgeon; *oral* test; *oral* contract.

Auditory refers to the sense of hearing or to the organs of hearing: *an auditory delight*; *slight loss of* *auditory* ability; *auditory* nerves; etc.

Auricular most commonly means *shaped like an ear*. See also VERBAL, ORAL.

author, *v.* Although the use of this word as a verb. (*authored many popular books*) is frowned upon by some writers, it is nevertheless fully acceptable in standard English.

authoress, *n.* See NOUN, 2A.

authoritarian, authoritative, *adj.* *Authoritarian:* behav-

ing in, or demanding, unquestioning obedience to government, power, or other authority. Dictatorships are characterized by *authoritarianism.*

Authoritative: based on, or coming from, a source considered official, reliable, expert, etc.

auto, automobile, *n.* See PHONE, TELEPHONE.

automaton, *n.* For plural, see NOUN, 6R.

autopsy, biopsy, *n.* An *autopsy* is performed, usually by a pathologist, coroner, or medical examiner, on a corpse to determine the cause of death.

A pathologist performs a *biopsy* on tissue or fluids removed from a live body. The examination is often done with a microscope, and the purpose is diagnostic.

auxiliary, *n.* A term in Structural Grammar that corresponds to *auxiliary verb* or *helping verb* in traditional grammar. See VERB, 6.

avenge, revenge, *v.* You *avenge* a wrong, usually done to someone else, by exacting just punishment.

You *revenge* (yourself) or seek *revenge* in a retaliatory, spiteful, or malicious manner, for some real or imagined wrong that you have suffered at the hands of another.

See also VENGEANCE, RE-
VENGE; VENGEFUL, REVENGEFUL.

averse, *adj.* See ADVERSE,
AVERSE.

aversion, *n.* See ADVERSE,
AVERSE.

avert, *v.* See AVOID, AVERT.

aviatrix, *n.* See NOUN, 2C;
NOUN, 6O2.

avoid, avert, *v.* When you
avoid someone or something,
you stay clear of her, him, or
it.

When you *avert* something,
you turn it away (*avert one's
gaze*) or prevent its occurrence (*avert punishment, failure, disaster,* etc.).

await, wait, wait on, *v.* *Await*
is a transitive verb: *you await
someone's arrival; a surprise
awaits you.*

Wait is intransitive: *you
wait for the train, wait on
tables, wait patiently, wait
at home.*

Do not use *wait on* as a
substitute for *wait for: wait
for* (not on) *the arrival of the
instructor.*

For transitive and intransitive verbs, see SENTENCE
PATTERNS.

awake, awaken, *v.* See WAKE,
AWAKE, AWAKEN, WAKEN.

award, reward, *n.* An *award*
(medal, plaque, certificate,
money, etc.) is given for some
accomplishment (as in athletics, sports, art, sciences, or
school success), usually in a
ceremony or officially, and
as a decision of a judge or
judges: *award for heroism.*

A *reward* is given in return or in compensation for
what one has done: *reward
for good behavior, for finding a lost dog, for providing
information that identifies
and/or convicts a criminal.*

By implication an *award*
is won; a *reward* is received,
offered, or given. Both words
also function as verbs.

aware, *adj.* See CONSCIOUS,
AWARE.

away, aweigh See WAY,
WEIGH.

awful, awfully Use *awfully*
(not *awful*) as a qualifier:
awfully (not *awful*) *unhappy.*
There is a certain illogic in
combining awfully with an
adjective that has a pleasant
connotation (*awfully deli-
cious; awfully fortunate*), and
such a construction should
be restricted to colloquial or
informal English.

awhile, a while *Awhile* is
an *adverb: stay awhile; rest
awhile;* etc.

Use the separated words
when a *noun* is required:
*rested for a while; it was a
while ago that; a while back;*
etc.

awkward, *adj.* Followed by
in or *at: awkward in movement; awkward at saying
good-byes;* etc.

axis, *n.* For plural form, see
NOUN, 6N.

B

backward, backwards, *adv.*
See -WARD, -WARDS.

bacterium, *n.* The plural is
bacteria. See NOUN, 6Q.

bad, badly Although *badly*
is indeed the adverbial form
of the adjective *bad,* it is nevertheless often used as an adjective to mean *emotionally
uncomfortable*: I feel *badly
about this misfortune.* When
current idiom contradicts a
so-called rule, the idiom is
correct; the rule is simply
not universal. See also GOOD,
WELL.

bade, *v.* See BID.

baited breath See BATED
BREATH, BAITED BREATH.

baluster, *n.* See BANISTER,
BALUSTRADE, BALUSTER.

bandeau, *n.* For plural, see
NOUN, 6S.

bandit, *n.* For plural forms,
see NOUN, 6L5. See also
THIEVERY.

banister, balustrade, baluster,
n. A *banister* or *balustrade*
(the former term is more common) is the railing held up by
a row of *balusters* or posts,
along one or both sides of a
staircase.

barbaric, barbarous, barbarian,
adj. Though these adjectives
are used synonymously by
many writers, there is a distinction worth preserving,
namely:
 Barbaric: pertaining to, or
describing, groups, tribes, etc.
(or their actions, customs,
etc.) that are wild, uncivi-
lized, primitive, etc.; also, descriptive of taste, style,
mannerisms, etc. that are
wild, unrestrained, crude, etc.
Noun: **barbarism**.
 Barbarous: cruel, savage,
brutal in actions. Noun:
barbarity.
 Barbarian (n.) may denote
either a *barbaric* person or a
barbarous person. *Barbarian*
(adj.) is a synonym of both
barbaric and *barbarous.*

barely See HARDLY, SCARCELY,
BARELY.

barren, *adj.* See STERILE, BAR-
REN, INFERTILE, IMPOTENT.

basis, *n.* For plural, see
NOUN, 6N.

bat, *v.* *Past tense*: **batted**;
participle: (has, was) **batted**.

bated breath, baited breath
One listens or waits with
bated (*not baited*) breath—i.e.,
in suspense, fear, anticipa-
tion, etc.

23

bathos, *n.* See PATHOS, BATHOS.

B.C. See A.D.

beastly, bestial, *adj.* To begin with, both adjectives mean, interchangeably, *pertaining to, characteristic or descriptive of, etc., a beast or animal.*

However, when applied to a person or to human behavior, *bestial* is much the stronger word. *Beastly* may mean no more than *very disagreeable, unpleasant, unkind,* etc. *(she is so beastly to her husband),* but bestial means *cruel, brutal, morally depraved.*

beat, beaten, *part.* The participle of the verb *beat* is *beaten,* not *beat*: *our team has never been beaten; he has beaten his dog unmercifully;* etc.

"I feel *beat* today!" (i.e., exhausted), "It can't be *beat!,*" and similar expressions are idiomatic but are reserved for informal speech and writing.

beau, *n.* For plural forms, see NOUN, 6S.

because of, See DUE TO.

become, get, *v.* See GET, BECOME, HAVE.

beef, *n.* For plural forms, see NOUN, 6G1.

befit, *v.* Past tense and participle are both *befitted: befitted the occasion; has*

befitted her dignity. See also FIT, FITTED.

beget, *v.* *Begat* is archaic or Biblical. *Past tense:* **begot**; *participle:* **begotten** or **begot** *(has* **begotten** *or has* **begot***).*

begin, *v.* The past tense is **began,** not **begun.** *Begun* is the participle only: *has* **begun***; was* **begun***;* etc.

behalf, *n.* *In behalf of* is generally used to indicate *for the benefit of* or *in the interest of: the money raised in behalf of Ethiopia.*

If you mean *acting as agent,* or *speaking for,* the correct preposition is *on: on behalf of the family, he accepted the settlement; the attorney responded on behalf of her clients.*

behind, *prep.* For personal pronoun following a preposition, see PRONOUN, 8B.

being as that, being as how Substandard substitute for *because* or *since.*

belabor, labor (a point) You may *belabor a point* or *labor a point;* in either case, you are doing the same thing: going on repetitiously.

Many writers prefer the shorter verb *(labor)* as being more precise, but *belabor* is also current in educated speech and writing.

benefactor, *n.* For feminine form, see NOUN, 2C.

bereaved, bereft *Bereaved*

generally describes someone who has lost a relative, close friend, etc. through death: *the bereaved widower.*

Bereft usually indicates loss or deprivation in other circumstances: *bereft of hope (friends,* etc.).

berserk See AMUCK, AMOK, BERSERK.

beseech, *v.* Preferable past tense and participle are *besought; beseeched* is also correct.

beside, besides *Beside* means *next to, at the side of: Beside the couch is an end table.*

Besides means *also, in addition to, furthermore,* etc:

Besides sugar, she uses cream in her coffee.

best, *v.* See WORST.

bestial, *adj.* See BEASTLY, BESTIAL.

better, best See COMPARISON

better, bettor *Better* is an adjective; *bettor* is *one who bets*—i.e., wagers.

better than, more than In dealing with numbers, *more than* seven out of every ten people is more precise and certainly more logical than *better than* seven out of every ten people.

between, *prep.* For personal pronoun following prepositions, see PRONOUN, 8B.

BETWEEN, AMONG, prep.

Although *between* generally refers to *two,* this preposition is standard usage when a one-to-one relationship is implied in reference to larger numbers or when each of the units of a group is thought of individually *(friction between Susan and her parents).*

Among is the preposition of choice if the group is thought of as a collective whole: *he felt isolated among all the hostile strangers; the profits will be divided among all the shareholders.*

Betwixt, as a substitute for *between,* is now archaic; it is used only for special literary effect, except in the phrase *betwixt and between*—i.e., *neither one thing nor another* or *in a totally indecisive state: felt betwixt and between.*

Amongst is a somewhat literary variant form of *among.*

Amid or *in the midst of* suggests being surrounded: *amid* (or *in the midst of) all the confusion; amid* (or *in the midst of) the fields of grain.*

Amidst, like *amongst,* is somewhat literary.

Amid, amidst, and *in the midst of,* then, are synonymous with *surrounded by.*

betwixt See BETWEEN, AMONG.

bi-, *prefix* Do not hyphenate words with this prefix: *bipartisan, biweekly,* etc. See also SEMI-, DEMI-, HEMI-.

biannual, biennial, *adj.* A problem occurs because *bi-* may mean either *two* or *twice.* Here are the solutions to various time periods if you wish to be precise:

Biannual: twice a year; biennial: every two years. Since *biannual* may be misunderstood, *semiannual* (i.e., *every half year*) is the unambiguous term for *twice a year.*

Bimonthly, biweekly: strictly *every two months* and *every two weeks,* respectively. If you mean *twice a month,* use *semimonthly; twice a week, semiweekly.*

bid, *v.* The past tense is *bade* (pronounced BAD) in expressions like *they bade him good-bye,* etc., but *bid* in reference to bidding at an auction: *she bid two spades in the bridge game. Bidden* is the preferable participle in the former instance *(have bidden her to enter),* but *bid* is the correct participle in reference to auctions *(has bid two hundred dollars).*

biennial See BIANNUAL, BIENNIAL.

bigamy, polygamy, polygyny, polyandry, *n. Bigamy* is the illegal act of marrying, or state of being married to, another person when a previous marriage is still in effect. Though *bi-* means *two,* any number of subsequent marriages are *bigamous* if one has not been divorced from a first, living spouse.

Polygamy is a custom or practice: *bigamy* is a crime. *Polygamy* denotes a plurality of women married to one husband.

Polygyny is the mating of one male animal with more than one female.

Polyandry is the custom in which a woman has a plurality of husbands.

bijou, *n.* For plural, see NOUN, 6S.

bimonthly See BIANNUAL, BIENNIAL.

bingeing See SINGEING.

biopsy See AUTOPSY, BIOPSY.

bisect, intersect, *v.* To *bisect* is *to cut* (something) *into two equal parts. Bisect* may also mean *branch* or *fork in two directions: the highway bisects at the crest of the hill.*

Intersect, on the other hand, means *cross: Whittier Boulevard intersects Greenleaf Avenue; there is a stop sign where the two streets intersect.*

bite, *v.* Past tense is *bit.* In the active voice, *bitten* is the preferred participle *(has bitten),* but *bit* is also acceptable *(has bit).* In passive constructions, *bitten* is the correct participle *(was **bitten** by the gambling bug).*

biweekly See BIANNUAL, BIENNIAL.

black (Black), *n.* This is the preferred ethnic designation today, as opposed to *Negro, Negress, colored person,* etc.

blame To be ultracorrect, we **blame** (a person, etc.) *for* something, rather than **blame** (something) *on* (a person, etc). Both constructions, however, are acceptable. When using the *noun,* you place the *blame on* (someone) *for* (something).

blasé, *adj.* See JADED, BLASÉ.

blatant, flagrant, glaring, *adj.* A **blatant** act, attitude, etc. is offensive, obtrusive, conspicuous, and in poor taste: *blatant* bragging.

A *flagrant* act, on the other hand, though also conspicuous, is both intentional and illegal, wrong, evil, or unethical: *flagrant* refusal to appear in court.

A **glaring** error, misspelling, miscalculation, or other impropriety need not be intentional, but is so obvious as to, so to speak, glare at you.

bloc, block, *n.* To refer to a group of people, nations, etc., united in some common interest and for mutual support, spell the word **bloc** not **block**: *elected by a large, conservative **bloc** of voters in the third district; the farm **bloc** in the legislature.*

blond, blonde Use either spelling as an adjective; the former is more common.

As a noun, *blond* may indicate either a male or female; a *blonde* is a female only.

bloody, gory, *adj.* Both words may refer to the shedding of blood, but **gory** more definitely indicates that the bloodshed is the result of a battle, serious accident, slaughter, etc. See also SANGUINARY, SANGUINE.

boast, brag, *v.* In the sense of *expressing pride,* the words are synonyms, but *brag* strongly suggests conceit, ostentation, perhaps even offensiveness. One *boasts about* or *of,* or *brags about* one's accomplishments, etc. (Do not use the preposition *on* after either verb.)

Boast *(v.)* takes a direct object in an expression such as *The city now boasts a newly constructed five-story municipal building.*

boat, ship, vessel, *n.* In general use, the words are interchangeable for a watercraft. People involved with the sea maintain, however, that a *boat* is small, and is generally used for pleasure, while a *ship* is a much larger craft, capable of long journeys and able to accommodate a great number of people.

born When indicating geographical birth, use a hyphen:

Chinese-**born** philosopher; American-**born** children of Russian immigrants.

both sides See EACH SIDE, EITHER SIDE.

-bound Words with this suffix are written solid (*snowbound*, *storm***bound**, *westbound*, etc.) except when they are proper nouns designating geographical location (*New York-***bound**, *Paris-***bound**, etc.).

bow, stern, *n.* In watercraft or aircraft, the *bow* is the front end, the *stern* the back end.

bowdlerize, *v.* See CENSOR, BOWDLERIZE, EXPURGATE.

brag, *v.* See BOAST, BRAG.

breach, breech A *breach* (n.) is a break or breaking (either physical or figurative): *breach in the wall*; *breach of promise*; etc. To *breach* (v.) is to make such a break or opening: *to breach the defense line, to breach his oath of loyalty*, etc.

A *breech* (n.) is the lower or back part of something, as a gun, etc.

breadth, bredth The latter is a misspelling: *a breadth of five miles.*

breakdown, breakthrough, breakup Write solid as *nouns: a breakdown; a breakthrough; a breakup of the relationship;* etc.

Write separately as *verbs: to break down; to break through; to break up.*

breath, breathe The first word is a noun: *a deep breath*; the second is a verb: *breathe deeply.*

bredth See BREADTH, BREDTH.

breed, *v.* Past tense and participle are both *bred*: *they bred animals; has bred.*

breed of See KIND OF.

bridal, bridle As adjective or noun, *bridal* refers to a bride or to a marriage ceremony.

Bridle is either a noun (*control, restraint*) or a verb (*to control, restrain, take offense, show anger*, etc.)

bridegroom, groom, *n.* It is one of the many myths of English usage that *groom* may not be used for the husband-to-be at a marriage ceremony. Such use is fully acceptable.

bridle See BRIDAL, BRIDLE.

bring, take, fetch, *v.* You *bring* (something or someone) *to* a place, *take* (something or someone) *from* a place.

When you *fetch* (someone or something), you go to a particular place and come back with the person or object requested.

broad- Adjective compounds are hyphenated: *broad-minded*, *broad-backed*, *broad-shouldered*.

broadcast, *v.* The preferable past tense or participle is *broadcast*, not *broadcasted*.

bromide, *n.* See CLICHÉ, BROMIDE, ANODYNE, PLATITUDE.

brother-in-law, *n.* For plural form, see IN-LAWS; NOUN, 6U.

brunet, brunette For the adjective, use either spelling. A *brunet* (*n.*) is a male or female, but a *brunette* (*n.*) is a female only.

build Past tense or participle of the verb is *built;* *builded* is archaic. The noun, referring to a person's figure, is *build,* pronounced BILD, not BILT.

bullet, cartridge, *n.* Strictly, the *bullet* is the small spear of lead or other metal; the *cartridge* is the casing around the bullet.

bullhorn, *n.* See MEGAPHONE, MICROPHONE, BULLHORN.

bump, bunk, *v.* You *bump,* not *bunk,* into someone or something.

bureau, *n.* For plural forms, see NOUN, 6S.

burglary, *n.* See THIEVERY.

burgle, burglarize, *v.* The former is nonstandard. See also ENTHUSE; THIEVERY.

bursar, purser, *n.* The person in charge of money (i.e., the treasurer), as in a college or other institution, is a *bursar;* on a ship, such an official is a *purser.* See also COMPTROLLER, CONTROLLER.

burst, bust, *v.* In the sense of *breaking open* or *apart,* the correct verb is *burst; bust* is slang. Past tense or participle of *burst: burst.*

But, *conj.* You may start a sentence with *But* or *And;* such usage is perfectly good style, high school composition teachers to the contrary notwithstanding.

but, *prep.* For pronoun following this preposition, see PRONOUN, 8B.

butle, *v.* See ENTHUSE.

C

cactus, *n.* For plural form, see NOUN, 6P.

cadaver, corpse, *n.* A *corpse* is called a *cadaver* when it is prepared for, or undergoes, medical dissection.

caduceus, *n.* For plural, see NOUN, 6P.

calendar, calender, colander, *n.* A *calendar* is a system of dates, etc.; a *calender* is a machine for pressing paper or cloth; a *colander* is a kitchen utensil for draining foods.

callous, callus, callosity In general use, *callous* is either an *adjective* meaning *hardhearted, unfeeling, insensitive* (*a callous attitude*), or a *verb* meaning *to make or become callous.*

However, *callous* (*adj.*) may also describe a hardened or thickened place on the skin, or skin containing *calluses.*

A *callus* (*n.*) is a hard or thick part of the skin. The word *callous* is not correctly used as a noun with this meaning.

Callosity is either the state of being hardhearted (i.e., *callousness,* the less ambiguous noun), or another word for *callus* (*n.*).

camaraderie, comradery, *n. Camaraderie,* a French im-port well established in English, is the preferable term. *Comradery* is also acceptable, though less frequently used in formal writing.

candelabra, candelabrum As a singular noun denoting *one* ornamental candlestick, *candelabra* is so commonly used that it is futile to insist that the singular is *candelabrum.* (Strictly, *candelabra* is a *plural* noun: *the candelabra are beautiful.*) Indeed, not only is *candelabra* used as *singular,* but the plural form is inevitably considered to be *candelabras.* Decide for yourself how conservative you wish to be about these words.

See also DATA, INSIGNIA; MEDIA; NOUN, 6Q.

candidate, *n.* See CONTESTANT, CANDIDATE, ASPIRANT.

can, may *aux.* That *can* shows ability (*tadpoles can become frogs*) and *may* indicates possibility or permission (*it may arrive; she said we may leave*) is a truth much emphasized by English teachers. But that *can* is also universally used, except, perhaps on the most formal level, for *possibility* or *permission* is a fact that *can* (or *may*) be confirmed by simple observation. In short, there is no real point in getting stuffy about the so-called distinction.

In negative questions challenging denials *(why can't I see my personnel file?)*, the use of *why mayn't I?* or *why may I not?* sounds overelegant.

cannot, can not Standard style is to write the word solid, unless you wish to emphasize the *not: Can not, repeat not.* . . .

cannot but Amateur grammarians argue against this usage, claiming that it is a double negative. However, idioms violate so-called rules, and *cannot but* is a common, firmly established idiom: *he cannot but envy her.*

canon, cannon, *n.* A *canon* is a law (religious or otherwise), rule, basis for judging, etc.: *canons of good taste.* A *cannon* is a piece of artillery. Incidentally, *cannon* is a plural form when the big guns are thought of as a group, *(the cannon were finally silent); cannons* is the plural when the reference is to individual separate guns.

cantatrice, *n.* See NOUN, 2C.

can't seem to An idiom that, like *cannot but,* is firmly established in the language; it need not be changed to *seem unable to,* unless you prefer the latter wording for reasons of style.

canvas, canvass *Canvas* is a kind of cloth; *canvass* is either a verb, i.e., go about seeking orders, votes, opinions, etc. *(canvass the neighborhood)* or a noun of similar meaning *(make a canvass of the voters).*

capful, *n.* For plural, see -FUL, -FULS.

capital, capitol, *n.* As here contrasted, the former is the *city* that is the seat of government of a state or nation; the latter is the *building* in which the legislature sits. *Capitol* is spelled with an upper-case *C* if a specific building is meant: *the Capitol in Washington, D.C.*

caponize, *v.* See CASTRATE, GELD, ALTER, FIX, CAPONIZE, EMASCULATE, SPAY.

carat, karat, caret, *n.* The unit of weight of a precious stone is a *carat.*

Karat refers to the proportion of gold in a metal or piece of jewelry: *14-karat gold.*

Caret is the symbol ∧, used when additional material is inserted in a line.

The three words, totally different in meaning, have identical pronunciations.

cardinal numbers See ORDINAL NUMBERS, CARDINAL NUMBERS.

cardsharp, cardshark, *n.* The former is the correct word for *one adept at cheating in card games.*

In colloquial usage, **card-shark** may also describe such a person, or may signify *one who is an unusually skillful card-player.*

careen, career. *v.* In general use, the two verbs are distinguished as follows:

Careen: speed along in a lurching, twisting, unsteady manner.

Career: rush headlong; move at top speed; speed wildly.

Careen has the additional meaning of *leaning or tilting to one side.*

carnage, slaughter, *n.* The words are closely synonymous, but *carnage* is more extensive, bloodier, wholesale slaughter, as in wars, battles, atomic bombing, etc. *Carnage* may also suggest the piling up of dead bodies.

carnivorous, herbivorous, omnivorous, *adj.* A *carnivorous* animal (tiger, lion, etc.) is a meat-eater; a *herbivorous* animal (cow, deer, elephant) subsists solely on grains and greens. Humans, rats, and domesticated cats and dogs are *omnivorous*—they eat both types of food.

cartridge, *n.* See BULLET, CARTRIDGE.

cast, *v.* Past tense and participle; **cast,** not **casted**.

castrate, geld, alter, fix, ca- **ponize, emasculate, spay,** *v.* In the literal sense, *to castrate* is to remove the testicles of (a male).

To geld is to *castrate* (a male horse). A **gelded** horse is a **gelding**.

Alter or *fix* is the euphemistic term for *castrate*, and may also mean *remove the ovaries* (of a female animal).

To **caponize** is to *castrate* (a rooster). A *castrated* rooster is a **capon**.

Emasculate may be used in the literal sense of *castrate*, but more often means *remove the power, force, effectiveness, strength, or virility of* (a person, thing, etc.). *Castrate*, too, may be, but less often is, used in this figurative sense.

To **spay** is to *remove the ovaries* (of a female animal), especially a cat or dog. The female thus treated has been **spayed**, not **spaded**.

casualty, fatality, mortality, *n.* As here contrasted, a *casualty* is a person injured or killed in an accident, or a member of the armed forces injured, killed, missing in action, or captured by the enemy.

A *fatality* refers only to the death of a person in an accident, battle, natural disaster, etc.

Both words are often, but not exclusively, used in the plural: *many casualties; fortunately, there were no fatalities.*

Mortality, as contrasted with *casualty* and *fatality*, is the number of deaths from any cause in a region, country, etc. in proportion to the size of the population—often used in the phrase *mortality rate* or *rate of mortality*.

casuistry, sophistry, *n*. These words are synonymous, meaning *clever and subtle reasoning or argumentation that sounds plausible but is in fact specious and misleading*. *Casuistry*, however, often deals with moral issues.

catalog, catalogue See -OGUE, -OG.

catch fire, catch on fire The former is the preferable usage.

catchup, *n*. See CATSUP, CATCHUP, KETCHUP.

cater-cornered, catty-cornered, cater-corner, kitty-cornered, *adj*. All these spellings are correct.

catsup, catchup, ketchup, *n*. *Ketchup* is the standard spelling; the other forms are acceptable variants. However you spell it, pronounce it KECH'-əp.

catty-cornered, *adj*. See CATER-CORNERED, CATTY-CORNERED, CATER-CORNER, KITTY-CORNERED.

caution, *v*. Followed by *against* (*cautioned* him against smoking), not to (*cautioned* him not to smoke), or that (*cautioned* him that he was not to smoke).

cave, cavern, *n*. A *cavern* is much larger than *cave*.

cello, 'cello, violoncello, *n*. The shortened form *cello* is in perfectly good repute and wide use. There is no need to use a preceding apostrophe; on the other hand, there is no law against doing so as long as you realize that *'cello* is not a popular spelling. *Violoncello* is the full word—note that *o*, not *i*, follows the first *l*.

Cello has two plural forms—the original Italian *(celli)* and the Anglicized version *(cellos)*. People professionally involved with music usually prefer *celli*.
See also NOUN 6L4.

censer, *n*. See CENSOR, CENSER, CENSURE.

censor, bowdlerize, expurgate, *v*. To *censor* is *to remove objectionable material from* (writing, etc.).

To *bowdlerize* to *to delete from* (a book, etc.) *material, language, or passages that may be offensive to a person of prudish tendencies*. (The word is derived from Thomas Bowdler, who in the 1800s published an edition of Shakespeare with all the "salty" parts removed.)

To *expurgate* is *to revise a published work by omitting* (i.e., purging) *parts considered obscene, sexually explicit*, etc. This verb is similar to *bowdlerize*, but is in more common use.

An *expurgated* edition may also, but less commonly, refer to a revision from which erroneous material has been deleted or changed.

See also UNABRIDGED, UNEXPURGATED.

censor, censer, censure, n. A *censor* is one who has the power to delete written material considered objectionable for whatever reason.

A *censer* is a container for incense.

Censure (n.) is stern disapproval, scolding, criticism, etc.

Censor and *censure* may also be used as verbs.

ceremonial, ceremonious, adj. Ceremonial occasions, activities, clothing, rites, etc. are those attended by, or proper for, a formal ceremony.

Ceremonious persons tend to make a ceremony or ritual out of an otherwise ordinary activity—they are rigidly formal, overly courteous, perhaps even pompous. *Ceremonious* may also apply to actions, attitudes, etc. that are unnecessarily or excessively formal, ritualistic, etc.

CHAIRMAN, CHAIRWOMAN, CHAIRPERSON, *n.*

The current trend is to reduce the gender identification of nouns.

If a woman is the head of a college department or of a committee of any sort, it is of course illogical to refer to her as the *chairman.* In many places, the term popularly used for either sex is *chairperson*—but this seems almost as awkward as replacing *repairman* with *repairperson* or *manhole* with *personhole.*

I see no need for neutering the office so completely. Personally, I prefer calling the male head of a group a *chairman* and the female head a *chairwoman.* (*Chairlady* sounds too much like a woman who sells, or perhaps is in charge of, chairs!)

Another way of avoiding problems is to use *the chair,* as in *"The chair recognizes the delegate from California."* However, it sounds faintly unidiomatic to say, for example, *"Carolyn Russell is the chair of the English Department."*

chaise longue, chaise lounge, *n.* The latter is considered by many authorities to be a nonword, mistakenly used, no doubt, because one *lounges* in a *chaise longue* (SHAYZ-lông), a chair that reclines. (The correct word is derived from the French for "long chair.") Nevertheless, so common is the substitution of *lounge* for *longue* in this term that it has gained entry in some dictionaries, and one can hardly afford to sneer at it. To be on the safe side, use the former spelling and pronunciation.

chanteuse, *n.* See NOUN, 2C.

chaperon, chaperone, *n.* Either spelling is correct, the former more popular. The word originally referred to an older married woman who accompanied an unmarried couple to make sure that all the proprieties were observed. Today, however, an older male may also be a *chaperon* (or *chaperone*), as at a high school dance, etc. All forms of the *verb* to *chaperon* are spelled with one *n* only.

characteristic of, peculiar to *Characteristic of*: *part of the intrinsic nature or character of.*
    Peculiar to: *found exclusively or almost exclusively in: guttural sounds peculiar to German speech.*

charlatan, quack, impostor, *n.* A *charlatan* pretends to training, skill, knowledge, or powers that, in fact, he or she does not possess.
    A *quack* is a charlatan in the field of medicine.
    An *impostor* pretends, for purposes of deceit or personal gain, to be someone other

than who he or she actually is.

chateau, *n.* For plural forms, see NOUN, 6S.

cherub, *n.* The plural is *cherubim* for the angelic beings of theology, *cherubs* for human children who look, or act, like angels.

chief of staff *n.* For plural, see NOUN, 6U.

childish, childlike, *adj.* *Childish*, when applied to adults, shows disapproval: *childish temper* (tantrum, etc.). *Childlike*, on the other hand, indicates approval and refers to the pleasant traits of children: *childlike innocence* (charm, frankness, delight, etc.)

Chinaman, Chink, Chinese, *n.* The first two terms are considered offensive. A person from China, male or female, is a *Chinese.*

chiropodist, *n.* See PODIATRIST, CHIROPODIST.

choice, *n.* See ALTERNATIVE, CHOICE.

choral, chorale *Choral* is an adjective: *choral* music, *choral* singing.
    Chorale is a *noun*, pronounced kə-RAL' or kô-RAL', and is either *the hymn or other musical composition to be sung by a choir* or the choir itself.
    A variant spelling of *chorale* (n.) is *choral* (n.) and in

this spelling the word is still pronounced with the accent on the second syllable.

chord, cord, *n.* It's *chord* in music, geometry, or one's emotions: *chord of a harp; played several chords on the piano; struck a sympathetic chord in her listeners.*

It's *cord* in *vocal cords; a cord of wood; tied with stout cord;* etc.

chronic, inveterate, *adj.* *Chronic* indicates continual recurrence, time after time: *chronic colds; chronic invalid; chronic liar.* The word often refers to recurring attacks of an illness or illnesses, and usually suggests something unpleasant.

Inveterate implies long-established habit and usually refers to unhealthful, unpleasant, socially unacceptable, or illegal activity: *inveterate thief (smoker, drinker, etc.).*

cicada, *n.* For plural, see NOUN, 6M.

cicatrix, *n.* For plural, see NOUN, 6O1.

cilium, *n.* For plural, see NOUN, 6Q.

cion, scion, *n.* For a *shoot of a plant,* either spelling is correct, the latter preferable.

For a *human descendant,* **scion** is the only spelling.

circular, more circular See EQUAL, MORE EQUAL.

class, *n.* See NOUN, 1.

classic, classical *Classic (adj.)* describes something that is of the highest quality or that serves as a model. *The classic group of the jazz era; a classic example of . . .*

Classic is also used as a noun: *that novel (movie, artwork, etc.) is a classic; enjoys reading the classics.*

Classical (adj.) refers either to the culture of ancient Greece or Rome *(classical architecture)* or to music that was composed in the latter part of the eighteenth century (or similar music), as opposed to modern, folk, popular, jazz, rock, etc., music: *enjoys classical music.*

clean, cleanse, *v.* *Clean* is used in the general sense of removing dirt, pollutants, impurities, errors, etc. *Cleanse* (KLENZ) is more specific, suggesting the use of strong *cleansing* agents (chemicals, purgatives, etc.). *Cleanse* also has a figurative meaning: *cleanse one's mind of evil thoughts.*

clench, *v.* See CLINCH, CLENCH.

clew, *n.* See CLUE, CLEW.

cliché, bromide, anodyne, platitude, *n.* These close synonyms all refer to any trite, stale, overused expression in speech or writing.

Cliché is the general, all-inclusive term.

A *bromide* is so dull and

obvious as to cause drowsiness or boredom.

An *anodyne* is intended to soothe, comfort, or allay one's fears or anxieties.

A *platitude* is said or written as if it were meaningful or important, but falls flat because of its triteness.

climatic, climactic, *adj.* *Climatic* is the adjective derived from *climate* (n.): *climatic conditions at the equator.*

Climactic (adj.) is derived from the noun *climax*: *the climactic scene of the play.*

Anticlimactic is the adjective from *anticlimax* (n.). Obviously, *anticlimatic* is meaningless and probably a misspelling of *anticlimactic*.

climb down Illogical though it may sound, *climb down* is standard usage. If the illogic bothers you, use *descend*.

clinch, clench, *v.* Both verbs mean *to fasten, tie, nail, etc. together,* but *clinch* is more frequently used in this sense. On the other hand, *clench* is the proper verb in phrases like *clench one's teeth* (*jaws, fingers, fist,* etc.) and *clench the ball in one's hands; clench the baby in one's arms;* etc.

closure, cloture, *n.* As a procedure by which debate is ended, as in the U.S. Senate, *cloture* is the preferable term. Though correct, *closure* is less commonly used in this sense.

clue, clew, *n.* *Clue* is the

usual spelling; *clew* is a variant spelling.

clumsy, maladroit, gauche, *adj.* *Clumsy* indicates awkwardness or ineffectiveness in movement, action, performance, etc.

Maladroit refers especially to social situations, as does *gauche;* but *gauche* additionally implies embarrassing tactlessness or boorishness in social relationships.

co-, *prefix* Generally written solid with its root (*coauthor, cohabit, coexist, coconspirator,* etc.), even if the first letter of the root is *o* (*cooperate, coordinate*). In the latter words, a hyphen may separate the two *o*'s but such spellings are less popular, as is *coöperate.*

coffee klatch (klatsch), *n.* See KAFFEE KLATSCH.

cohabit, *v.* By etymology, this verb simply means *live together;* however, the word may explicitly refer to a male and female living together in a sexual relationship although not legally married to each other.

cohort, *n.* See COMPANION, COHORT.

coiffeur, coiffeuse, *n.* *Coiffeur* is an elegant term for a hairdresser who is a male, *coiffeuse* for a hairdresser who is a female; the terms are mostly used in writing about style and fashion.

coincident, coincidence *Coincident* is one of the adjectives derived from the noun *coincidence*. The more commonly used adjective form is *coincidental*—and the adverb is *coincidentally*, not *coincidently*.

Hence: *What a coincidence* (n.)!; *a coincidental* (or, alternatively, but not commonly, *coincident*) *occurrence; coincidental* (or *coincident*) *with his arrival.*

See also *incidence, incident.*

colander, *n.* See CALENDAR, CALENDER, COLANDER.

coleslaw, cole slaw, coldslaw, *n.* *Coldslaw* is a misusage, understandable since this shredded cabbage dish is served cold. *Cole* is derived from the Dutch *cole,* "cabbage." *Coleslaw* is the preferable spelling; *cole slaw* (two words) is a variant spelling.

coliseum, Colosseum Both words are pronounced the same: kol'-ə-SEE'-əm. A *coliseum* is a building used for sports events, exhibitions, etc. The *Colosseum* (always with a capital *C*), refers to the huge amphitheater in Rome built in the first century A.D. Occasionally, but infrequently, the second word, with a small *c*, is used to refer to a present-day sports arena.

collection, *n.* See NOUN, 1.

collide, collision If you want to be strict and overly fussy, you will insist that a *collision* can occur only when *both* objects are in motion. However, this restriction is largely ignored; even in formal English, a car can *collide* with a stone wall. Furthermore, the words are often used figuratively in the sense of *being in conflict: their needs collide; their aims are on a collision course;* etc.

colloquium, *n.* For plural, see NOUN, 6Q.

collusion, *n.* This word is generally used to mean *a secret agreement* or *cooperation in an illegal* or *fraudulent act.* Verb: *collude* (with).

The noun is usually preceded by *in* (acting in collusion) and is followed by the preposition *with: in collusion with the rebels.*

colored person See BLACK.

Colosseum, *n.* See COLISEUM, COLOSSEUM.

combine together This is a redundancy—omit *together* when using the verb *combine.*

comedian, comedienne, *n.* The trend in current English usage is to avoid gender identification in occupations. The distinction, however, between *comedian* (masculine) and *comedienne* (feminine) is still prevalent. The feminine noun is pronounced kə-mee'-dee-EN'.

comic, comical, comedic, *adj.* *Comic* and *comedic* both refer to the noun *comedy: comic opera; comedic writings.*

Comical may also refer to *comedy,* but is more likely to mean *funny, laughable, amusing,* etc.

And, though *comic* has the added meaning of *funny, humorous,* etc., *comical* is more frequently used in this sense.

commander in chief, *n.* For plural, see NOUN, 6U.

commando, *n.* For plural, see NOUN, 6L2.

comment, commentate, *v.* No need for the longer, awkward form. However, the person who delivers, or *comments* on, the news on TV or radio is a *commentator.*

commerce, industry, *n.* *Commerce* is the distribution of goods, *industry* the manufacture *and* distribution, usually to wholesalers or retailers.

commiseration, condolence, *n.* Both nouns indicate an expression of sympathy for the grief or misfortune of another; *condolence* is perhaps the more formal expression and is especially used when someone has suffered the death of a loved one. *Condolences (n. pl.)* is generally the form used in such instances. *Verbs: commiserate (with), condole (with).*

common sense Two separate words as a noun: *plenty of common sense;* hyphenated in the adjective position: *a common-sense* approach. Alternate adjective form: *common-sensical.*

communicable, *adj.* See CONTAGIOUS, INFECTIOUS, COMMUNICABLE.

companion, cohort, *n.* *Cohort* is frowned upon by some authorities as a substitute for *companion, supporter, associate,* etc., except when used for humorous or derogatory effect. *Cohort* was a military group in ancient Rome.

compare, contrast, *v.* *Compare* things, people, etc. to note similarities or differences; *contrast* them to *emphasize* the differences.

The *nouns comparison* and *contrast* are followed by *between: no comparison can be made between; such a contrast between.*

The *verb contrast* is followed by *with* if you point out *differences;* by *to* if you imply that one is completely *opposite* to the other.

The phrase *in contrast* is followed by *with* or *to* following the distinction described above.

compare to, compare with You *compare* one *to* another in order to express a point or points of similarity between things that are essentially unlike: *compared her voice to a* *violin*; you *compare* one *with* another to note points of similarities and/or differences:

compare his reaction with that of his wife.

COMPARISON, n.

After the phrase *in comparison*, use either *to* or *with* as explained in COMPARE TO, COMPARE WITH. You make a *comparison* between things, abstractions, or persons.

When *two* are compared (as opposed to three or more), use the -ER (or *comparative*) form, rather than the -EST (or *superlative*) form of the adjective.

Hence:

She is the *older* (not *oldest*) of his two daughters.
This is the *lesser* (not *least*) of the two evils.
He is the *slower* (not *slowest*) of the two runners.
Of the two cars, which is *higher* (not *highest*) in price?
This is the *more comfortable* (not *most comfortable*) of the two rooms.

complacent, complaisant, *adj.* Although the two words are sometimes used interchangeably, the distinction between them is certainly worth preserving.

A *complacent* person is self-satisfied, even smug.

A *complaisant* person is eager to please others, easy to get along with, agreeable and cheerful.

Most people also observe a distinction in pronunciation: *complacent*: kəm-PLAY'-sənt; *complaisant*: kəm-PLAY'-zənt.

complected, *adj.* See COMPLEXIONED, COMPLECTED.

complement, compliment, supplement, *n.* A *comple-*

ment, derived from the verb *to complete*, is what makes something *complete*. In grammatical terminology, a *complement* is a word or group of words that follows a verb and *completes* a sentence.

A *compliment* is a word, phrase, or act that shows admiration, expresses praise, etc.

A *supplement* is what is *added*, with no implication of causing completeness.

All three words may also be used as verbs.

complexioned, complected, *adj.* These words are hyphenated with a tone, shade, or color: *dark-complexioned*, *light-complected*, etc. However, *complected* is not formal usage.

compliment, *n*. See COMPLE-MENT, COMPLIMENT, SUPPLE-MENT.

comprehend, *v*. See APPRE-HEND, COMPREHEND.

comptroller, controller, *n*. The two words are pronounced identically (kən-TRŌL'-ər). *Comptroller* is the official title for the head financial officer of an institution, government agency, etc.—in short, a treasurer. In many business firms or other organizations, *controller* is the title used for the financial officer. See also BURSAR, PURSER.

compulsion, obsession, fixation, *n*. As terms in psychology:

A *compulsion* is an irresistible need to perform some act, whether rational or irrational.

An *obsession* is a feeling, idea, or urge, normal or abnormal, that persists in the mind despite all efforts to reason it away.

A *fixation* is a persistent attachment to an object or person that derives from arrested psychosexual development at an early age.

comradery, *n*. See CAMARA-DERIE, COMRADERY.

concave, convex, *adj*. Something *concave* has a side that is curved *inward* (think of the opening of a cave); something *convex* has a side that curves or bulges *outward*.

concert, recital, *n*. In reference to a musical presentation, a *concert* is given by a number of performers (up to and including a symphony orchestra), a *recital* by a soloist or a small ensemble. Nevertheless, so delightfully illogical is our language, a soloist who gives recitals professionally is paid to *concertize*. (You figure it out. No, there is no such word as *recitalize*.)

concerto, *n*. For plural form, see NOUN, 6L4.

concur, *v*. You *concur with* someone *in* that person's plan, opinion, statement, etc.—that is, you express agreement. You *concur in* an arrangement, plan, action, etc.—that is, you approve of, or even act in concert to effect, such an arrangement, etc.

Circumstances, events, etc. *concur to* bring about a result—that is, act in combination to produce such a result: *the corruption of the government and the decadence of the people concurred to bring about the fall of ancient Rome.*

condolence, *n*. See COMMIS-ERATION, CONDOLENCE.

confess, *v*. See ADMIT, CON-FESS.

confidant, confidante, *n*. You tell your secrets or personal feelings to a *confidant*, male or female. If you wish to stress the gender of your female listener, she is your *confi-dante*. (Bear in mind that there is less and less emphasis on gender in current speech and writing.)

confide in, confide to You *confide in* someone—i.e., share secrets, personal matters, etc. with that person. You *confide* such secrets, etc. *to* someone you trust. *You may confide in me; you may confide your se-crets to me; the unlisted phone number was confided to me.*

Confide may also mean *entrust for safekeeping: we are willing to confide our child to a reliable baby-sitter.*

conform, *v.* Followed by the preposition *to.*

conformance, conformity, n. Followed by the preposition *to,* except in the phrase *in conformance* (or *conformity*) *with the rules* (*obliga-tions of office,* etc.).

congenial, genial, *adj. Con-genial* people have similar likes and dislikes, attitudes, temperaments, etc. A *con-genial* person is easy to get along with, sympathetic to one's needs and desires, etc. *Congenial* work, atmo-sphere, or other abstractions suit one's likes, needs, tem-perament, or life style.

A *genial* person is cheer-ful, sociable, kind, gracious, etc.: *our genial master of ceremonies.*

Both words indicate friend-liness, each in its own way.

congenital, *adj.* See GENETIC, CONGENITAL.

connive at, connive with When you ignore a wrong or illegal act on the part of an-other, thus by silence seem-ing to encourage it, you *connive at* (the thievery, fraud, etc.). When you secretly cooperate in another's action, you *connive with* that per-son. Hence, the noun *con-nivance* is followed by ei-ther *at* or *with,* depending on its use as explained above.

CONNOISSEUR, EPICURE, EPICUREAN, GOURMET, GOURMAND, n.

A *connoisseur* is a discriminating judge and expert in some field—especially, but not exclusively, the fine arts: *a connoisseur of painting* (*poetry, music, literature, food, wine, women,* etc.).

An *epicure* and a *gourmet* are both excellent judges of high-quality food and drink. The *epicure,* however, is more involved with the *pleasure* of eating than is the *gourmet.* The latter is concerned with the excellence of flavor and/or the expertness of preparation of what is served. (Less frequently used synonyms of *gourmet* are *gastronome* and *gastronomer*.)

An *epicurean* is dedicated to the pursuit of pleasures in general, including those of eating and drinking, so long as these pleasures stay within the bounds of morality.

A *gourmand* enjoys eating good food as a pleasurable activity, and often has the waistline to prove it. A *gourmand* is not as fussy or finicky as the *gourmet*. (A variant spelling of *gourmand* is *gormand*.)

The verb *gormandize*, derived from *gourmand*, is derogatory and means *gorge on food*—"*pig out*," as it were.

---

connotation, *n.* See DENO-TATION, CONNOTATION.

conscious, aware, *adj.* In the sense in which these words are contrasted, one is *conscious* of sensations or of what one feels, thinks, etc.—in short, of one's inner world. One is *aware* of what is happening outside oneself, either by using one's senses of perception or by receiving information in some other way. So one is *conscious* of pain, guilt, fear, happiness, etc. and *aware* of frost in the air, etc.

consensus of opinion Many authorities consider *consensus of opinion* an unnecessary redundancy, since *consensus* means *general agreement of opinion.* In short, *consensus,* by itself, is enough. See also GENERAL CONSENSUS.

consent See ASSENT, CONSENT.

conservative, reactionary, *n.* Politically speaking, a *conservative* prefers to keep things as they are (i.e., con-serve what one has) and is usually opposed to broad changes in government policy.

A *reactionary,* on the other hand, prefers to return to the political and economic policies of the past. A *reactionary* has been called a far-right or extreme *conservative,* and is thoroughly, if not violently, opposed to liberal or progressive government. See also LIBERAL, RADICAL.

consider, consider as *Consider* is followed by *as* only when it means *examine* or *analyze: when you consider Poe as a poet, you must bear in mind . . .*

Omit *as* in other constructions: *consider him a fool; consider her intelligent;* etc.

consist of, consist in Use *of* when speaking of the parts that make up the whole: *the U.S. consists of fifty states.*

Use *in* when giving a positive or negative definition of inherent qualities: *complete honesty consists in a deliberate refusal to deceive or* to use even minor forms of deception; beauty does not **consist** only **in** outward appearance.

consul, *n.* See COUNCIL, COUNSEL, CONSUL.

consul general For plural form, see NOUN, 6U.

consultative, consultatory, consultive, *adj.* These are interchangeable adjectives; the first is the most frequently used.

contact, *v.* Some authorities still frown on the use of this word as a verb *(I will **contact** you tomorrow)*. However, such usage is certainly prevalent in educated speech and writing; it is a sign of pedantry, perhaps, to condemn it.

contagious, infectious, communicable, *adj.* A **contagious** disease is transmitted from one person or animal to another or others by either direct or indirect contact.

An **infectious** disease results from the invasion of the body by bacteria, viruses, or other pathogens—i.e., disease-causing microorganisms. An **infection** *(n.)* can spread with or without contact.

A **communicable** disease can be passed (communicated) from one person or animal to another or others. **Communicable** is the general term, encompassing both **contagious** and **infectious.**

contaminate, pollute, *v.* Food can be **contaminated**; water can be **contaminated** or **polluted. Pollution** is the stronger term, indicating a much greater degree of impurity.

contemporary, contemporaneous, *adj.* Both words indicate *existence during the same time.* **Contemporary** more often refers to people or their artistic products, **contemporaneous** to events that occur during the same period. Only **contemporary** can also be used as a noun: *a **contemporary** of Mozart.*

Contemporary *(adj.)* may also mean *modern* or *present-day.*

contempt, *n.* See CONTEMPTIBLE, CONTEMPTUOUS.

contemptible, contemptuous, *adj.* A person, thing, action, etc. that is **contemptible** is *deserving of contempt*; a person who is **contemptuous** feels or expresses contempt for someone or something. One feels **contempt** for or *toward* and is **contemptuous** *of.*

contestant, candidate, aspirant, *n.* A **contestant** takes part in a contest: *a **contestant** in a footrace.*

A **candidate** has formally filed, or been nominated, for an office or position: **candidate** *for the presidency* (for *treasurer of the club, for the available teaching position, etc.).*

An *aspirant* is ambitious or eager to reach some high goal: *aspirant after the presidency (the Pulitzer Prize, great financial rewards,* etc.). One *aspires* to become wealthy; *to* or *after* wealth, success, etc..

CONTINUOUS, CONTINUAL, *adj.*

Anything that goes on without interruption, from start to finish, is *continuous*: *continuous rain for two days* (i.e., during the two days there was no letup); *continuous silence for five minutes* (not a sound during that period).

Anything *continual* recurs, or is repeated: *continual rainfall during the summer months* (the rain comes down again and again, but there are dry spells, perhaps of short duration, occurring every so often); *his continual ill-health* (occasionally he is well). A kitchen needs *continual* cleaning—that is, again and again.

Continuous care, on the other hand (as for a very ill patient) is round the clock.

For space, only *continuous* is used: *a continuous line; a continuous expanse of wilderness;* etc.

Observe the same distinctions in using the adverbs *continuously* and *continually*.

CONTRACTIONS

The apostrophe (') takes the place of missing letters when two words are contracted into one:

I've = I have	you're = you are	doesn't = does not
I'm = I am	it's = it is	don't = do not
I'd = I would	he'll = he will	isn't = is not
who's = who is	they're = they are	aren't = are not
won't = will not	shouldn't = should not	can't = cannot
		shan't = shall not

Contractions are fully acceptable, even in formal writing. (The apostrophe is also used in possessive nouns *[men's]*, pronouns other than personal pronouns *[someone's, no one's]*, and optionally in the plurals of figures *[8's]* or individual letters *[A's, B's]*.)

contralto, *n.* For plural, see NOUN, 6L4.

contrast, *v.* See COMPARE, CONTRAST.

controller, *n.* See COMPTROLLER, CONTROLLER.

convenient for, convenient to Meaning *easy, not causing trouble,* etc., followed by *for*: *whenever it is convenient for you to call.*

Meaning *near,* followed by *to*: *convenient to shopping, freeways.*

convex, *adj.* See CONCAVE, CONVEX.

convince, persuade, *v.* You *convince* someone *that* (something is true, etc.); you *convince* someone *of* (the truth, etc.).

You *persuade* people *that* (they should, etc.); you *persuade* people *to* (go, take, etc.).

In passive constructions, the same patterns hold. For passive voice, see VERB, 9.

cooperate, co-operate, coöperate, *v.* Current style is to write the word solid, rather than with a hyphen or a dieresis (the two dots over the second *o* to show that the two *o*'s are pronounced separately). See also CO-.

coordinate See CO-.

copyright, copywright The correct spelling is *copyright.* *Wright* refers to a person who makes or does (something),

as *playwright, millwright, wheelwright,* etc. *Copyright* refers to the *right* to exclusive use granted an author, composer, publisher, etc.

cord, *n.* See CHORD, CORD.

corespondent, *n.* See CORRESPONDENT, CORESPONDENT.

coroner, *n.* See PATHOLOGIST, MEDICAL EXAMINER, CORONER.

corporal, corporeal, *adj.* *Corporal* is used to indicate the effect of something on the body (*corporal punishment,* for example); *corporeal,* as opposed to *spiritual,* refers to the body as a physical entity: *corporeal existence* (*needs,* etc.). *Corporeal* also means *material* or *tangible* rather than *abstract.*

corps, corpse, corpus, *n.* A *corps* (KŌR) is any body or unit of people working together: *Marine Corps, corps de ballet,* etc.; a *corpse* is a dead body.

A *corpus* may also be a dead body, but is currently used only humorously with this meaning; more frequently it refers to a comprehensive collection of some kind, as *corpus juris,* the body of laws of a nation, state, etc., or the whole body of writings on a particular subject.

See also CADAVER, CORPSE.

correspondent, corespondent, *n.* A *correspondent* is one who writes, as letters, reports, etc.

A *corespondent* (kō'-rə-SPOND'-ənt) is the person charged with having had sexual relations with the defendant in a divorce action. With no-fault divorce acceptable in many states, this term will, no doubt, eventually become obsolete.

corrigendum, corrigenda Mostly used in the plural (*corrigenda*) to refer to a list of errors, with the proper corrections, published in a book and inserted because the pages were printed before the errors were caught. One *corrigendum* is one printer's error that is to be corrected. See also NOUN, 6Q.

cosmonaut, *n.* See ASTRONAUT, COSMONAUT.

could have, could of *Could have* (gone, eaten, seen, etc.) is correct—two auxiliaries before a participle. In the normal flow of speech, *could have* sounds very much like *could of*, hence the understandable error in writing.

Similarly, *may of, might of, must of, ought to of, seems to of, should of, would of,* etc. are writing errors—replace *of* with *have*.

council, counsel, consul, *n.* A *council* is a *governing body,* one member of which is a *councilor.*

Counsel is *advice;* also, *a lawyer or group of lawyers.* A *counselor* is *one who advises,* as in a school, camp,

etc.; also, *a lawyer.* To *counsel* (v.) is *to advise.*

A *consul* is *a member of the foreign service of a country.*

counselor, *n.* See PSYCHIATRIST, PSYCHOANALYST, PSYCHOLOGIST, PSYCHOTHERAPIST, COUNSELOR, ALIENIST

counselor-at-law, *n.* For plural, see NOUN, 6U.

couple, *n.* When thought of as a single entity, the word is singular: *that couple is weird!*

Considered as two individuals, the word is plural: *the couple are spending their honeymoon at Lake Tahoe; the couple were rarely seen together;* etc.

Couple of is treated as a plural: *a couple of my friends were with me.*

See also DUO, DUET, DUAD, DYAD; NOUN, 1.

court-martial, *n.* Plural form is *courts-martial. Martial* is an *adjective* meaning *military;* the *noun court* is pluralized. See also NOUN, 6U.

craft, *n.* When referring to planes, ships, or boats, *craft* is either singular or plural, depending on the number: *the craft* (i.e., *one*) *was approaching; the craft* (i.e., *many*) *were approaching; the aircraft* (i.e., *two*) *were on a collision course; the aircraft* (i.e., *one*) *was landing.* It is an error to use *crafts* as the plural for airplanes or *watercraft.*

craps, *n.* The gambling game is singular, despite the *-s* ending; *craps is his favorite game.* See also DICE.

credible, plausible, creditable, *adj.* *Credible,* quite simply, means *believable: a credible witness* (*story, explanation,* etc.).

A *plausible* story, excuse, explanation, etc. is reasonable and *seems* or *sounds* true; but you imply, when you use this word, that you are not totally convinced.

Creditable, on the other hand, describes some action, performance, accomplishment, etc. that is worthy of credit—i.e., commendation, approval, or slight praise.

See also CREDULOUS, GULLIBLE.

credo, creed, *n.* *Credo* refers to one's personal philosophical belief or beliefs, *creed* to one's religious faith or to any system of ethics, morals, principles, etc.

credulous, gullible, *adj.* *Credulous* persons readily believe whatever they are told, no matter how far-fetched or unreasonable the statement may be. *Nouns: credulity, credulousness.*

Gullible persons are easily tricked, cheated, or duped.

See also CREDIBLE, PLAUSIBLE, CREDITABLE.

creed, *n.* See CREDO, CREED.

creep, *v.* *Crept* (not *creeped*) is both the past tense and the

participle: *they crept; they have crept.*

crematorium, *n.* For plural, see NOUN, 6Q.

cretinous, *adj.* See FEEBLE-MINDED, CRETINOUS, MORONIC, IMBECILIC, IDIOTIC.

criminal, scofflaw, *n.* A *criminal* has committed a (usually serious) crime.

A *scofflaw* habitually violates traffic regulations, flagrantly disobeys city ordinances, etc., and then either ignores summonses to court or refuses to pay the fines levied for the misdemeanors.

cringe, *v.* The *-ING* form is *cringing* (KRINJ'-ing) *not cringeing.*

crisis, *n.* For plural form, see NOUN, 6N.

criteria, *n.* This is the plural form of *criterion: these criteria are ... Criterions* is a variant plural form. See NOUN, 6R.

critical, criticism, criticize, critique The first three words may be used in the pejorative sense of showing disapproval; in other contexts, however, they may refer to making judgments and evaluations of literary or other artistic works or of public performances, and do not automatically imply adverse reactions: *a critical analysis of Tolstoy's novels,* etc.

A *critique* (*n.*), on the other

hand, is solely such an objective evaluation; to *critique* (v.) is to give or write such an evaluation.

cul-de-sac, *n.* Plural is *cul-de-sacs*.

culminate, *v.* See END, CULMINATE.

cumulative, *adj.* See ACCUMULATIVE, CUMULATIVE.

cumulus, *n.* For plural, see NOUN, 6P.

cupfuls, cups full, cupsful See -FUL, -FULS.

curriculum, *n.* For plural, see NOUN, 6Q.

curriculum, syllabus, *n.* A *curriculum* in an institution of learning consists of the courses required, as for graduation, certification, etc.

A *syllabus* is an outline of material to be covered in a particular course.

For plurals, see NOUN, 6P, 6Q.

curriculum vita, *n.* See VITA.

czar, tsar, tzar, *n.* The first spelling is preferable, whether referring to an emperor of Russia or to someone in full control *(baseball czar)*. *Tsar* is frequently used by scholars of Slavic life. *Tzar* is a variant spelling, seldom used.

czarina, tsarina, tzarina, *n.* Feminine form of *czar*, denoting either the wife of a Russian czar or a Russian empress. *Tsarina* and *tzarina* are variant spellings.

D

dais, podium, lectern, *n.* A *dais* is a large raised platform where special guests are seated during a formal dinner. Such a platform may also be called a *podium*.

Podium, more commonly, indicates the platform on which the conductor of an orchestra stands or from which someone delivers a speech or lecture to a group of listeners. Pluralize the word normally (*podiums*) or, if you prefer the Latin form, *podia*.

A *lectern*, on the other hand, is a speaker's stand with a slanted top for a lecturer's or teacher's notes, books, or other paraphernalia.

damp, dampen, *v.* Either verb means *make damp: damp* (or *dampen*) *the shirt before ironing it.* Only *dampen* means *become damp: the air will dampen as the humidity rises.*

dare, *v.* *Dare* is used with a singular subject in constructions like *how* *dare* *she do that?; he dare not disturb her.*

Otherwise a singular subject is followed by *dares: anyone who dares enter; he dares his friend to enter;* etc.

Archaic past tense: durst; modern form: *dared.*

dash, hyphen, *n.* A *dash* (–) is longer than a *hyphen*.

The *hyphen* (-), not the *dash*, indicates that a word continues on the next line of writing, typing, or print.

data *Data* is a plural noun; the singular form is *datum*— *one* fact or piece of information.

Strictly, then, one should say or write *the data are; these data do not prove;* etc.

In current usage, however, this distinction is not always observed; you will often see *data is, data has, this data,* etc. in newspapers, magazines, and books. (Scientific writing, on the other hand, usually treats *data* as a plural.)

Language changes, and the concept of *data* as a *list* or *collection* of facts, hence singular, is becoming more and more prevalent.

See also CANDELABRA, CANDELABRUM; INSIGNIA; MEDIA; NOUN, 6Q.

date Despite pedantic objections, *date (n.)* is common in speech and writing to mean *an appointment to meet* or *someone of the opposite sex with whom one goes out; date (v.)* is likewise frequently used to mean *see* (a member of the opposite sex) *on a regular basis*, usually with romantic intentions.

daughter-in-law, *n.* See IN-LAWS.

DAY, DAY-

These compounds are written solid:

daybook	dayfly	daystar
daybreak	daylight	daytime
daydream	daylong	daywork

These compounds are written as separate words:

day bed	day in court	day nursery
day coach	day laborer	day school

Day-to-day, as an adjective, is hyphenated, as is *daylight-savings time*.

---

day's pay See STONE'S THROW.

de-, *prefix* When adding this prefix, hyphenate if the word starts with the letter *e*: *de-electrify, de-emulsify, de-emphasize, de-escalate.* Otherwise, write solid: *desegregate, deplane, deregulate.*

deadly, deathly, *adj.* Meaning *causing death*, the adjectives are interchangeable, but the former is in more common use. Meaning *like death* (*deathly* pallor), the second adjective is the correct word.

deal, *v.* *Dealt* is both the past tense and the participle: *she dealt; she has dealt.*

Dear . . . , My dear . . . As a salutation in a letter, *My dear* (plus a person's name) is more formal.

deathly, *adj.* See DEADLY, DEATHLY.

debut, *v.* Many authorities reject the use of *debut* as a verb. However, since it appears frequently in publicity handouts, ads, newspapers, and magazines, it must certainly be considered acceptable in informal English.

decimate, *v.* See DESTROY, DEMOLISH, DECIMATE.

decry, descry, *v.* Both verbs are used more in formal writing than in everyday speech, and though similar in appearance, are totally unrelated in meaning.

To *decry* is to denounce strongly (i.e., to cry down): *decried* his brutality. Noun: *decrial.*

To **descry** is to *catch sight of*, usually from a distance, or *to discover*, especially after careful examination: *descried the ship nearing the horizon*. There is no derived noun form of *descry*.

deductive, inductive *(reasoning, learning, teaching, etc.)*— **Deductive** reasoning, etc. draws conclusions, from general principles, about specific items governed by these principles. *Verb:* **deduce.** *Noun:* **deduction.**

Inductive reasoning, etc. considers specific items to arrive at a general principle. *Verb:* **induce.** *Noun:* **induction.**

deer, *n.* For plural, see NOUN, 6J.

defalcation, *n.* See THIEVERY.

defeatist, futilitarian, *adj.* A **defeatist** attitude permits one to accept defeat, failure, etc. without any attempt to change circumstances or conditions.

A **futilitarian** attitude expresses the feeling that all life is futile, so why bother?

The words are certainly similar in connotation, though differing in denotation.

Each word may also be used as a noun to designate a person.

defect, deficiency, *n.* A **defect** is a flaw, fault, or imperfection, as in the structure or design of a thing or in the character or personality of a person.

A **deficiency** refers to a lower degree, amount, or quality than is expected or desired.

deference, deferment, deferral, *n.* The verb *defer* has two unrelated meanings:

1. *yield, out of courtesy, respect, acknowledgment of superiority, greater knowledge*, etc. With this meaning, the verb is followed by *to*: **defer** *to the senator from Illinois;* **defer** *to your greater experience in such matters.*

The noun derived from this meaning of the verb is **deference**: *out of* **deference** *to her parents' wishes; your* **deference** *to his demands is understandable.* The adjective form is **deferential.**

2. *put off to a later time; postpone.* In this instance the noun form is either **deferment** or **deferral.**

deficiency, *n.* See DEFECT, DEFICIENCY.

definite, definitive, *adj.* Something (or someone) **definite** is clear, certain, explicit, etc.: **definite** *limits* (*answer,* etc.).

Something **definitive**, on the other hand, is either:

1. *so far the most complete and most accurate: the* **definitive** *history of the fall of Rome;* or

2. *so authoritative and final as to allow no change or*

*appeal: **definitive** decision by the U.S. Supreme Court.*

deism, *n.* See THEISM, MONOTHEISM, POLYTHEISM, PANTHEISM, DEISM.

delegate-at-large, *n.* For plural, see NOUN, 6U.

delight, *v.* Meaning *get pleasure or joy from,* **delight** is usually followed by *in* plus a noun or the *-ING* form of a verb: *delights in gourmet foods; delights in eating at gourmet restaurants.* Less frequently, it is followed by an infinitive: *delights to eat at . . .*

delighted, *adj.* Followed by *at, with,* or *by* in reference to a fact, occurrence, etc.: *delighted at (with, by) the change of weather;* followed by *with* in reference to a person or animal: *delighted with the child.*

delirium, *n.* For plural, see NOUN, 6Q.

deliverance, delivery, *n.* *Deliverance* is specifically *a setting free or rescuing (or the fact or state of being set free or rescued) from slavery, imprisonment, danger,* etc. This noun should not be confused with *delivery,* which has a number of related meanings having to do with giving, sending, etc.: *delivery of the message (speech, furniture,* etc.).

The verb for either noun is *deliver.* In the sense of *rescuing* or *setting free,* **deliver** is followed by the preposition *from: deliver us from bondage; was delivered from peril;* etc.

delusion, illusion, *n.* A *delusion* is a false belief, firmly held despite all objective evidence to the contrary: *delusions of grandeur; delusion that she was a Russian empress.* (*Delusion* is the noun form of the verb *delude—to deceive, fool, trick,* etc.)

An *illusion* is either an erroneous perception of what has objective existence (*illusion of depth; optical illusion;* etc.), or a misapprehension or misimpression, usually based on what one wishes or expects (*illusion that she would marry him; an illusion that she would win the election; illusions about her friend's integrity;* etc.).

demi- See SEMI-, DEMI-, HEMI-.

demolish, *v.* See DESTROY, DEMOLISH, DECIMATE.

denotation, connotation, *n.* The *denotation* is the actual, explicit, or literal meaning of a word or phrase. *Motherly,* for example, *denotes* like, pertaining to, descriptive of, etc. *a mother,* but *connotes* warm, affectionate, tender, protective, etc.

So the *connotation* is the *implied* meaning or *emotional flavor* of a word or phrase.

deprecate, depreciate, v. In the sense of *belittling, disparaging,* or *putting down,* these verbs are interchangeable, despite some pedantic objections. They are often used reflexively: *self-deprecate* or *self-depreciate.*

Deprecate may also mean *show* or *express disapproval of. Depreciate* also means *make,* or *become, lower in price or value: her portfolio of bonds depreciated.*

descend, v. See CLIMB DOWN.

descry, v. See DECRY, DESCRY.

desert, dessert *Desert,* the verb, is pronounced də-ZURT'.

Desert, the noun (note the single s), is a more or less barren region *(the Sahara Desert).* Pronounced DEZ'-ərt.

Deserts, the plural noun *(punishment or retribution that is well deserved),* occurs mainly in the cliché *just deserts.* Pronounced də-ZURTS'.

Dessert, a noun (note the double s), is a sweet (ice cream, pie, etc.) at the end of a meal. Pronounced də-ZURT'.

desideratum, n. For plural, see NOUN, 6Q.

desirable, desirous, adj. *Desirable* describes that which, or one who, is worth having, getting, achieving, desiring, etc.: *a desirable goal.*

Desirous, followed by *of,* describes a person who has a desire, need, wish, aim, etc.: *desirous of attaining her goal.*

despair, desperation, n. *Despair* is *lack of all hope: in despair of ever finding love.* The verb is also followed by *of: despaired of finding love.*

Desperation suggests foolish, reckless, or wild action as the result of complete loss of hope: *in desperation, he committed suicide; committed suicide out of desperation.* (Note that *desperation* may be preceded by *in* or *out of.)* *Adjective: desperate.*

despatch See DISPATCH, DESPATCH.

dessert See DESERT, DESSERT.

destined, fated, adj. As indicated in the next entry, *destined* usually has a pleasant, *fated* an unpleasant, connotation.

destiny, fate, n. The words are synonymous, but *destiny* is usually pleasant in connotation, *fate* unpleasant.

destroy, demolish, decimate, v. *Destroy* and *demolish* are synonymous, but *demolish* may also mean *destroy by smashing to pieces,* as when a wrecking ball *demolishes* a building. When the verb has this specific meaning, the noun form is *demolition;* otherwise the noun form is *demolishment.*

Destroy completely and *demolish completely* are redundancies, for *destruction* and *demolishment* (or *demolition)* are by definition complete.

To *decimate*, on the other hand, does not indicate completeness, but rather means to *destroy* (or *kill*) a great portion of: *the Black Plague decimated the population of England; the hurricane decimated the structures along the coast.*

So *to decimate completely* would be a contradiction.

destruct, *v.* See ENTHUSE.

DETERMINER

1. Determiners, in Structural Grammar, include all the words that, in traditional grammar, are called *articles (a, an, the)*, *possessive adjectives (my, his, her, its, our, your, their, whose)*, *demonstrative adjectives (this, that, these, those)*, *distributive adjectives (each, every)*, plus many similar words, including *cardinal numbers (one, two, three)* and *ordinal numbers (first, second, third)*.

2. Determiners precede nouns but, unlike adjectives, do not fit into the adjective pattern (see ADJECTIVE, 1) and, with a very few exceptions, do not have comparative and superlative inflections.

3. One or more determiners may precede a noun: *every book; my many other books.*

4. Adjectives are often found between determiners and nouns: *his large inheritance; many interesting people.* DETERMINER + ADJECTIVE(S) + NOUN is a common pattern in English and constitutes a *noun phrase.*

5. If a determiner is found in a sentence *without* its understood noun, such a determiner functions as a pronoun: *both* (det.) *books are missing; both* (pron.) *are missing.*

6. Here is a list of commonly used determiners:

one, two, *etc.*	few, fewer, fewest
first, second, *etc.*	other
a, an	some
the	all
this, that, these, those	many, more, most
either, neither	such
my, his, her, *etc.*	less, lesser, least
each, every	much
enough	several
no	both
	same

device, devise *Device* (də-VĪS') is a noun: *an unusual device.*

Devise (də-VĪZ') is a verb: *devised a new way.*

(However, *devise* is a noun in legal terminology, referring to real property bequeathed to another or others in a will; or a will, or clause in a will, bequeathing such property.)

devout, pious, *adj.* *Devout* people are most sincere in their devotion to a religion, cause, belief, etc.

Pious describes those who practice strict adherence to the doctrines of a religion. The word is sometimes used derogatively to connote hypocritical practices.

See also RELIGIOSITY, RELIGIOUSNESS, RELIGIONISM.

dexterous, adroit, ambidextrous, *adj.* *Dexterous* and *adroit* both mean *skillful*. *Dexterous* often refers to manual skill *(a dexterous surgeon)*, while *adroit* more often refers to skill involving mental processes *(adroit debater; adroitly parried the questions).*

Ambidextrous indicates equal skill in both the right and left hands.

diagnosis, prognosis, *n.* In reference to illness, a *diagnosis* is the conclusion reached by a doctor as to the nature of a patient's affliction; a *prognosis* is the doctor's prediction as to the outcome of the patient's disease, whether or when the patient will recover, etc.

dialogue, duologue, *n.* A *dialogue* is a conversation between *two or more* people, as in a play, movie, or real life.

A *duologue* is a conversation between *only two* people, especially in a play or movie. *Duologue*, not a commonly used word, stresses that only two people are talking.

dialysis, *n.* For plural, see NOUN, 6N.

dialyze, *v.* See -YZE.

dice, *n.* This is the plural form of *die*, one of the pair of cubes used in the game of craps or some other game of chance. The game itself may also be called *dice* and is then considered a singular: *dice is a game of luck rather than skill; let's play dice.* See also CRAPS; DIE.

diction, enunciation, *n.* These words are often used synonymously; strictly, however, *diction* refers to the choice and use of words in speech or writing, while *enunciation* stresses the sounds made in speaking or singing.

dictum, *n.* For plural form, see NOUN, 6Q.

didactic, *adj.* See PEDANTIC, DIDACTIC, PURISTIC, PEDAGOGICAL, PEDAGOGUISH.

dido, *n.* For plural see NOUN, 6L2.

die, *n.* As one of the cubes used in craps and other games of chance, the plural is *dice.* In other contexts, the plural is *dies.*

dieing See DYING, DYEING, DIEING.

die of, die from One *dies of* (or *as a result of*), not *from,* a disease, heart failure, etc.

dieresis, *n.* For plural, see NOUN, 6N.

dietetics, *n.* See -ICS.

dietitian, dietician, *n.* Both spellings are correct; the former is more commonly used.

differ from, differ with Things or people *differ from* one another when they are unlike. People *differ with* one another when they disagree.

different than, different from, different to In formal usage, *from* is the preferable preposition following *different* (*different from yesterday's report*); *different than* is widely used but frowned upon by some authorities; *different to* is British English.

dilation, dilatation, *n.* Both words are noun forms of the verb *dilate; dilatation,* however, is chiefly used in medical terminology.

dilettante, *n.* For plural form, see NOUN, 6L5.

diminishment, diminution, *n.* Either word is the noun form of the verb *diminish.*

dinghy, dingey, dingy, *n.* Three spellings of the word for a small boat, pronounced DING'-ee or DING'-gee. If the *-ey* spelling is used, the plural ends in *-eys;* otherwise, *-ies.*

Dingy, pronounced DIN'-jee, is also an adjective meaning *shabby, grimy,* etc.

direct object See SENTENCE PATTERNS

directly, *adv.* See PRESENTLY, DIRECTLY, SOON.

disassociate, dissociate, *v.* These verbs may be used interchangeably. The latter is more common; both are correct.

disc, *n.* See DISK, DISC.

discomfit, discomfort, *v.* To *discomfit* is *to frustrate, confuse, make uneasy, embarrass.* Noun: *discomfiture.*

To **Discomfort** is *to make uncomfortable in any general sense,* and is much milder in connotation than *discomfit.* The words are not exact synonyms.

discreet, discrete, *adj.* **Discreet**: *careful in what one says or does, especially in avoiding dangerous situations or the exposure of another's confidences.* Noun: *discretion, discreetness.*

Discrete: *separate, unconnected.* Noun: *discreteness.*

disect, *v.* See DISSECT, DISECT.

disenfranchise, disfranchise, *v.* These verbs are identical in meaning and use; the latter form is more common.

diseuse, *n.* See NOUN, 2C.

dishful, *n.* For plural, see -FUL, -FULS.

disinterested, uninterested, *adj. Disinterested* means *objective, neutral, impartial, unbiased*—i.e., not personally involved and therefore capable of being fair. *Noun: disinterest.*

    Uninterested, obviously, is simply *not interested, indifferent, bored.*

    Authorities frown on the use of *disinterested* to mean *indifferent.*

disk, disc, *n. Disc* is chiefly used to mean *a phonograph record; an internal anatomical part;* or *a blade on a disc harrow.* Otherwise the preferable spelling is *disk.*

disorient, disorientate, *v.* The former is much the preferable word; *disorientate* is a variant form. See also: ORIENT, ORIENTATE.

dispatch, despatch, *n. and v. Dispatch* is the preferable spelling.

dispute, disputation, *n. Dispute* is an argument, quarrel, controversy, etc. One who argues, quarrels, etc. is a *disputer.*

    Disputation is the art of debate or discussion. One who engages in the art of debate or discussion is a *disputant.*

    Though *disputation* is occasionally used as a synonym of *dispute,* the distinction between the two words is worth preserving.

disremember, *v.* See MISREMEMBER, DISREMEMBER.

dissatisfied, unsatisfied, *adj.* One who is *dissatisfied* is displeased, unhappy, etc. One who is *unsatisfied* has not yet received enough, wants or needs more, etc.

dissect, disect, *v.* The latter is a misspelling.

dissociate, *v.* See DISASSOCIATE, DISSOCIATE.

distrust, mistrust, *v.* These words, as well as their adjective derivatives (*distrustful, mistrustful*), may be used interchangeably.

dived, dove, *v. Dived* is the preferable past tense of *dive (v).* The participle is *dived (has dived).*

divers, diverse, *adj. Divers* (DI-vərz) means *various, sundry, several: divers causes (relationships,* etc.).

    Things or people *diverse* (də-VURS') *from* one another are distinctly different or separate.

    A *diverse* supply, accumulation, etc. is made up of various different kinds—i.e., *diversified* or *varied.*

divertimento, *n.* For plural form, see NOUN, 6L4.

divorcé, divorcée, divorcee, *n.* With the French accent, a *divorcé* (də-vôr-SAY') is a divorced male, *divorcée* (də-vôr-SAY') a divorced female. Without the accent (and this is the most commonly used term), a *divorcee* (də-vôr-SEÉ, də-vôr-SAY', də-VÔR'-see, or də-VÔR'-say), refers to either sex.

dock, *n.* See PIER, DOCK, MARINA, QUAY, WHARF.

doddering, dottering, *adj.* The latter word is a misspelling.

doe, *n.* See NOUN, 2D.

doesn't, don't *Doesn't* is used with a singular subject: *he* (*she, it, a book,* etc) *doesn't. Don't* is used with the pronoun *you* or *I* or a plural subject: *you* (*I, they, the people,* etc.) *don't.*

dogma, *n.* The plural is either *dogmas* or *dogmata*; the former is more commonly used.

dogmatic, *adj.* See ARBITRARY, DOGMATIC.

dominate, domineer, *v.* To *dominate* is *to exercise one's power over: dominated her husband.*

To *domineer* (over) is *to exercise such power harshly or tyranically.*

don't, doesn't See DOESN'T, DON'T.

don't let's Nonstandard usage when *let's not* is meant.

dormant, latent, potential, *adj. Dormant* abilities, powers, talents, etc. are those that are slumbering, as it were, and have not yet been awakened for use. *Noun: dormancy.*

Latent abilities, powers, talents, etc. exist but are hidden and await discovery or development. *Noun: latency.*

Potential abilities, powers, talents, etc. are in a rudimentary state awaiting full development. *Noun: potentiality.*

Obviously, these adjectives are more or less synonymous; the distinctions are rather fine.

dottering, *adj.* See DODDERING, DOTTERING.

DOUBLE NEGATIVE

Grammatical term for the incorrect use of *two* negative words for a negative meaning. Here are some typical examples, with the correct use in parentheses:

can't hardly   *(can hardly)*
can't barely   *(can barely)*

won't never	(will never)
didn't do nothing	(didn't do anything or did nothing)
didn't see no one	(didn't see anyone or saw no one)
wasn't nowhere	(wasn't anywhere or was nowhere)

DOUBT

Many constructions are possible with *doubt* as either a noun or a verb:

There is some *doubt* that . . .	(It is not certain . . .)
We *doubt* that . . .	(We do not expect . . .)
We *doubt* whether . . .	(We're not sure . . .)
We *doubt* if . . .	(We're not sure . . .)

[*Doubt if* is less acceptable than *doubt whether*.]

In negative constructions:

There is no *doubt* that . . .	(It is fairly certain . . .)
I do not *doubt* that . . .	(I am fairly certain . . .)
There is no *doubt* but that . . .	(It is fairly certain . . .)
I do not *doubt* but that . . .	(I am fairly certain . . .)

The same comments apply to constructions with the adjective *doubtful*.

There is no doubt but what, and *I do not doubt but what* are nonstandard usages.

---

doubtless, no doubt, *adj.* As adverbs, these words express somewhat less assurance or certainty than *indubitably*, *undoubtedly*, or *without doubt*, and are thus close in meaning to *probably* or *in all likelihood*.

douse, dowse, *v.* To *douse* is *to plunge* (someone or something) *into water*, or *to make or become thoroughly wet*.

To *dowse* is *to use a divining rod in search of under-* ground water or minerals. *Dowse* may also be spelled *douse*, but this is a variant form and infrequently used.

dove, *v.* See DIVED, DOVE.

downward, downwards See -WARD, -WARDS.

dozen, dozens *Dozen* is both the singular and plural form in the sense of: *a dozen* rolls (i.e., twelve; *five dozen* eggs (i.e., sixty).

But *dozens* is the plural form in the sense of *a large*

but indeterminate number: *dozens* of customers; many *dozens* of people; *dozens* responded to our ad.

draft, draught, *n.* The latter is the British spelling.

dramatics, *n.* This noun is singular when it refers to the art of the theater, acting, etc.: *Dramatics was his chosen career.* It is plural when it means *dramatic* or *emotional behavior: your dramatics do not impress me.* See also -ICS.

draught, *n.* See DRAFT, DRAUGHT.

dread, *adj.* A somewhat literary or poetic form of *dreadful* in the sense of *fearsome, terrifying,* etc.: *dread diseases of ancient times.*

dream, *v.* Past tense or participle is *dreamed* or *dreamt: I dreamed, I dreamt; I have dreamed, I have dreamt.*

drink, *v.* Past tense is *drank.* The participle is *drunk: we have drunk.*

drive, *v.* Past tense is *drove.* The participle is *driven: has driven.*

drought, drouth, *n.* Both words are correct, but the latter is seldom used in formal English.

drown, *v.* The past tense and the participle are *drowned,* not *drownded.*

druggist, pharmacist, *n. Pharmacist* is the official

word, as is *pharmacy* (as opposed to *drug store*). But *druggist* and *drug store* are fully acceptable terms.

drugs, pharmaceuticals, *n. pl. Pharmaceuticals* is the official word to mean *the medications and drugs dispensed by a pharmacist.*

drunk, drunken *Drunk* is both the participle of the verb *drink* and an adjective (*they were very drunk*). *Drunken* is the adjective used before a noun: *a drunken bum; a drunken driver.* However, the terms *drunk driver* and *drunk driving* are today so commonly used as to be fully acceptable.

duad, *n.* See DUO, DUET, DUAD, DYAD.

duck, *n.* See NOUN, 2D.

due to In careful usage, *due to* is used only after a form of the verb *to be: the accident was due to carelessness,* etc.

  Due to the late hour, we will have to leave, or *due to the carelessness of the driver, the bus skidded off the road,* is, for no truly logical reason, unacceptable in formal writing. Preferable usage: *owing to, because of,* or *on account of.*

duet, *n.* See DUO, DUET, DUAD, DYAD.

dumfound, dumbfound, *v.* Both spellings are correct.

duo, duet, duad, dyad, twain,

n. Two people who act, appear, do something, etc. together, or have some connection or relationship, may be called, in general, a *couple*, a *pair*, a *twosome*, or a *duo*.

A *duo* may also signify the two performers of a musical *duet*.

A *duet* may be either a musical composition for two performers, or the two performers of such a composition.

Duad is the less common term for either *couple* or *pair*.

Two people who interact in a psychological or sociological group are a *dyad*: *the leader asked the group to break into dyads to discuss the problem.*

Twain is the poetic or archaic word for *two*: *"never the twain shall meet."*

duologue, *n.* See DIALOGUE, DUOLOGUE.

durst, *v.* See DARE.

dwarf, midget, *n.* In reference to persons, a *dwarf* is not only much smaller than average but also may be misshapen. *Plural*: **dwarfs** or **dwarves**.

A *midget*, on the other hand, is a normally formed human, but is unusually small. *Midgets* prefer to be called "little people."

dwell, *v. Past tense* or *participle*: **dwelt** or **dwelled**.

dyad, *n.* See DUO, DUET, DUAD, DYAD.

dying, dyeing, dieing These are -ING forms of different verbs. *Dying*, of course, comes from the verb *die*—i.e., lose one's life.

Dyeing is from the verb *dye*—i.e., color with *dye*. Other forms of the verb *dye* are *dyes, dyed.*

Dieing is from the verb *die*—i.e., to stamp out with a die or master pattern. Other forms are *dies* and *died.*

All three -ING forms are pronounced identically.

E

each, each one As a pronoun, *each* means *each one* and is singular: *each* of the *prisoners has been searched.* In the example cited, *each* is the subject of the verb phrase *has been searched*—*prisoners* is the object of the preposition *of.*

Each may also be used as a determiner, and of course is followed by a singular noun: *each woman; each person;* etc. A problem then arises: do we say *each person took his seat? his or her seat? their seat?* Strict rules require either *his, her,* or *his or her.*

Each one is obviously singular also. So strictly correct usage requires *each one was on time; each one took his, her,* or *his or her seat.*

For a further discussion of this problem, see ANYBODY.

each other, one another Some authorities and writers make a distinction between the two, using *each other* when referring to two people, *one another* when referring to more than two. In current usage, however, the terms are interchangeable.

each side, either side The distinction here is a matter of clarity rather than grammar. *On each side,* logically and obviously, means *on every side. On either side* means on one side or the other and implies that there are only two sides. So *His bodyguards walked on either side of the gangster* says, but perhaps was not intended to mean, that the bodyguards protected the gangster on only *one* of his two sides, an unlikely situation.

To be absolutely clear, use *both sides* if that is what you mean.

eager, anxious, *adj.* See ANXIOUS, EAGER.

East, east; Eastern, eastern Capitalize *East* or *Eastern* if the word is part of the official name: *East Indies, East Berlin, Eastern Orthodox Church,* etc. Use lowercase *e* for direction: *traveling east; an eastern wind.*

The *East* (capital *E*) refers to the eastern part of the United States, or to Asiatic areas as opposed to Europe and countries in the Western Hemisphere (i.e., the West).

Capitalize the initial *E* of *Eastern* if the word refers to the Asiatic area or to the Orient: *Eastern customs (philosophy,* etc.).

See also NORTH, SOUTH, WEST.

eastward, eastwards. See -WARD, -WARDS.

eatable See EDIBLE, EATABLE.

eaves, *n. pl.* This is a plural noun for which a singular form does not exist: *the eaves are in need of repair.*

economic, economical, *adj.* *Economic* refers to the economy, to economics, money management, etc.: *economic downturn; economic philosophy; economic problems.*

Economical means *thrifty, sparing, frugal,* etc. (Rarely, though not incorrectly, this form of the adjective is used to refer to economics or the economy.)

economics, *n.* Use this word as a singular: *economics is a dreary subject; economics is taught by Professor Howard.* See also -ICS.

edible, eatable Whether noun or adjective, the words are interchangeable. *Edible* is the more popular form.

editor in chief, *n.* The plural form is *editors in chief.* The term is preferably written without hyphens. See also NOUN, 6U.

editress, *n.* See NOUN, 5A.

effect, affect See AFFECT, EFFECT.

effluvium, *n.* For plural, see NOUN, 6Q.

e.g., i.e. These are abbreviations of Latin phrases: *e.g.* *(exempli gratia)* means *for example; i.e. (id est)* means *that is.*

egoism, egotism, egocentricity, egomania, *n.* Though *egoism* and *egotism* are sometimes used interchangeably, there is a distinction observed by careful writers and speakers, namely:

Egoism is the quality of thinking only of one's own needs, desires, etc., without taking into consideration the needs or desires of others—in short, a philosophy of extreme selfishness or "me first."

Egotism is the tendency to boast about oneself, one's abilities, achievements, etc. —in short, *conceit* or *self-aggrandizement.* ("I love myself, I think I'm great. . . .")

Egocentricity (or *egocentrism*) is self-centeredness, a viewing of the world only as it relates to oneself.

Egomania is a pathological and obsessive concern with oneself—it is the extreme form of *egocentricity.*

EITHER OF, NEITHER OF (plus verb)

Either and *neither*, when followed by *of*, are *singular pronouns* and mean, respectively, *either one* and *neither one.*

As grammatical subjects, therefore, they require a verb or auxiliary in the S-FORM (called *singular verbs* in traditional grammar).

Check the correct verb form in these sentences:

1. *(Has, Have)* either of your friends arrived?
2. Neither of the two projects *(was, were)* finished on time.
3. Neither of the two applicants *(is, are)* fully qualified.
4. *(Does, Do)* either of my suggestions meet with your approval?
5. Neither of her parents *(wishes, wish)* to attend the P.T.A. meeting.
6. Neither of them *(is, are)* available.

KEY: 1. *Has;* 2. *was;* 3. *is;* 4. *Does;* 5. *wishes;* 6. *is.*

EITHER ... OR, NEITHER ... NOR

These are *correlative conjunctions.* When they join the subjects of a verb, the subject *closer* to the verb governs the verb form.

Check the correct verb form in these sentences:

1. Either a pen or a pencil *(is, are)* necessary.
2. Neither money nor fame *(was, were)* available to her.
3. Either her aunt or her sisters *(is, are)* willing to help you.
4. Neither the staff members nor the president, *(has, have)* arrived.
5. Neither he nor I *(is, are, am)* ready.
6. Neither she nor her children *(has, have)* ever spent much time with me.
7. Neither they nor she *(is, are)* willing to help.
8. *(Is, Are)* either the president or his secretaries available?

KEY: 1. *is;* 2. *was;* 3. *are;* 4. *has;* 5. *am;* 6. *have;* 7. *is;* 8. *is.*

The agreement of the verb form with the closer subject may result in awkwardness of style. If so, recast your sentence. For example, sentence 5 may be rephrased as *He is not ready, and neither am I;* sentence 7: *They are not willing to help, and neither is she.*

See also SUBJECT, VERB AGREEMENT, 4.

---

either side See EACH SIDE, EITHER SIDE.

elder, eldest/older, oldest As an adjective describing a person, the words are inter-changeable: *her elder* (or *older*) *brother; his eldest* (or *oldest*) *sister.*

Elder and *eldest* describe persons only: *the older animal; the oldest of all trees.*

Elder (*adj.*) may also indicate seniority in a group: *an elder statesman; one of the elder members of the committee.*

Used as a noun, *elder* may refer also to an ancestor, or to an older and influential member of a community, church, or other organization. See also COMPARISON.

elderly, old, aged These words may show one's subjective attitude toward advancing years. If you use *elderly*, you suggest that one is getting on in years, but not yet *old*. *Old*, then, is older than *elderly*, and *aged* is very old. Call people *aged* (AY'-jəd) and you imply that they have not only lost the vigor of youth but may be laboring under the so-called handicaps of old age. (No mental infirmities are suggested by any of these words.) Possibly, *elderly* is used by some speakers or writers to soften the blow of the word *old*. With the increase in longevity, some persons may be called *elderly* in their seventies, *old* in their eighties, and *very old* (or *aged*) in their nineties or beyond. (Lately *senior citizen* has come into vogue as a catch-all term for anyone over sixty.)

Electra complex See OEDIPUS COMPLEX, ELECTRA COMPLEX.

electrolyze, *v.* See -YZE.

electronics, *n.* See -ICS.

ellipsis, *n.* For plural, see NOUN, 6N.

else Following a pronoun (*anyone else, someone else,* etc.), the possessive is formed by adding *'s* to *else* (*anyone else's, someone else's,* etc.).

In the case of *who else,* you have a choice: *who else's* or *whose else.* The former construction is more popular.

elsewhere, elsewheres, *adv.* See -WHERE, -WHERES.

emasculate, *v.* See CASTRATE, GELD, ALTER, FIX, CAPONIZE, EMASCULATE, SPAY.

embargo, *n.* For plural, see NOUN, 6L1.

embezzlement, *n.* See THIEVERY.

embryo, *n.* See FETUS, EMBRYO. For plural, see NOUN, 6K.

emigrate, *v.* See IMMIGRATE, EMIGRATE.

émigré, *n.* See IMMIGRATE, EMIGRATE.

eminent, *adj.* See IMMINENT, IMMANENT, EMINENT.

emote, *v.* See ENTHUSE.

empathize, sympathize, *v.* When you *empathize* with

someone, you not only share that person's feeling or feelings, but identify so completely with him or her that you experience the feeling or feelings yourself. It's as if you were that person for the time being.

Sympathize with another, and you accept and understand that person's feelings, but without the identification connoted by *empathize*.

emporium, *n.* For plural form, see NOUN, 6Q.

enamored of, enamored with Either preposition may be used.

encephalon, *n.* For plural, see NOUN, 6R.

enchantress, *n.* See NOUN, 2C.

enclave, *n.* See EXCLAVE, ENCLAVE.

enclose, inclose, *v.* The former is the more common spelling; both are correct.

enclude, include, *v.* *Include* is the correct spelling.

encomium, *n.* For plural, see NOUN, 6Q.

end, culminate, *v.* When something *culminates*, it reaches a climax or its highest point—it does not necessarily *end*: *Her appointment as president of the corporation was the* culmination *of her career.*

Culminate is followed by

the preposition *in*, and may be used informally as a synonym of the verb *result*: *culminated in disaster.*

end (v.), **end** (v.) **up** *End up* is at best colloquial or very informal. It is better usage to omit *up.*

endemic, epidemic, pandemic In reference to diseases, the distinction is as follows:

An *endemic* disease occurs over a protracted period in a particular, usually restricted, region: *pellagra was once endemic in some parts of the South.*

An *epidemic* disease is generally contagious, spreads quickly, and afflicts large numbers of people or animals.

A *pandemic* disease is an *epidemic* disease that has spread over a wide area, an entire country, or most of the world.

All three words are both adjectives and nouns.

endorse, indorse, *v.* *Indorse* is the variant spelling.

energize, *v.* See ENERVATE, INNERVATE, ENERGIZE.

enervate, innervate, energize, *v.* To *enervate* (EN'-ər-vayt') is *to leave totally exhausted, mentally and physically.* (The derivation is Latin *enervis*, "nerveless, weak.") It is quite the opposite of *energize*: *to give vigor, strength, or energy to.* *Innervate* (ə-NUR'-vayt') is a medical term, meaning *to stimulate* (a nerve, muscle, etc.).

engage, *v.* Meaning *to be active, busy, occupied* or *involved,* or *to take part,* the verb in any form is followed by the preposition *in: engaged in a lengthy investigation.*

Meaning *to set forth, get started on,* etc. the verb is followed by *upon,* or less frequently, *on: engaged upon a new and difficult project.*

Meaning *to agree* or *promise,* the verb is followed by an infinitive: *He engaged to cooperate with the committee.*

enhance, *v.* See AUGMENT, ENHANCE.

enormity, enormousness, *n.* *Enormity* is best restricted to the meaning of *outrageousness, heinousness, wickedness,* etc.: *the enormity of the insult* (*crime,* etc.). If you wish to indicate a very large size or amount, vastness of area, etc., *enormousness* is the preferable word to use. See also MONSTER, MONSTROUS.

enquire, inquire, *v.* See INQUIRE, ENQUIRE.

en route Write always as two words.

ensue, follow, *v.* Many writers insist that *ensue* means *follow immediately* or *as a direct result.* The distinction may be worth preserving.

ensure, *v.* See ASSURE, ENSURE, INSURE.

enthuse, *v.* This verb is a so-called back-formation from the noun *enthusiasm,,* and is not acceptable in formal speech or writing.

Similarly, the verbs *burgle, butle, emote,* and *opine*—back-formations from *burglar, butler, emotion,* and *opinion* —are also nonstandard and are generally used only for humorous effect.

To *destruct* and to *self-destruct* (i.e., to automatically destroy itself) have become established and acceptable American idioms.

Locomote (*v.*), on the other hand, is considered a nonword.

The verbs *sculpt* and *sculp,* however, are acceptable, though some writers prefer the verb *sculpture.*

entrée, entree, entry, *n.* The first two words (you may, or need not, use the French accent) are pronounced AHN'-tray. All three words are interchangeable in the sense of *physically entering* or *permission* or *right to enter.* **Entrée** (or *entree*) has an added figurative meaning of *having access (to): would like to gain entrée to the inner circle of power; finally possessed entrée to the presidential advisers.*

Of course, the main dish of a meal is also called the *entrée* or *entree.*

entrust, intrust, *v.* *Entrust* is the more popular spelling.

entry, *n.* See ENTRÉE, ENTREE, ENTRY.

enunciation, *n.* See DICTION, ENUNCIATION.

enure, *v.* See INURE, ENURE.

envious, jealous, *adj.* In the sense of *wishing to have what another possesses,* **envious** and **jealous** are synonymous —**jealous** is perhaps the stronger word, often implying some resentment.

Jealous may also mean *determined to keep or guard what one has: a jealous husband; jealous of her good reputation, she would do nothing to tarnish it.*

epicure, epicurean, *n.* See CONNOISSEUR, EPICURE, EPICUREAN, GOURMET, GOURMAND.

epidemic See ENDEMIC, EPIDEMIC, PANDEMIC.

epilogue, prologue, *n.* An *epilogue follows* the end of a novel or play; a *prologue precedes* the start of a novel, play, or poem.

epithet, *n.* Though **epithet** has the general meaning of *any term used to characterize a person or a place* (e.g., *Richard the Lionhearted*), the word is mostly used today to mean a derogatory or disparaging term (e.g., *dope, idiot, loudmouth*).

equal, more equal Certain adjectives do not, logically and strictly, have degrees—for example *equal, circular, fatal, square, perfect, unique, round, even.* That is, things

are either *equal* or *unequal, perfect* or *imperfect, even* or *uneven,* etc.

So, to call things or people *more equal* or *less equal, more perfect* or *less perfect,* etc. contradicts the definitions of such words.

To avoid illogicality, especially in formal speech or writing, use phrases like *more nearly equal, more nearly unique, less than equal, less than perfect,* etc.

equally, equally as *Equally as* is considered nonstandard style; say or write *they are* **equally** *valuable, not equally as valuable,* etc.

In other comparisons, use *as,* not *equally as*—i.e., *she runs as fast as I,* not *she runs equally as fast as I.*

equestrienne, *n.* See NOUN, 2C.

equilibrium, *n.* For plural, see NOUN, 6Q.

equivocal, *adj.* See AMBIGUOUS, EQUIVOCAL, EQUIVOCABLE.

-er, -re Many words that we spell with terminal *-er* end in *-re* in British English. These are some typical words, with the British spelling in parentheses: *caliber (calibre); center (centre); meter (metre); theater (theatre).*

After a *c,* however, the *-re* ending is required: *acre, lucre, massacre, mediocre, nacre,* etc.

Ogre is the correct and only spelling of this word.

See also -OR, -OUR.

erratum, *n.* For plural, see NOUN, 6Q.

escape You *escape (v.)* or *make an escape (n.) from* a place of confinement or imprisonment; you *escape* danger, pursuit, punishment, the consequences of your misdeeds. You *escape*, or *make an escape, from* the police or *from* your pursuers.

esophagus, *n.* For plural, see NOUN, 6P.

esoteric, exoteric, *adj.* *Exoteric* is the opposite of *esoteric.*

Esoteric knowledge, ideas, etc. can be understood by the limited number of special people for whom they are intended; hence, such knowledge or ideas are unusually abstruse, or comprehensible only to the initiated.

Exoteric material, on the other hand, is not so limited and is easily understood by the general public.

especial, special, *adj.;* **especially, specially,** *adv.* In general, the paired words are more or less synonymous.

However, *especial* or *especially* is the preferable term when you wish to emphasize *exclusive(ly), exceptional(ly),* or *to a very high degree: an especial attraction for sophisticated people; especially for you and your family; an especial gift for relating to children; dogs especially* well

trained to sniff out hidden drugs; etc.

espresso, expresso, *n.* The specially brewed type of coffee is *espresso; expresso* is a nonword.

essay See ASSAY, ESSAY.

esthete, esthetic See AESTHETE, ESTHETE; AESTHETIC, ESTHETIC.

esthetics, *n.* See AESTHETICS, ESTHETICS.

etc. See AND ETC.

ethics, *n.* See -ICS.

evacuate, vacate, *v.* Both verbs mean *to empty;* also, *to leave,* or *to remove people from* (a place).

When you *evacuate* an area, or when the police *evacuate* the residents of an area, the purpose is to avoid present or imminent danger.

When you *vacate* an office, apartment, house, etc., you leave it, give up residency, etc., for various other reasons. The office, apartment, or house is now vacant.

even, more even See EQUAL, MORE EQUAL.

everybody, everyone, every body, every one Write solid as a pronoun referring to a person: *everybody is here; everyone has left.* These words are singular pronouns, and in strict usage are followed by singular forms—i.e., *he, she; his, her; him, her;* not *they,* them, or *their*. (For a fuller discussion of this point see ANYBODY.)

Write as separate words in contexts such as: *every body in the morgue has been accounted for; every one of you must appear on time; every one of the bags had been opened*.

everybody else's   See ELSE.

everyday, every day   As an adjective preceding a noun, the word is written solid; *an everyday* occurrence. In other constructions, the words are separated, *every day* of the month has been rainy; *left early every day*.

everyone, *pron.*   See ANY-BODY.

everyone, every one   See EVERYBODY.

everyone else's   See ELSE.

everyplace, every place, *adverbial*   This adverbial is preferably written as two words: *she made friends every place she visited*. Even as separate words, however, *every place* (*adverbial*) is considered colloquial or informal; *everywhere* or *wherever* is a better choice as an adverb in formal usage.

When *place* is a *noun, every place* is standard English: *we looked for the book in every place that you suggested*.

For *adverbial*, see ADVERB, 4.

everywhere, everywheres

See EVERYPLACE, EVERY PLACE; -WHERE, -WHERES.

ewe, *n.*   See NOUN, 2D.

exaggeration, hyperbole, *n. Hyperbole* is *exaggeration* for effect, not meant, nor to be taken, literally.

example, *n.*   See PRECEPT, EXAMPLE.

except, *prep.*   Followed by an objective personal pronoun. See PRONOUN, 8, 8B.

exceptional, exceptionable, *adj.*   These similar words should not be confused.

Anyone or anything *exceptional* is unusual, different from others of its kind, above average, etc.

Anything *exceptionable* can be taken exception to or objected to.

exclave, enclave, *n.*   West Berlin is an *enclave in* East Germany—an area belonging to West Germany but surrounded by the territory of the eastern sector.

However, West Berlin is an *exclave of* West Germany—a western area surrounded by East German territory.

In short, the distinction depends on whether you are talking or writing from the point of view of East Germany or of West Germany. (The same distinction, of course, applies to other territories.)

excuse, *n.*   See ALIBI, EXCUSE.

excuse, forgive, *v.* Generally, you *excuse* a minor error,
discourtesy, etc., and *forgive*
a major type of misconduct,
transgression, sin, etc. (Additionally, when you *forgive*,
you do not harbor resentment
or anger.)

But *forgive me* is correctly
used in expressions like
*Forgive me if I sound uncer-
tain,* etc.

**executer, executioner, exec-
utor, executrix,** *n.* An *executer* (EKS'-ə-kyōō'-tər) is simply one who executes certain
duties or responsibilities, and
in this sense may also be
called an *executor,* pronounced the same way as
executer. Too, someone who
carries out an execution may
be termed as *executer,* but
the preferable term for such a
person is *executioner,* especially if the death penalty
has been imposed by a court
of law.

Executor, on the other hand
(pronounced əg-ZEK'-yə-tər) is
the person appointed to carry
out the provisions of someone's last will and testament.
If such a person is a female,
she is the *executrix* (əg-
ZEK'-yə-triks). (For the plural form of *executrix,* see
NOUN, 6O.

exhibit, exhibition, *n.* As
here contrasted, both words
indicate a formal public showing of various kinds—art,
technology, plants and flowers, etc. However, when you

mean *one* item in such a display, call it an *exhibit.* The
person or group responsible
for one or more of the *exhibits*
is an *exhibitor* (or, less often, *exhibiter*), not an *exhibitionist,* who makes a
practice of, and gets sexual
gratification from, showing
in public parts of the body
usually kept covered; or who,
perhaps offensively, shows off
his or her talent, skill, clev-
erness, etc.

exhibitionist, *n.* See EXHIBIT,
EXHIBITION.

exhilarator, *n.* See ACCELER-
ATOR, EXHILARATOR.

exoteric, *adj.* See ESOTERIC,
EXOTERIC.

expect, anticipate, *v.* Strictly, when you *anticipate*
something, you are keenly
aware of the pleasure or pain
that will accompany it; or, in
a somewhat different sense,
you *expect* that something
may happen and take proper
measures to handle it.

However, *anticipate* is often used simply as a direct
synonym of *expect,* and such
use is completely acceptable.

expect (that) *I expect that
. . . ,* meaning *I suppose, believe,* or *assume (that) . . . ,*
is colloquial rather than formal English.

expedite, *v.* See FACILITATE,
EXPEDITE, ACCELERATE.

explicit, *adj.* See IMPLICIT,
EXPLICIT.

exploitative, exploitive, *adj.* The former is the more popular adjective form derived from the verb *exploit*. Both are correct.

expresso, *n.* See ESPRESSO, EXPRESSO.

expurgate, *v.* See CENSOR, BOWDLERIZE, EXPURGATE.

exray, ex-ray See X RAY, X-RAY, X RAY, X-RAY.

extenuate, mitigate, *v.* Certain factors, conditions, or circumstances may *extenuate* a transgression, sin, crime, etc. by serving as excuses that make the action less serious or blameworthy. *Adjective:* **extenuating, extenuatory,** or **extenuative.**

To **mitigate** is *to make or become milder, less harsh, or less severe.* A judge can *mitigate* a penalty; weather *mitigates* when a harsh winter is over; a parent, taking *extenuating* factors into consideration, *mitigates* a child's punishment. **Mitigating** factors make a crime less serious than it would otherwise seem. *Other adjective forms:* **mitigative, mitigatory.**

extra- All words starting with this prefix are written solid, including *extraordinary.*

extravert, extrovert, *n.* The latter spelling is preferable; *extroverted* (*adj.*) and *extroversion* (*n.*) are similarly preferable to *extraverted* and *extraversion.*

eyeglasses, *n.* See GLASSES.

F

fable, allegory, n. As here contrasted, both are stories containing morals; the characters of a *fable*, however, are usually animals, as in Aesop's *Fables*.

facilitate, expedite, accelerate, v. When you *facilitate* a process, solution, etc., you make it *easier*. When you *expedite* something, you make progress *easier* and also *faster*, especially by removing obstacles. When you *accelerate* something, you speed it up.

fact, actual fact, true fact Since all facts, by definition, are actual and true, *actual fact* and *true fact* are redundancies —omit *actual* or *true*.

fail to Strictly, *she failed to arrive on time* indicates that she tried and did not succeed. *Fail to*, in informal usage, often means, simply, *did not*.

family, n. Consider *family* a *singular noun* if the concept is that of a unit: *The family was seated at the table; her family was more important to her than anyone else.*

Construe *family* as a *plural noun* if the concept is that of a number of individual members: *the family were all waiting for her to arrive before they sat down to dinner; "her large family of grown children besiege her with their woes"* (quoted from a movie review in *Newsweek*).

See also NOUN, 1.

famous, notorious, adj. *Notorious*, unlike *famous*, indicates strong disapproval: *notorious gambler*, (*racketeer, criminal*, etc.); *notorious crime* (*murder*, etc.).

fantasize, fantasy, v. *Fantasize* is in popular and accepted use because it *sounds* like a verb, owing to its *-ize* suffix.

Many careful writers, however, prefer the verb *fantasy*, which is, of course, also the noun form. *Past tense and participle: fantasied; -ING form: fantasying.*

fantasm, phantasm, phantasy, n. As a ghost, supernatural presence, or illusion, *phantasm* is the preferable spelling; *fantasm* is a variant spelling.

Phantasy, on the other hand, is a variant spelling of *fantasy* (n.).

fantasy See FANTASIZE, FANTASY; FANTASM, PHANTASM, PHANTASY.

fantom, *n.* See PHANTOM, FANTOM.

farther, further For physical distances, *farther* is the preferable word: *China is farther away than Minneapolis. Further* is not incorrect, however, as an indication of literal distance.

To mean *figurative distance, more, to a greater extent, in addition,* etc., *further* is the preferable word: *further details; nothing could be further from my mind; spoke further about her experiences.*

The same distinctions hold for *farthest* and *furthest.*

fatal, fateful, *adj.* Something *fatal* causes death, disaster, or destruction: *a fatal blow, fatal error.*

Fateful primarily means *having an important effect* (*fateful day in her life*), but has additional, although less frequently used, secondary meanings: *ominous; prophetic,* or, synonymously with *fatal, capable of causing death or disaster.*

fatal, more fatal In the sense of *causing death,* something is either *fatal* or not *fatal*—it cannot be *more fatal* or *less fatal,* death being final. *Fatal* is a word like *equal, unique, perfect,* etc. that does not, logically, have degrees. See also EQUAL, MORE EQUAL; FATAL, FATEFUL.

fate, *n.* See DESTINY, FATE.

fated See DESTINED, FATED.

fateful, *adj.* See FATAL, FATEFUL.

father-in-law, *n.* For plural, see IN-LAWS.

faun, fawn, *n.* A *faun* is the mythological Roman minor deity; a *fawn* is a young deer.

fauna, flora, *n.* *Fauna* refers to the animal life of a region, *flora* to the plant life.

fawn, *n.* See FAUN, FAWN.

fearful, fearsome, *adj.* These words are synonymous, and, strangely enough, each one means both *feeling fear* and *causing fear. Fearsome,* however, is more commonly used in the latter sense.

FEEBLEMINDED, CRETINOUS, MORONIC, IMBECILIC, IDIOTIC, *adj.*

Feebleminded is the general, all-inclusive term.

The other adjectives are synonymous in everyday use; they are interchangeable as terms of disparagement for anyone or anything we consider stupid.

There is, however, a scientific distinction between the nouns from which the last four adjectives are formed, namely:

A *cretin* has congenitally very low intelligence as well as arrested physical development, owing to a thyroid deficiency.

A *moron* has an I.Q. of 50 to 70.

An *imbecile* has an I.Q. of 25 to less than 50.

An *idiot* has an I.Q. lower than 25.

Except scientifically, the nouns, too, are generally used merely as epithets to show one's annoyance or contempt.

---

feel bad, feel badly See BAD, BADLY.

feel good, feel well See GOOD, WELL.

felony, misdemeanor, *n.* In law, a *felony* is a major crime (murder, arson, burglary, armed robbery, etc.), for which the penalty in most states is more than a year of imprisonment.

A *misdemeanor* is a minor illegal act (a traffic violation, spitting on the sidewalk, etc.) for which the punishment is less severe—usually a fine or, at worst, less than a year in jail or prison.

feminine nouns—See NOUN, 2.

fertile, prolific, *adj.* *Fertile* indicates the capability of being productive: *fertile soil, fertile period, fertile imagination.*

Prolific describes either one who has been unusually productive in any way (*prolific parents; a prolific writer, composer, artist, poet,* etc.) or may refer to the creations of such a person (*her most prolific period*).

fetch, *v.* See BRING, TAKE, FETCH.

fetus, embryo, *n.* The unborn child is a *fetus* after the third month of the mother's pregnancy; through the third month, it is an *embryo. Foetus* is a variant spelling of *fetus.*

fewer, less See LESS, FEWER.

fiancé, fiancée, *n.* The man to whom a woman is engaged is her *fiancé;* the woman is the man's *fiancée.* The words are pronounced identically, preferably fee-ahn-SAY'.

fictional, fictitious, fictive, *adj.* When you describe a character, form, style, etc. as *fictional,* you stress that you are referring to fiction—i.e., a novel, short story, etc.; *fictional style.* But *fictional* may also mean *pretended* or *untrue.*

Call anything *fictitious* and you are saying it is pretended, imagined, not real, not true, etc.: *fictitious name* (*anger, statement,* etc.).

Fictive, a less common word, is synonymous with *fictional* or *fictitious.*

fight with, fight against
Fight with someone and you may be either on the same or on the opposing side. *Fight against* a person or thing, and the two of you are unambiguously opposed. The preposition may be omitted when the combatants are in opposition: *we fought the enemy; she fought a cold for several days.*

figuratively, *adv.* See LITERALLY, FIGURATIVELY.

figure, suppose, *v.* *"Do you figure they'll be on time?"* is informal or colloquial for "do you *suppose* (imagine, think, believe . . .)." Such use of *figure (v.)* is unacceptable in formal English.

filch, *v.* See THIEVERY.

Filipino, *n.* See PHILIPPINE ISLANDS, PHILIPPINES.

filly, *n.* See NOUN, 2D.

finalize, *v.* Some critics object to this verb in standard English, but for no good reason. Verbs are often derived from adjectives ending in *-al* by adding *-ize: normalize, neutralize, generalize, verbalize, vocalize,* etc. The word is of comparatively recent coinage, but is nonetheless perfectly proper.

firebug, *n.* See ARSONIST, INCENDIARY, PYROMANIAC, FIREBUG.

first, firstly Either word is correct to mean *in the first*

place. First may be used as an adverb, even in starting a list which contains a second, third, etc. item. Similarly, **second, third, fourth,** etc., in such a list, may correctly substitute for **secondly, thirdly, fourthly,** etc., and, in fact, usually does.

fish, fishes, *n. pl.* The normal plural form of *fish* is *fish; fishes* may be used to emphasize different species. See also NOUN, 61.

fit, fitted The past tense of *fit* is either *fitted* or *fit;* the former is somewhat preferable. The participle, however, is *fitted,* not *fit: the sweater has not fitted him for some time; her training has not fitted her for her new job.*

fix, predicament, *n.* Meaning *a difficult* or *puzzling situation, fix (what a fix to be in!)* is acceptable in informal speech or writing. **Predicament** is the preferable term in formal language.

fix, prepare, *v.* To *fix* breakfast is as standard a usage as to **prepare** breakfast—or lunch, dinner, a snack, etc. Use the verb that appeals to you. See also CASTRATE, GELD, ALTER, FIX, CAPONIZE, EMASCULATE, SPAY.

fixation, *n.* See COMPULSION, OBSESSION, FIXATION.

flagon, flacon, *n.* A *flagon* is a container, with a spout and a handle, for some liquid, often wine or spirits. A *flacon* is a small container or bottle, with a stopper or other closure, generally for perfume.

flagrant, *adj.* See BLATANT, FLAGRANT, GLARING.

flail, flay, *v.* To *flail* is to whip, as if with a *flail* (n.), a device used to thresh grain manually. (One also *flails* one's arms—i.e., moves them back and forth forcefully.)

To *flay*, on the other hand, is to strip the skin from, by whipping. (One also, in a figurative sense, *flays* a person with strong or biting criticism, censure, scolding, etc.)

flair, flare. A *flair* (n.) is a natural talent: *flair for poetry*.

For any other meanings, use *flare*, which is both a noun and a verb.

flammable, inflammable, nonflammable, *adj.* *Flammable* and *inflammable* are identical in meaning: *easily set on fire*. (The *in-* of *inflammable* is not a negative prefix.) The negative of *flammable* or *inflammable* is *nonflammable* or *noninflammable*.

In figurative usage, *inflammable* is more common than *flammable*: *his inflammable temper*.

flare See FLAIR, FLARE.

flaunt, flout, *v.* To *flaunt* is to display conspicuously, ostentatiously, defiantly, etc.: *flaunted his wealth*.

To *flout* is to show glaring contempt for: *flout the law; flout the rules, flout authority*.

flautist, flutist, *n.* One who plays the flute is either a *flautist* or a *flutist*. The former term is more likely to be heard in musical circles.

flay, *v.* See FLAIL, FLAY.

fleet, *n.* Generally used as a singular noun: *a fleet of ships was in the harbor*. See also NOUN, 1; SUBJECT, VERB AGREEMENT, 5.

fleet, flotilla, *n.* A *flotilla* is either a small *fleet* or a *fleet* of small ships.

flier, flyer, *n.* Both spellings are correct for one who flies, but *flier* is preferable.

Use *flier* for a handbill, circular, etc.

flora, *n.* See FAUNA, FLORA.

flotilla, *n.* See FLEET, FLOTILLA.

flotsam, jetsam, *n.* Generally, the words are used in combination to refer to useless or unimportant things (*the flotsam and jetsam of his life*) or to down-and-out and homeless people (*the flotsam and jetsam of humanity*). *Flotsam*, strictly, is the wreckage of a ship, or a wrecked ship's cargo, found floating in the sea, while *jetsam* is cargo or anything else *thrown overboard* from a ship.

flout, *v.* See FLAUNT, FLOUT.

fluid, liquid, *n.* A *fluid* is any substance that can flow, as gas, air, water, milk; *liquid* is commonly restricted to a substance that not only is capable of flowing but is also wet to the touch. A *liquid*, then, is also a *fluid*, but not all *fluids* are *liquids*.

flutist, *n.* See FLAUTIST, FLUTIST.

focus, *n.* For plural form, see NOUN, 6P.

foetus, *n.* See FETUS, EMBRYO.

folklore, *n.* See LEGEND, MYTH, FOLKLORE.

follow, *v.* See ENSUE, FOLLOW.

for Followed by a noun or pronoun to form a phrase, *for* is a preposition: *for the moment; for everyone.* The preposition *for* is followed by an objective personal pronoun: *for him and me, for you and her.*

    Followed by a clause, *for* is a *conjunction*, or to use the term in Structural Grammar, a *connector: Things are out of hand, for no one is in control.* (Note that a comma generally precedes the connector *for*.)

    See also PRONOUN, 8B.

forbear, *v.* Past tense is *forbore;* participle is *forborne.*

forbid, prohibit, *v.* Past tense of *forbid* is *forbade* (or, infrequently, *forbad*); the participle is *forbidden.* This verb is followed by an infinitive, or the -ING form, of another verb: *forbade him to go; forbids loitering* (*smoking,* etc.). It is not followed by the preposition *from* (i.e., not "*forbids* him from going").

    To **prohibit** is to *forbid officially, or by authority,* and is followed by a noun (*prohibits the sale of alcoholic beverages*); by the -ING form of another verb (*prohibits loitering on or near school grounds*); or by *from* plus the -ING form of a verb (*prohibits them from working*). The noun *prohibition* is followed by the preposition *against: a prohibition against drinking.*

forceful, forcible, *adj.* Though the words are in many ways synonymous, this distinction is usually observed:

    Forceful—full of force; effective; powerful; strong: a forceful speaker; forceful argument; forceful blow.

    Forcible—accomplished through force: forcible entry by the police; forcibly pushed out of line.

FORE-, FOR

Fore- is the spelling when the prefix indicates *early; before or beforehand; front;* etc. These words, as examples, are spelled *fore-*:

forearm	forename
forebear, *n.* (*i.e., ancestor; also*	foreordain
spelled forbear)	forepart
forebode	forequarter
forecast	forerunner
foreclose	foresee
forecourt	foreshadow
foredoom	foreshorten
forefather	foresight
forefront	forestall
foreground	foretell
forehead	forethought
foreleg	foretoken
foreman	forewarn
foremost	foreword

The following words, among others, have no implication of time or frontal position, so they are spelled *for-*.

forbear, *v.*	forgive, *v.*
forbid, *v.*	forlorn, *adj.*
forgather, *v.*	forsake, *v.*
forget, *v.*	forswear, *v.*

forecast, *v.* The preferable past tense or participle is *forecast*: *he forecast (has forecast) snow.*

foreword, forward The preface to a piece of writing is a *foreword*—i.e., words preceding the main text. *Forward* is an adjective, adverb or verb indicating direction.

forget, *v.* Participle is *forgotten*, or, less commonly,

forgot: *he has forgotten* (or *has forgot*).

forgive, *v.* See EXCUSE, FORGIVE.

forgiveness, *n.* This is one of the very rare instances in which the noun suffix -*ness* is added directly to a verb— i.e., *forgive* plus -*ness*.

former, latter, *adj.* Use these words when *only two* people, groups, things, items, etc. are referred to; if there are three or more, use *first* and *last*.

formula, *n.* For plural form, see NOUN, 6M.

fortuitous, *adj.* Strictly, this adjective means *happening by chance, accident,* or *coincidence.* The word is, however, coming into vogue with the added meaning of *fortunate.* (Many writers, it should be noted, object to this new meaning.)

forward See FOREWORD, FORWARD.

forward, forwards, *adv.* See -WARD, -WARDS.

forward, froward, *adj.* A *forward* person is bold, impertinent, etc.; a *froward* person is obstinate or disobedient.

Frankenstein, Frankenstein's monster *Frankenstein* was the *creator* of the monster in the old horror story, so it is a *Frankenstein's monster,* not a *Frankenstein,* that is created and then gets out of hand to cause no end of harm and trouble.

free gift An obvious redundancy, since a *gift* is *free.* The phrase is, however, common in advertising.

frenetic, phrenetic, *adj.* The latter is a variant spelling.

frenzy, phrensy, *n.* The second form is a variant and earlier spelling.

from whence, whence Since *whence* means *from where,* *from* is redundant. *Whence* itself is a rather elegant and old-fashioned-sounding term.

frontward, frontwards, *adv.* See -WARD, WARDS.

froward, *adj.* See FORWARD, FROWARD.

-ful, -fuls As terms of measurement, nouns like *spoonful, cupful, glassful, armful, handful, shovelful,* etc. are pluralized by adding -*s*: *spoonfuls, cupfuls, handfuls,* etc. *Spoonsful, cupsful, armsful,* etc. are nonstandard English. The point is that you are using one spoon, cup, glass, etc. and filling it two, three, four or more times— hence -*fuls*.

However, if you actually have two or more spoons, cups, shovels, etc. and *each one* is full, you write *five spoons full* (of whatever), *two cups full,* three *shovels full,* etc., using separate words in each instance.

fulsome, full, *adj.* *Fulsome* does not mean *full* or *abundant* but rather *excessive to an offensive degree* or *excessive and insincere.* See also NOISOME, NOISY.

fun, *adj.* A *fun* time, a *fun* class, etc., in which *fun* means *enjoyable,* is acceptable only as a colloquialism, not to be used in formal English.

funerary, funereal, *adj.* Both words mean *referring or pertaining to, or suitable for, a funeral,* but **funereal** is more commonly used in the sense of *sad, gloomy, mournful*— i.e., *looking as if one were attending a funeral.*

fungus, *n.* For plural, see NOUN, 6P.

further See FARTHER, FURTHER.

futilitarian, *adj.* See DEFEAT-IST, FUTILITARIAN.

G

gage, gauge Meaning *a standard* or *measure* or *to measure*, *gauge* is the preferred spelling.

gallant The adjective is usually pronounced gə-LANT' or gə-LAHNT' when it means *chivalrous; pleasingly courteous and attentive to women;* with other meanings (*brave, noble*, etc.), it is pronounced GAL'-ənt. *Gallantry* is the noun form for all meanings.

A man who is chivalrous is a *gallant* (n.), also pronounced gə-LANT' or gə-LAHNT'.

galore Expressions like *money galore, clothing galore*, etc., meaning *in great quantities*, are more suitable to informal than to formal usage.

ganglion, *n.* For plural, see NOUN, 6R.

gantlet, gauntlet, *n.* Whether a glove or a challenge, *gauntlet* is the preferable spelling.

garnish, garnishee, *v.* To *garnish* is to *decorate* in various ways. *Garnishee* is a term in law meaning *to attach by legal procedures (the salary of a debtor to satisfy a debt.)*

The noun *garnishment* derives from either verb; *garniture (n.)* is whatever is used as a decoration.

gastronome, gastronomer, *n.* See CONNOISSEUR, EPICURE, EPICUREAN, GOURMET, GOURMAND.

gauche, *adj.* See CLUMSY, MALADROIT, GAUCHE.

gauge See GAGE, GAUGE.

gauntlet, *n.* See GANTLET, GAUNTLET.

gay See HOMOSEXUAL, GAY, LESBIAN.

geegaw, gewgaw, *n.* See GEWGAW, GEEGAW.

geld, *v.* See CASTRATE, GELD, ALTER, FIX, CAPONIZE, EMASCULATE, SPAY.

genealogy, *n.* See GENETICS, GENEALOGY.

general consensus Like *consensus of opinion*, **general consensus** is redundant, since *consensus* is a general agreement. See also CONSENSUS OF OPINION.

genetic, congenital, *adj.* A *genetic* trait, characteristic, etc. is inherited—i.e., is produced by the particular genes in one's cells and is established at the time of conception.

A *congenital* defect, disease, deformity, etc. is one that occurs at any time *after* conception (that is, during the mother's pregnancy) until the infant is born—i.e., has emerged from the birth canal.

genetics, genealogy, *n.* *Genetics* is the biological science of heredity—i.e., the transmission of characteristics through the genes from parents to offspring.

Genealogy, on the other hand, deals with one's family tree, tracing one's descent from various ancestors. Biological characteristics are not involved.

See also -ICS.

genial, *adj.* See CONGENIAL, GENIAL.

genus, *n.* For plural, see NOUN, 6P.

geriatrics, gerontology, *n.* *Geriatrics* is the medical specialty dealing with the diseases and pathological physical problems of old age.

Gerontology is the nonmedical science that deals with other problems of aging. A *gerontologist* is not a physician; a *geriatrician* is.

See also -ICS.

gerund, *n.* A term in traditional grammar designating the -ING form of a verb used as a noun: *walking is fun; she enjoys swimming.* See also VERB, 3.

gesticulate, gesture, *v.* These verbs are synonymous, though *gesticulate* may imply the use of hands or arms and may indicate more forceful movements.

get, become, have, *v.* Purists and pedants are unhappy about the many uses of *get* (*v.*) that have become acceptable and prevalent in standard English, but the fact is that *get* may mean *become* (he **got** rich), possess (we've **got** the answer), secure, obtain (we will **get** what you ordered), etc.

(However, do not use the past tense, *got*, to indicate possession in the present tense. *I got the money* meaning *I have the money* is nonstandard English.)

The participle is either *got* or, especially in the sense of *obtain*, **gotten**: *has he* **gotten** *the necessary supplies yet?*

gewgaw, geegaw, *n.* *Gewgaw* is the only correct spelling. Pronounced GYŌŌ'-gô.

gibe, jibe, *v.* *Gibe* is the preferable spelling meaning *to ridicule, mock,* etc. *Jibe* is the only spelling meaning *to agree, be in accord.* The nautical term is *jibe* or *gybe.*

gift, *v.* Meaning *to give a present to* (someone), this verb is acceptable only in colloquial speech or informal writing. In formal usage, avoid sentences like *She gifted him with a new necktie.*

glad, *adj.* Followed by an infinitive (**glad** *to accept*); a clause or *that* plus a clause (**glad** *[that] he was on time*); the preposition *of* (**glad** *of that*); or the preposition *about* (**glad** *about your success*). You are not **glad** *at* someone or something.

gladiolus, *n.* For plural, see NOUN, 6P.

glamour, glamor, *n.* The preferable spelling is **glamour**. Other forms, however, drop the *u*: **glamorous** *(adj.)*; **glamorize** *(v.)*.

glaring, *adj.* See BLATANT, FLAGRANT, GLARING.

glasses *(i.e.,* **eyeglasses**)*, n.* Though a single item, the word is plural: *Her* **glasses** *(eyeglasses) are in need of repair.*

glassful, *n.* For the plural form, see -FUL, -FULS.

go, *v.* The participle **gone** may follow either the auxiliary *be (it was* **gone**) or a form of *have (she has* **gone** *away).*

good, well Technically, **good** is an *adjective,* **well** an *adverb: that is* **good**; *spent money* **well** *but not wisely.* However, **well** may be used as an *adjective* in reference to health: *she feels* **well**; *she is* **well**; *he is not a* **well** *person.* (Someone who is sick is **unwell**.) Recently, the noun **wellness** has been coined and is found in standard usage as a synonym of **good** *health.* (*Feel* **good** less often refers to health.) *Do* **good** is acceptable in informal English, but *we work* **good** *together, they do it* **good**, *he runs* **good**, and similar usages border on the illiterate. See also BAD, BADLY.

good and ... *Good and hot, good and lazy,* etc., are acceptable only in informal usage.

good will, goodwill The noun is preferably written as two words: *a gesture of* **good will**; the adjective is written solid: *a* **goodwill** *gesture.*

goodby, goodbye The two spellings are equally correct, and you may, if you wish, hyphenate the word: **goodby** or **good-bye**. Plural form is **goodbys** (not *goodbies*), **goodbyes, good-bys**, or **good-byes**.

goose, *n.* The plural for the bird is, of course, **geese**. But the word also refers to a kind of iron formerly used by tailors to press garments, and in such instance the plural is **gooses**! See also NOUN, 2D.

gormand, gormandize See CONNOISSEUR, EPICURE, EPICUREAN, GOURMET, GOURMAND.

gory, *adj.* See BLOODY, GORY.

got, gotten See GET, BECOME, HAVE.

got to, have got to In the

sense of *must* or *need to, got to* is nonstandard. Not *I got to go*, but *I've got* to go.

gourmand, *n.* See CONNOIS-SEUR, EPICURE, EPICUREAN, GOURMET, GOURMAND.

gourmet, *n.* See CONNOIS-SEUR, EPICURE, EPICUREAN, GOURMET, GOURMAND.

graduate, *v.* Either *she graduated from Yale* or *she was graduated from Yale*—both usages are correct, the former somewhat more popular.

On the other hand, *she graduated Yale* is considered nonstandard.

In short, you either *graduate from*, or *are graduated from*, a school, college, etc.

graffiti, *n. pl.*; **graffito,** *n. sing.*
Graffiti, since it is a plural word, strictly designates several drawings, scribblings, slogans, etc., on a wall, the side of a building, or any other public structure. One such scrawl, drawing, etc., is a **graffito** (*n. sing.*): *The wall was covered by one large graffito; there were graffiti all over the side of the building.*

gramophone, *n.* See PHONO-GRAPH, GRAMOPHONE, RECORD PLAYER, TURNTABLE, VICTROLA.

gray, grey The first spelling is American, the second British.

grisly, grizzly, gristly, *adj.* The first two words are pronounced identically (GRIZ'-lee). **Grisly** means *horrifying, ghastly, cruelly inhuman*, etc.; **grizzly** is *grayish*: **grizzly** whiskers; **grizzly** bear. (**Grizzly** is also a noun, designating the bear.)
Gristly (GRIS'-lee) means *full of gristle*, as meat, etc.

groom, *n.* See BRIDEGROOM, GROOM.

group, *n.* See NOUN, 1.

gruesome, grewsome, *adj.* **Grewsome** is a rare and variant spelling.

guarantee, *n.* See WAR-RANTY, GUARANTEE.

gullible, *adj.* See CREDU-LOUS, GULLIBLE.

gybe, *v.* See GIBE, JIBE.

gymnasium, *n.* For plural form, see NOUN, 6Q.

gymnastics, *n.* See -ICS.

gynecology, obstetrics, *n.* *Gynecology* is the medical specialty dealing with the reproductive system and the physiological problems of females, *obstetrics* with pregnancy and child-delivery. Most *gynecologists* are also *obstetricians*, and vice versa.

H

habit, habitude, *n.* A *habit* refers to an act or activity frequently performed or engaged in, and therefore reflexive or second-nature.

Habitude, on the other hand, is one's usual manner of acting or one's tendency to act in a certain way.

habitat, habitation, *n.* The *habitat* of an animal, plant, or less frequently, a person or thing is the region in which such animal, etc. is generally found.

A *habitation*, most commonly, is a home or a place in which to live.

had better (best) go, *etc.* A well established and fully acceptable idiom.

had his (her) arm broken, had his (her) hair cut, *etc.*
She *had her arm broken*, meaning that her arm was broken in an accident, sounds illogical but this and similar idioms have become established in informal English. *Had his (her) hair cut* makes more sense, of course, since the act was voluntary.

had ought to Illiterate or slang substitute for *ought to.*

had rather, would rather *(plus verb)* Both *had rather* go, etc.

and *would rather* go, etc. are acceptable, but *would rather* is somewhat more current.

hail, hale, haul *Hail* is a *noun* or *verb. Hail (n.)* is frozen raindrops or small ice pellets; it is also a call or cheer. *Hail (v.)* may refer to weather *(it hailed all night)*, or may mean *to call or summon (hailed a taxi), come from (hails from Texas),* or *pour down* (on or upon) *(hailed epithets upon them.)*

Hale is an *adjective* or *verb. Hale (adj.)* means *healthy* or *still vigorous,* and is especially used to describe an old person. *Hale (v.)* means *require* or *force to go: was haled into court.*

Haul is a *verb* or *noun. Haul (v.)* is *to drag, pull,* etc. *(hauled into the room, into court,* etc.). *Haul (n.)* refers to *dragging, pulling, transporting,* etc., or to the distance pulled or traveled *(a long haul to Reno).*

hairbrained, harebrained, *adj.* Only the second spelling is correct, and describes someone or something foolish, rash, giddy, etc.—i.e., having, or coming from, the brain of a hare.

The word is not very complimentary to hares, which are by no means stupid creatures.

hairbreadth, hairsbreadth, hair's-breadth Spell the word in any of these three ways, all equally correct.

hale See HAIL, HALE, HAUL.

half a (an), a half *Half* an hour or *a half* hour? *Half a* loaf or *a half* loaf? *Half a* dollar or *a half* dollar? *Half a (an)* implies a portion of a whole; *a half* hour (loaf, dollar, etc.) indicates a separate unit. See also IN HALF, INTO HALVES.

half, step *Half* brothers or *sisters* have only one parent in common; that is, they may have the same mother but different fathers, or the other way around.

A *stepchild* is the daughter or son of one's spouse by a previous marriage. One's *stepsister* or *stepbrother* is, in essence, related in the same way as one's *half* sister or *half* brother. What is the distinction, then? By using the word *step*, you are stressing the remarriage of a parent to a new spouse. And, of course, one can have a *stepparent* without having any *stepsisters* or *stepbrothers*.

Note, also, that *half* brother and *half* sister are *separate* words, while *stepsister, stepbrother, stepmother, stepfather, stepparent*, etc. are solid words.

handful For plural, see -FUL, -FULS.

hangar, hanger, *n.* A place for storing aircraft is a *hangar*, not *hanger*. The two words are pronounced identically.

hanged, hung See HUNG, HANGED.

hanger, *n.* See HANGAR, HANGER.

hanger-on, *n.* Plural is *hangers-on.* See NOUN, 6U.

happen, transpire, *v.* See TRANSPIRE.

hardly, scarcely, barely These words are negative in connotation, so use them with affirmative verbs: *have* (not *haven't*) *hardly* any; *saw* (not *didn't see*) *scarcely* anyone; *was* (not *wasn't*) *barely* out of the house when . . .

Introduce a clause following *hardly, scarcely,* or *barely* with *when,* not *than:* had *hardly* (*scarcely, barely*) *closed the door when* (not *than*) *the phone rang.*

See also DOUBLE NEGATIVE.

harebrained, *adj.* See HAIRBRAINED, HAREBRAINED.

has (have) got Acceptable for *has (have), possess,* etc., especially in the form of a contraction: *he's got* a bad cold; *she's got* very little to complain about; etc. See also GET, BECOME, HAVE.

has (have) got to Acceptable for *must* or *has (have) to,* especially in the form of a contraction: *I've got to* do it. See also GET, BECOME, HAVE; GOT TO, HAVE GOT TO

haul See HAIL, HALE, HAUL.

have, *v.* See GET, BECOME, HAVE.

have got to See GOT TO, HAVE GOT TO.

HE/SHE

Some people react negatively to the use of *he* (or *his* or *him*) to refer to an indefinite person, claiming that *he, his,* and *him* are masculine words. In actuality, *he (his, him)* is convenient and well-established word for both sexes in expressions like *everyone took his seat; no one raised his hand;* etc.

The current trend in writing, it is true, is to de-emphasize gender-related terms. So you have a number of choices when a problem arises:

1. Write a disclaimer in a preface to a paper, book, etc. explaining that in your vocabulary the generalized *he, his,* or *him* refers to both sexes.
2. Use the slash mark: *he/she, his/her, him/her;* or, go the whole hog: *she/he, her/his, her/him.*
3. Use *or: he or she,* etc. (*she or he?*).
4. When possible, use *you* in place of *anyone, someone, everyone,* etc.

See also ANYBODY.

headquarters, *n.* Use this word as either a singular (*the police headquarters was located*) or a plural (*their headquarters were raided*).

healthy, healthful, *adj.* In strict usage, *healthy* means possessing health: *a healthy person; healthful* means producing or promoting health: *healthful food* (*climate, conditions,* etc.).

hear tell This is a regionalism, rarely used in standard writing.

heathen, *n.* The plural is *heathens* if you are referring to individuals, *heathen* if you mean such people as a group. See also NOUN, 1.

heave, *v.* Past tense or participle is *heaved,* except in nautical usage, in which instance it is *hove.*

heighth, *n.* Misspelling of *height.*

heir, *n.* The feminine is *heiress,* but *heir* may refer to either sex. See also NOUN, 2C.

help but Like *cannot but*, *cannot help but* is an established idiom.

hemi See SEMI-, HEMI-, DEMI-.

hence, *conj.* For correct punctuation when this conjunction introduces a clause, see HOWEVER.

herbivorous, *adj.* See CARNIVOROUS, HERBIVOROUS, OMNIVOROUS.

hero, *n.* The plural is *heroes*, not *heros*. The feminine form is *heroine*. See also NOUN, 2C; NOUN, 6L1.

herpes, *n.* See MEASLES.

her's, hers *Hers* is a possessive pronoun and needs no apostrophe—*her's* is a misspelling. (See PRONOUN, 8.)

herself, *pron.* See HIMSELF, HIS SELF, HISSELF; SELF.

hew, *v.* The past tense is *hewed*; the participle used as an adjective is *hewn*: *rough-hewn* rock (*features, etc.*); otherwise, the participle is either *hewn* or *hewed*: *has hewn, hewed; was hewn, hewed.*

hiatus, *n.* For plural, see NOUN, 6K.

hiccup, hiccough The first form is the preferred spelling. However you spell it, say HIK'-əp.

hid, hidden, *part.* *Hidden* is the preferred participle (*has hidden, was hidden*) of the verb *hide.* *Hid* is the past tense.

highlight, *n.* or *v.* Preferably written as a solid word, unless the noun means *a light that is up high,* in which case, of course, the words are separated.

hijack, highjack, *v.* The former spelling is preferred.

himself, his self, hisself The reflexive pronoun is *himself* (*he hurt himself*); *his self* emphasizes that *self* is a noun: *he feared that his self* (*i.e., identity, essential nature, etc.*) *was being smothered.* With such a meaning, *self-hood* or *identity* or *personality* would be a better term. The same distinction applies to *herself* and *her self.*

  Hisself is an illiterate substitute for *himself.*

  See also SELF.

hippopotamus, *n.* For plural form, see NOUN, 6P.

his/her See HE/SHE.

historic, historical, *adj.* Use *historic* to connote *important, significant,* or *famous in history*: *historic battle* (*occasion, etc.*); *historical* to refer to history—i.e., past times: *historical studies* (*novels, movies, documents, etc.*).

histrionics, *n.* See -ICS.

hives, *n.* A plural noun when you refer to multiplicity of insect *hives* (i.e., beehives); a singular noun when you mean an allergic reaction, for which the medical term is *urticaria*. See also MEASLES.

hoard, horde, *n.* *Hoard* is a reserve supply, *horde* a crowd, swarm, etc. A *horde* is usually on the move, may consist of people or animals, and often implies attack: *horde of insects: horde of predatory barbarians; a horde of shoppers stormed the store.*

hoi polloi, *n.* Mistakenly used by some speakers or writers to refer to those of higher social or intellectual standing, when, in fact, the term means *the common people; the masses.* Even though *hoi* in Greek, from which language the term is derived, means "the," it is correct, though obviously redundant, to say or write *the hoi polloi.*

People of high social or intellectual stature are, in fact, the *hoi aristoi* (again, redundant, but correct).

hold, ahold, *n.* See AHOLD, HOLD.

holy, holey, *adj.* If you mean *full of holes*, spell it *holey*.

homeward See -WARD, -WARDS.

homicide, manslaughter, murder, assassination, *n.* The all-inclusive, general term in law for the killing of one person by another is *homi-*

cide. If the killing was without malice or premeditation (as by a drunk driver), the legal term is **manslaughter**.

Murder is premeditated, with intent and malice, etc. In law there are various degrees of **murder**, depending on the circumstances.

Assassination is the sudden and surprise **murder** of a political figure, usually (but not necessarily) by someone hired by others.

homogenous, homogeneous, *adj.* *Homogenous* describes a group, area, etc. that is composed of people of the same ethnic background.

Homogeneous refers to similarity of any kind in grouping (age, intelligence, wealth, etc.), including ethnic descent.

homonym, homophone, *n.* *There* and *their* are **homonyms**, or, to use the term preferred in linguistics, *homophones*—words spelled differently, and with different meanings, but pronounced alike.

homosexual, gay, lesbian, *n.* A *homosexual* or a *gay* is either a male or a female; *lesbian* is a female *homosexual*. All three words are also adjectives.

Gay is a recent addition to standard English, having once been considered slang. Today, one has to be careful, when using *gay* as an adjective to mean *merry, happy,* etc., that no ambiguity is possible.

honey, n. For plural, see NOUN, 6F.

honeyed, honied, adj. See MONEYED, MONIED.

honorific, title, n. An *honorific* is a *title* of special respect: *your excellency; his worship;* etc.

hoof, n. For plural, see NOUN, 6G1.

hopefully, adv. Some authorities frown on the use of this adverb to mean *it is to be hoped that . . .*, as in *hopefully, she will arrive on time.* However, such usage is now so prevalent that one has little choice but to consider it acceptable in standard speech and writing.

hopeless, more hopeless Like *equal, correct, unique, perfect,* and other words that do not logically permit comparison, one cannot be *less hopeless* nor *more hopeless.* The same rule applies to words like *painless, useless, fearless, worthless,* etc. See also EQUAL, MORE EQUAL.

horde, hoard, n. See HOARD, HORDE.

horror, terror, n. See TERROR, HORROR.

hose, hosiery, n. It is an oddity of usage that *hose*—i.e., *stockings* or *socks*—looks like a *singular* noun and in fact is construed as a *plural: her hose were made of nylon.*

Hosiery, a collective noun for *stockings* or *socks in general,* is a singular noun: *good hosiery is very expensive.*

host, v. *Host* as a verb (*hosted the celebration*) is so widely current that it is now fully acceptable, despite pedantic objections to the contrary.

hostess, n. See NOUN, 2C.

hot cup (*of coffee,* etc.) What is meant, of course, is *hot coffee in a cup*—i.e., a cup of hot coffee; but, illogical or not, wide usage makes for acceptability.

hove, v. This is the past tense or participle in nautical usage of the verb *heave.* See also HEAVE.

how come? This sounds slangy, but is correct in informal usage.

however, conj. Use a semicolon or period, not a comma, when this conjunction connects two clauses: *we'll accept it; however, we are not happy about it.* If *however* appears later in the clause, it is set off by commas, and the two clauses are still punctuated with a semicolon: *we'll accept it; we are not, however, happy about it.*

Other conjunctions that require similar punctuation are *hence, moreover, nevertheless, nonetheless, therefore,* and *thus.*

however, how ever The solid word is a conjunction, as noted in the entry above, or an adverb (*however* you do it). Separate words are used in questions like *How ever did you accomplish such a feat?*

how's about . . .? Used only in colloquial or very informal English.

human, *n.* Standard and fully acceptable in the sense of *human being* or *person.*

humane, humanitarian, *adj. Humane* persons, treatment, attitudes, etc. are kind or merciful—not cruel or brutal.
Humanitarian describes people who are concerned with, or involved in, the alleviation of suffering, poverty, and other such ills that may afflict humanity.
Humanitarian is also a noun designating a person so concerned or involved.

humid, moist, *adj. Humid* generally refers to weather or air, *moist* to other things.

humpback, hunchback, *n.* The words are interchangeable.

hung, hanged *Hanged* is preferable as the past tense or participle of *hang* when execution or suicide is the purpose or result. *They* **hanged** *(have* **hanged***) the murderer; he* **hanged** *(has* **hanged***) himself; a horse thief was* **hanged** *in the early days of the American West.*
   Otherwise, when *suspended* is meant, **hung** is the past tense and the participle: *they* **hung** *(have* **hung***) the pictures; the stockings were* **hung** *by the chimney.*

HYPER-, HYPO-, *prefix*

Hyper- means *above, over, more than normal,* etc.; **hypo-** is just the opposite—*below, under, less than normal.* (Words with these prefixes are written solid, not hyphenated.)
   Examples are:

hyper-	*hypo-*
hyperactive	hypochondria
hypercritical	hypodermic
hypersensitive	hypotension
hypertension	hypothyroid
hyperthyroid	

---

hyperbole, *n.* See EXAGGERATION, HYPERBOLE.

hyphen, *n.* See DASH, HYPHEN.

hyphenating The general rule is this: when two or more words are combined to form an *adjective*, especially if this *adjective* precedes its noun, *hyphenate*: *water-cooled (engine)*; *run-of-the-mill (quality)*; *happy-go-lucky (attitude)*; *uncalled-for (remark)*.

However, there are exceptions; also, many *noun* compounds are hyphenated, as are some *verb* compounds. Find the particular compound you are looking for in its alphabetical position.

hypnotism, hypnosis, mesmerism, *n.* Strictly, *hypnotism* is the *study, theory,* *practice* or *act* of inducing *hypnosis*; the latter is the *state* or *condition* one is in after being *hypnotized*.

Mesmerism is *hypnotism* as practiced by Franz Mesmer in the late 1700s and early 1800s, and is occasionally used as a synonym of *hypnotism*.

Mesmerize (v.) may mean *to hypnotize*, but more often is used figuratively in the sense of *fascinate, spellbind, hold one's attention as if by hypnotism*, etc.

hypothesis, *n.* For plural form, see NOUN, 6N.

I

-ICS

A word ending in **-ICS** usually refers to a science, art, specialty, body of knowledge, or a course of study in school or college. For example:

acoustics	histrionics
acrobatics	linguistics
aesthetics (or esthetics)	logistics
athletics	mathematics
dietetics	mnemonics
dramatics	numismatics
economics	obstetrics
electronics	physics
ethics	politics
genetics	semantics
geriatrics	statistics
gymnastics	tactics

Such words, when they refer to a science, art, course of study, etc. are treated as *singular* nouns:

Acoustics (electronics, physics) is required for a degree in engineering.

Acrobatics (athletics, dramatics, economics, gymnastics) was an elective course.

Aesthetics (ethics) is taught by the philosophy department of the university.

Dietetics (genetics, geriatrics, obstetrics, politics) is her specialty.

Mathematics (statistics, tactics) is a demanding course.

When such a word does *not* refer to a science, art, etc., it is treated as a *plural* noun:

The *acoustics* in this room *are* poor.

Their *dramatics (histrionics, acrobatics, gymnastics) were* amazing.

Your *genetics are* the source of your blue eyes.

His *ethics are* very strict.

Mnemonics are useful in learning correct spelling.

Our *politics do* not interest her.

The *tactics* they used *were* not effective.

His sudden *hysterics* *were* hard to account for.

The *logistics* of preparing for the attack *were* more difficult than we had at first thought.

---

identical, *adj.* Followed by to: *identical to the one you have.*

idiotic, *adj.* See FEEBLE-MINDED, CRETINOUS, MORONIC, IMBECILIC, IDIOTIC.

i.e. See E.G., I.E.

if, whether, *conj.* *Whether* is the preferable conjunction to express affirmative or negative possibility: *I don't know whether (or not) I should go; we are not sure whether (or not) the package will arrive today; find out whether (or not) he is in.*

if I would have Awkward substitute for *If I had* (*gone, seen,* etc.).

if only ... was, if only ... were If only ... expresses a wish, and when you must decide between *was* and *were* with a singular subject, use *were: If only he were here! If only she were taller! If only it were true!* See also AS IF ... WAS, WERE; IF ... WAS, IF ... WERE; WISH ... WAS, WISH ... WERE.

if ... was, if ... were When the clause introduced by *if* states a condition *contrary to fact,* use *were* rather than *was,* with a singular subject. The main clause, in such in-

stances, will usually contain the auxiliary *would, could,* or *might.* For example:

If your wife *were* here, you *wouldn't* dare say such things. (Your wife is *not* here.)

If it *weren't* raining, we *could* drive faster. (It *is* raining.)

If she *were* penniless, I *could* understand her applying for welfare. (She is *not* penniless.)

If she *was* planning to be late, why didn't she call? (Apparently, she *was* planning to be late.)

See also AS IF ... WAS, AS IF ... WERE; IF ONLY ... WAS, IF ONLY ... WERE; WISH ... WAS, WISH ... WERE.

ill, *adj.* See SICK, ILL.

ill- Use a hyphen to combine *ill* with an *adjective* or *verb: ill-advised, ill-bred, ill-fated, ill-treat, ill-treated, ill-use, ill-used.* Write separately if the next word is a noun: *ill fame, ill humor, ill nature, ill will.* Exception: *ill-usage and ill-use,* nouns. See also WELL-.

illegal, illicit, *adj.* *Illicit* may be used as a synonym of *illegal,* or it may mean, depending on the context, *con-*

trary to morality, prevalent custom, or acceptable rules of conduct. Embezzlement and other forms of thievery are clearly *illegal*, while an affair with one's friend's spouse is generally considered *illicit*.

illuminate, illumine, *v.* In the sense of *giving light to* or *glowing*, the words are synonymous, but *illumine* is more commonly used in poetry than in straightforward prose.

In the sense of *clarifying, enlightening,* or *decorating a page or initial letter with a design, illuminate* is the correct verb.

illusion, *n.* See DELUSION, ILLUSION.

illy, *adv.* Nonstandard English for *poorly* or *badly*.

imbecilic, *adj.* See FEEBLE-MINDED, CRETINOUS, MORONIC, IMBECILIC, IDIOTIC.

immanent, *adj.* See IMMI-NENT, IMMANENT, EMINENT.

immigrate, emigrate You *immigrate to* a country, intending to settle there permanently. When you reach your destination, you are an *immigrant* in your new homeland.

You *emigrate from* the country you are permanently leaving, and you are then an *emigrant* from that country. If you have been forced to flee your country for politi-cal reasons, you are an **émigré** (EM'-ə-gray'), also spelled **emigré.**

Every *immigrant* is, of course, also an *emigrant*; the word you use depends on whether you are referring to the country *to* which one comes (*immigrant*) or *from* which one leaves (*emigrant*).

imminent, immanent, emi-nent, *adj.* **Imminent**: *about to happen (imminent arrival).*

Immanent: *inherent; subjective (immanent reactions of wild animals to danger).*

Eminent: *of people: renowned for superiority or excellence (eminent composer of the nineteenth century); of things: towering above others of the same kind,* most frequently used in the noun form *(a rocky eminence along the coast).*

immoral, *adj.* See AMORAL, NONMORAL, UNMORAL, IM-MORAL.

immune, *adj.* Preferably followed by the preposition *to: immune to certain diseases.*

immunity, *n.* May be followed by *to, against,* or *from: immunity to (against, from) measles.*

impact (on), *v.* In the sense of *have an effect or figurative impact (on),* this verb is awkward and not fully acceptable; it is found mostly in educational or business jargon. The usage, however, is gradually spilling over into everyday writing and may eventually be recognized as standard English.

impassable, impassible, *adj.* See PASSABLE, PASSIBLE.

impious, sacrilegious, irreligious, nonreligious, *adj.* An *impious* person, statement, act, etc. shows a lack of respect or reverence for God.

A *sacrilegious* act is a deliberate violation of, or disrespect for, whatever is considered holy, sacred, etc.

Irreligious describes a person who follows no religion, or who is opposed to organized religion.

Nonreligious indicates that no question of religion is involved.

implicit, explicit, *adj.* Something *implicit* is merely suggested, hinted at, or expressed indirectly; something *explicit* is clearly and directly stated.

imply, infer, *v.* When you *imply*, or make an *implication* (*n.*), you send an indirect message, whether by word or deed. *Imply* is followed by *that* plus a clause: *implied that I was at fault.*

When you *infer* or draw an *inference* (*n.*), you *receive* the indirect message that someone is sending. In short, you *infer* what another person *implies*. *Infer* is followed by *from* (*I infer from what you said*) or by *that*

plus a clause (*I inferred from his guilty look that he had indeed stolen the ring.*)

impostor, *n.* See CHARLATAN, QUACK, IMPOSTOR.

impotent, *adj.* See STERILE, BARREN, INFERTILE, IMPOTENT.

impracticable, impractical, *adj.* See PRACTICABLE, PRACTICAL.

in, into, *prep.* If you enter a house from outside, you walk *into* the house; if you are already in the house, you walk *in* the house by striding around. Similarly, something is already *in* the file, but you put it *into* the file when it is not yet there.

in accord with, in accordance with See ACCORD, ACCORDANCE.

in addition to, *prep.* See AS WELL AS.

in behalf of See BEHALF.

in contrast to, in contrast with See COMPARE, CONTRAST.

in half, into halves The two phrases are identical in meaning. *Into halves* is preferable to *in halves*. See also HALF A (AN), A HALF.

in line, on line You wait *in line* or *on line*; the phrase you use depends on the part of the country in which you live.

in regard(s) to See REGARD, REGARDS.

inasmuch as The first word is written solid.

incendiary, *n.* See ARSON-IST, INCENDIARY, PYROMANIAC, FIREBUG.

incidence, incident, *n.* *Incidence* denotes the range or frequency of occurrence: *the incidence of arthritis among the elderly.*

An *incident* is a single or particular occurrence: *an incident he would not forget.*

See also COINCIDENT, COINCIDENCE.

incident, incidental, *adj.* The adjective, *incident* means *likely to happen* and is followed by *to: certain hazards incident to committing a burglary.*

Incidental (*adj.*) is derived from the noun *incident* (see INCIDENCE, INCIDENT) and may mean either *casual, minor,* or *associated* (with): *incidental remark; costs incidental to filing a claim.*

incidental, *n.* Often found in the plural: *certain incidentals we hadn't counted on.*

incidently, incidentally, *adv.* Only *incidentally* is the correct spelling.

inclose, *v.* See ENCLOSE, INCLOSE.

include, *v.* See ENCLUDE, INCLUDE.

incognito, *n.* See ALIAS, PSEUDONYM, PEN NAME, NOM DE PLUME, INCOGNITO.

incongruity, *n.* See ANACHRONISM, INCONGRUITY.

incredible, *adj.* The negative of *credible.* See also CREDIBLE, PLAUSIBLE, CREDITABLE.

incredulous, *adj.* The negative of *credulous.* See also CREDULOUS, GULLIBLE.

incubus, succubus, *n.* According to the mythology of the medieval ages, an **incubus** was a male demon or evil spirit who visited a sleeping woman and lay on top of her to consummate sexual intercourse; a **succubus** was a female demon or evil spirit who visited a sleeping man and had intercourse with him. (A variant form for **succubus** is *succuba.*)

Hence, **incubus** also designates *an oppressive burden* or *nightmare*; **succubus** also designates *any demon* or *evil spirit.*

For the plural of **incubus** or **succubus,** see NOUN, 6P; for the plural of **succuba,** see NOUN, 6M1.

incumber, encumber, *v.* The latter spelling is more popular.

indescribable, ineffable, unspeakable, unmentionable, *adj.* All these adjectives say that, for whatever reason, words cannot or should not describe or explain (something or someone).

Indescribable is the general, all-inclusive and neutral term: *indescribable* delight; *indescribable* terror.

Ineffable is generally used in a pleasant or complimentary sense: *ineffable* charm (beauty, wonders, etc.)

Unspeakable usually refers to things or qualities that are too evil, reprehensible, etc. to permit description: *unspeakable* crimes (violence, wickedness, ugliness, etc.)

Anything *unmentionable* is not the sort of thing one expresses or mentions in polite circles lest some people take offense.

index, *n*. See APPENDIX, INDEX. For plural form, see NOUN, 6O.

indicium, *n*. For plural, see NOUN, 6Q.

indict, indite, *v*. To *indict* is to *accuse* (someone); to *indite* is to *write* (a letter, etc.) The words are pronounced identically.

indirect object See SENTENCE PATTERNS, 4.

indiscreet, indiscrete, *adj*. These are the negative forms of *discreet* and *discrete*. See also DISCREET, DISCRETE.

indite, *v*. See INDICT, INDITE.

indorse, *v*. See ENDORSE, INDORSE.

indubitable, *adv*. See DOUBTLESS, NO DOUBT.

inductive See DEDUCTIVE, INDUCTIVE.

industrial, industrious, *adj*. **Industrial**: referring to, pertaining to, containing, etc., industries i.e., factories, businesses, etc.

Industrious: busy, hardworking, etc. The noun form is either *industriousness* or *industry*: shows commendable industriousness (industry).

industry, *n*. See COMMERCE, INDUSTRY; INDUSTRIAL, INDUSTRIOUS.

inedible, uneatable, *adj*. Synonymous words, but *inedible* is in far more common use.

ineffable, *adj*. See INDESCRIBABLE, INEFFABLE, UNSPEAKABLE, UNMENTIONABLE.

ineluctable, *adj*. See INEVITABLE, INELUCTABLE, UNAVOIDABLE.

inequity, iniquity, *n*. **Inequity** is lack of fairness or justice: life is full of *inequities*.

Iniquity is wickedness, sinfulness, immorality, etc.: den of *iniquity*; a life of *iniquity*.

The adjective forms are, respectively: *inequitable*, *iniquitous*.

inevitable, ineluctable, unavoidable, *adj*. The three words are synonymous in the sense of certain to happen; cannot be avoided nor prevented. *Ineluctable* is largely a literary term, and *unavoidable* does not have quite the force or finality of *inevitable*.

infection, n. See AFFECTION, INFECTION.

infectious, adj. See CONTAGIOUS, INFECTIOUS, COMMUNICABLE.

infer, v. See IMPLY, INFER.

infertile, adj. See STERILE, BARREN, INFERTILE, IMPOTENT.

infinitive, n. This term in grammar designates the un-inflected form of a verb preceded by the word to: to swim, to run, to spend. In Structural Grammar, to, in such instances, is the sign of the infinitive, not a preposition.

infinitive, splitting the See SPLITTING THE INFINITIVE.

infinitive, subject of In a sentence such as I want him to be the captain, him is the subject of the infinitive to be (him to be the captain is the object of the verb want). The subject pronoun of an infinitive is in the objective case, though the subject pronoun of any inflected form of a verb is in the nominative case (he is the captain). In you want me to be him, the objective pronoun him links to the objective me. So we use an objective pronoun after the

infinitive to be if to be has a subject.

Consequently, in the problem (who, whom) did you think him to be?, we read the sentence as: Did you think him to be him?, and correctly write, Whom did you think him to be?

See also INFINITIVE; WHO, WHOM.

inflammable, adj. See FLAMMABLE, INFLAMMABLE, NONFLAMMABLE.

inflection A term in Structural Grammar referring to one of the several forms of a noun, adjective, pronoun, or verb. Some inflections of a noun are the singular, plural, possessive; of an adjective, comparative, superlative; of a verb, past, present, participle, etc. See also: ADJECTIVE; NOUN; PRONOUN; VERB.

inform, v. See ADVISE, INFORM.

informant, informer, n. Informant is generally used in a neutral sense. Informer, on the other hand, is one who secretly gives information that implicates another in some wrongdoing, crime, or other illegal or improper activity: a police informer.

-ING FORM OF A VERB USED IN THE NOUN POSITION

When the -ING form of a verb (eating, working, telling) is used in the noun position (eating is important; he enjoys working; telling off-color jokes is his specialty), a preceding pronoun is preferably in the possessive inflection. For example:

> I cannot understand *his* (not *him*) eating so little.
> She appreciated *our* (not *us*) working so hard on her project.
> I resent *your* (not *you*) telling off-color jokes.

(Such use of the -ING form of a verb is called a *gerund* in traditional grammar, a *nominal* in Structural Grammar.)

On the other hand, if the -ING form is used as an adjective, the preceding pronoun is correctly in the objective inflection. For example:

> I watched *him* eating his dinner.
> They want *us* working harder.
> We listened to *them* telling funny stories.

---

ingenious, ingenuous, *adj.* See NAIVE, INGENUOUS, IN-GENIOUS.

iniquity, *n.* See INEQUITY, INIQUITY.

IN-LAWS

Note these plural forms:

| (mother-in-law) | mothers-in-law, *pl.* |
| (father-in-law) | fathers-in-law, *pl.* |

The same rule applies for *brothers-in-law, sisters-in-law, sons-in-law, daughters-in-law,*, etc. There is a single law that makes a mother a *mother-in-law* to the spouse of her son or daughter. If several such mothers are referred to, *mother* is of course pluralized, as is *father, brother, sister,* etc. One such person you are related to by marriage is your *in-law;* plural form: *in-laws.*

To make these words *possessive,* we follow the usual rules: **mother-in-law's** *(n. sing. pos.);* **mothers-in-law's** *(n. pl. pos.);* **in-law's** *(n. sing. pos.);* **in-laws'** *(n. pl. pos.).*

See also NOUN, 7.

---

innervate, *v.* See ENERVATE, INNERVATE, ENERGIZE.

innuendo, insinuation, *n.* Both are *subtly indirect state-* ments, but an *innuendo* is more likely to be derogatory or insulting. The plural of *innuendo* is preferably *innuendoes,* but *innuendos* is also correct. See also NOUN, 6L2.

inoculate, vaccinate, *v.* Though the words are sometimes used interchangeably in the sense of *protecting* (a person, etc.) *against disease by the introduction of a specific serum or vaccine into the blood,* **inoculate** is the general term; **vaccinate** usually refers specifically to protection against smallpox.

inquire, enquire, *v.* *Inquire* is the preferable spelling.

insanitary, unsanitary, *adj.* *Insanitary* is the preferable word.

insensible, insensate, unconscious, *adj.* Though each word has specific meanings of its own, in the sense of *left temporarily without feeling or consciousness,* the three terms are synonymous: *knocked insensible (insensate or unconscious) by the blow.* *Insensate* is less frequently used with this meaning than *insensible* or *unconscious;* and *unconscious* is the term of choice when referring to the effect of a general anesthetic.

See also SENSORY, SENTIENT, SENSATE.

insentient, *adj.* See SENSORY, SENTIENT, SENSATE.

inside, inside of Use *inside* for location: *inside the school.* Use *inside of* for time or distance: *inside of*

a week; *inside of* ten miles.

insignia, *n.* Strictly, this is a *plural* noun (the **insignia** were displayed); however, it is commonly and acceptably used as a singular (he wears a different **insignia**).

Indeed, **insignia** is so firmly established in popular use as a singular that the plural **insignias** is now considered correct.

The precise, though infrequently used, singular for a badge or emblem is **insigne,** pronounced in-SIG'-nee.

See also CANDELABRA, CANDELABRUM; DATA; MEDIA.

insinuation *n.* See INNUENDO, INSINUATION.

insofar as Written as indicated, the separation occurring only before *as.*

insoluble, insolvable, unsolvable, *adj.* All three words mean *cannot be solved,* and the choice is purely a personal one. However, only **insoluble** has the additional meaning *cannot be dissolved: some minerals are* **insoluble** *in water.*

install, *v.* Meaning *to place formally in office,* this verb is followed by *in: she was* **installed** *in the presidency; the executive committee formally* **installed** *her in the presidency.*

Meaning *to formally confer the title and duties of office on,* **install** is followed by *as: was installed as president; the executive committee installed her as president.*

The noun form is *installation,* followed by *in* or *as,* according to the distinction in meaning described above.

Instal is a variant spelling, infrequently used.

instinct, intuition, *n.* *Instinct* is a genetic factor, common to a species. Certain behavior patterns in animals are *instinctive*—i.e., present at birth rather than acquired or learned. (The adjective *instinctual* means *pertaining to instinct* or *instincts.*)

Intuition, on the other hand, is knowledge or understanding that arises from feelings rather than from logic, conscious reasoning, or analysis. *Verb: intuit* (in-TOO'-it); *adjective: intuitive.*

instruct, *v.* To teach—followed by *in: instructed her in music.*

To tell, order—followed by the infinitive; *instructed them to turn left.*

instructress, *n.* See NOUN, 2A.

insufferable, unsufferable, *adj.* These adjectives are interchangeable, but the former is in more common use.

insupportable, unsupportable, *adj.* Both adjectives mean *incapable of being supported or upheld,* but *unsupportable*

is the better choice in this context. Only *insupportable* signifies *intolerable, unendurable,* etc.

insure *v.* See ASSURE, ENSURE, INSURE.

inter-, intra-, *prefix* *Inter-* means *between: intercontinental,* between continents; *interurban,* between cities; *intermural,* between schools; etc.

Intra- means *within: intraurban,* within one city; *intramuscular,* within the muscle; *intramural,* within a school; *intravenous,* within the vein or veins; etc.

Words using either prefix are written solid.

intercede, *v.* You *intercede with* (someone who has authority) *for* or *in behalf of* (the person who has made a request, needs permission, etc.): *please intercede for me* (or *in my behalf*) *with the governor.*

intern, internist, *n.* An *intern* (also spelled *interne*) is a physician serving an apprenticeship, under supervision, in a hospital. An *internist* is a specialist in internal medicine.

interpretive, interpretative, *adj.* The shorter adjective is preferable.

intersect, bisect *v.* See BISECT, INTERSECT.

into, in, *prep.* See IN, INTO.

intra-, inter- *prefix.* See INTER-, INTRA-.

intradermal, *adj.* See INTRAMUSCULAR, INTRAVENOUS, SUBCUTANEOUS, INTRADERMAL.

intramuscular, intravenous, subcutaneous, intradermal, *adj.* *Intramuscular*: *into or within the muscles.*
Intravenous: *directly into a vein or veins.*
Subcutaneous: *under the skin.*
Intradermal: *between the layers of the skin.*
These adjectives generally refer to different types of injections.

intransitive verbs See SENTENCE PATTERNS, 2, 6.

intravenous, *adj.* See INTRAMUSCULAR, INTRAVENOUS, SUBCUTANEOUS, INTRADERMAL.

intrust, *v.* See ENTRUST, INTRUST.

intuition, *n.* See INSTINCT, INTUITION.

inure, enure, *v.* *Enure* is the variant spelling.

invaluable, *adj.* See VALUABLE, INVALUABLE.

inveterate, *adj.* See CHRONIC, INVETERATE.

invite Preferably used only as a *verb*. The correct *noun* form is *invitation*.

IOU For plural, see NOUN, 6T.

irony, sarcasm, *n.* As here contrasted, *irony* is more subtle than sarcasm, and often humorous. *Sarcasm*, additionally, is usually biting, sneering, taunting, and/or derogatory.

irregardless, *adv.* A misuse for *regardless* or *irrespective*.

irreligious, *adj.* See IMPIOUS, SACRILEGIOUS, IRRELIGIOUS, NONRELIGIOUS.

irremediable, irremedial, *adj.* See REMEDIABLE, REMEDIAL.

irreparable, unrepairable, *adj.* See REPAIRABLE, REPARABLE.

irritate, aggravate, *v.* See AGGRAVATE, IRRITATE.

is when, is where See WHEN, WHERE (IS WHEN, IS WHERE).

it is I; it is me See PRONOUN, 8, 8A, 8B; SENTENCE PATTERNS, 3.

iterate, *v.* See REPEAT, ITERATE, REITERATE.

its, it's, its' *Its* is possessive: *the baby refused its food. It's* is a contraction of *it is: It's raining outside.*
Its' is a nonword.
See also CONTRACTIONS; PRONOUN, 8.

J

jaded, blasé, *adj.* As here compared, persons are *jaded* (or their appetites are *jaded*) if they have had such an excess of pleasure or thrills that it is hard or impossible to find something new to appeal to them. *Jaded* often refers to *a particular thing*, and is followed by the preposition *with*: *jaded with gourmet dining.*

People who are *blasé* have also overindulged, have continually traveled in the fast lane of life, or have seen and done so much that they are bored by what others may consider exciting. (The two words are fairly synonymous.) *Blasé* is followed by the preposition *about*: *blasé about life* (*love, money*, etc.).

jail, prison, penitentiary, *n.* Any place of confinement is a *prison*.

Specifically, a *jail* is a place of confinement for people awaiting trial or who have been convicted of minor offenses. Such people are committed to *jail* for comparatively short periods of time. Usually a *jail* is run by the city or county government.

A *penitentiary* (or *prison*)

is a state or federal institution for those convicted of major crimes.

Jap, Japanese, Nipponese, *n.* The first term, like *Chink* or *Chinaman*, is considered offensive. *Nippon* is the Japanese term for Japan, so *Nipponese* and *Japanese* are interchangeable.

jealous, *adj.* See ENVIOUS, JEALOUS.

jetsam, *n.* See FLOTSAM, JETSAM.

Jewess, *n.* This term may be considered condescending or offensive. As English becomes less gender-oriented, words like *authoress, poetess, Negress, Jewess*, etc. are falling into disuse. See also NOUN, 2B.

jibe, *v.* See GIBE, JIBE.

job, position, *n.* Some people consider a *job* in a business firm to be of lower rank than a *position*.

join together A redundancy —omit *together*.

judicial, judiciary, judicious, juridical, *adj. Judicial*: referring to *courts of law, judges,* etc.

Judiciary: as an adjective,

interchangeable with *judicial*; as a noun, either *the governmental agencies involved in the administration of justice*—i.e., the whole system of law courts—or *judges*, collectively.

Judicious: *wise or sound in judgment; prudent.*

Juridical: *pertaining to the law, to proceedings in a court of law, or to the science of law.*

Jugoslavia, n. See YUGOSLAVIA, JUGOSLAVIA.

juridical, *adj.* See JUDICIAL, JUDICIARY, JUDICIOUS, JURIDICAL.

K

kaffee klatsch, *n.* Write as two words or as a solid word; if you prefer the Anglicized spelling, write **coffee klatch** or **coffee klatsch**. The Anglicized and Germanic versions are equally popular.

karat, *n.* See CARAT, KARAT, CARET.

ketchup, *n.* See CATSUP, CATCHUP, KETCHUP.

kibbutz, *n.* The plural form is *kibbutzim.*

kilt, kilts, *n.* A *kilt* is a Scottish skirtlike, male garment; a Scotsman would doubtless wear only one kilt at a time, so using the plural *kilts* to denote such a garment is illogical and, if you wish to be strict about it, incorrect.

In the language of fashion, however, *kilts* is a woman's skirt similar to a Scottish *kilt.*

kin, *n.* One's relatives collectively are one's *kin;* this noun is treated as a plural, and is the same as *kinsfolk, kinfolk,* or *kinfolks.* All these words are plurals and interchangeable. See also NOUN, 61.

kind, kinds, *n.* If you will bear in mind that *kind* is a singular noun, you will not be tempted to say or write *these* (or *those*) *kind* of people. Correct usage: *this kind* of people; *that kind* of men; *these kinds* of people; *those kinds* of men.

When *kind* is the subject of a verb, use the form of the verb or auxiliary that agrees with a singular subject: *this kind* of books is rare; *that kind* of people has not been popular.

The same rules apply also to *sort* (*n.*) and *type* (*n.*).

kind of *Kind of* happy or *sort of* bored, meaning somewhat happy (or bored) is colloquial rather than formal English.

Kind of, sort of, type of, or **breed of** is followed directly by the noun: *that kind* (*sort, type, breed*) of person, not *that* **kind** (*sort, type, breed*) of a person.

kinfolk, kinsfolk, kinfolks, *n.* See KIN.

kitty-cornered, *adj.* See CATER-CORNERED, CATTY-CORNERED, CATER-CORNER, KITTY-CORNERED.

kleptomania, *n.* See THIEVERY.

108

kneel, *v.* You have a choice of *knelt* or *kneeled* for both the past tense and the participle.

kudo, *n.* This is a nonword, mistakenly thought to be the singular form of *kudos*—despite, the -*s* ending, *kudos* is a singular noun, and the only acceptable form of the word.

L

labor (a point) See BELABOR, LABOR (A POINT).

lachrymal, lachrymose, *adj.* *Lachrymal* (also spelled *lacrymal*) refers to tears, and is a term in anatomy: *lachrymal ducts of the eye.*

  Lachrymose means *tearful, teary-eyed,,* or *so sad* (as a story, event, etc.) *as to cause one to shed tears.*

lacuna, *n.* For plural, see NOUN, 6M.

laden *Laden* is either an adjective—i.e., *loaded, burdened, oppressed (laden with baggage)*—or one of the participles of the verb *lade*—i.e., *to load,* or *to dip* or *bail out.* The alternate participle of *lade* is *laded* (has, was *laded*). *Lade* as a verb meaning *to load* is somewhat literary in tone.

lady-in-waiting, *n.* For plural, see NOUN, 6U.

laissez faire, *n.* Two words as a noun: *believes in laissez faire;* hyphenated as an adjective; *a laissez-faire policy.* The noun is also spelled *laisser faire.*

lama, llama, *n.* With one *l,* a Buddhist monk; with double *l,* a South American mammal.

larceny, *n.* See THIEVERY.

larva, *n.* For plural, see NOUN, 6M.

lasso, *n.* For plural, see NOUN, 6L2.

latent, *adj.* See DORMANT, LATENT, POTENTIAL.

lath, lathe, *n.* A *lath* is a strip of wood; a *lathe* is a machine. *Lath* rhymes with *bath,* *Lathe* with *bathe.* Either word is also used as a verb.

latter, *adj.* See FORMER, LATTER.

lay, lie, *v.* See LIE, LAY.

lead, *v.* Past tense and participle are *led.*

lean, *v.* Past tense and participle are *leaned. Leant* is an alternate form.

leap, *v.* Past tense and participle are *leaped; leapt* is an alternate form. *Lept* is a misspelling.

least, *adj.* See COMPARISON

leave, let, *v.* To *leave* means, or implies, *to go away; to depart.* You *leave* your money to your heirs (after you depart this life); you *leave* for Europe; you *leave* the money

110

on the table (and go off to wherever you're bound).

Let means *allow*. *Let me help you; let the cat out of the bag; let us do the driving;* etc. *Let me alone* suggests *don't bother me; leave me alone* suggests *go away so I can be alone.* (However, idiomatically, the last two usages are interchangeable.)

Past tense or participle of *leave* is *left: the plane left* (or *has left*) *on time.* Past tense or participle of *let* is *let; he let* (or *has let*) *me work on the crossword puzzle with him.*

Oddly enough, the *noun let* means *an obstacle* in the legal phrase *without let or hindrance.*

lectern, *n.* See DAIS, PODIUM, LECTERN.

legend, myth, folklore, *n.* A *legend* is a story known and believed by generations of people and supposedly factual but impossible to verify.

A person whose accomplishments have made her or him famous not only during her or his lifetime but for many years later may be called a *legend;* hence, the interesting and deliberately contradictory characterization, *a legend in her* (or *his*) *own time. Adjective: legendary.*

A *myth* may be either a *legend* that explains natural phenomena or that deals with gods, goddesses, and/or ancient heroes, and that is unlikely to have any factual basis; or a wholly fictitious story or statement. *Adjective: mythical* or *mythic.*

Folklore refers to the traditions, beliefs, customs and *legends* of a people. *Adjective: folkloric.*

legislator, Solon (*solon*), *n.* A *legislator* is a member of any law-making body—i.e., of a *legislature.*

Solon (or *solon*) is used as a deliberately impressive and laudatory term that attributes wisdom and power to a *legislator.*

leisurely *Leisurely* is used both as an *adjective* and *adverb* (obviously, *leisurelily* is a nonword). So *you take a leisurely stroll,* or *you stroll leisurely.*

lend, loan *Lend* is a *verb* (*past tense and participle: lent*); *loan* is preferably a *noun.* In business parlance, *loan* is often used as a verb, and such usage cannot be dismissed out of hand as incorrect. It is best, in careful writing, to observe the distinction.

lesbian, *n.* See HOMOSEXUAL, GAY, LESBIAN.

less Incorrect substitute for *unless: we'll go unless* (not *less*) *the weather turns stormy.*

less, fewer In formal speech and writing, use *less* with a singular noun, *fewer* with a plural noun: *less joy, less information; fewer people,* *fewer* problems; *fewer* than five people; etc.

lesser, least See COMPARISON.

let, *n.* See LEAVE, LET.

let, *v.* See LEAVE, LET.

let, *v. (plus pronoun)* Since *let* is a verb, the personal pronouns that follow it are the direct objects, and therefore in the objective case: *let* him and me do it for you. See also PRONOUN, 8B.

letter *(of the alphabet)* For plural of *A*, *B*, etc., see NOUN, 6T.

liable (to) See LIKELY (TO), LIABLE (TO), APT (TO), PRONE (TO).

liaise, *v.* A back-formation from the noun *liaison*, this verb is considered by most authorities to be on a par with *enthuse*, *emote*, etc. Although suggested for informal rather than formal English, the term has lately attained increased currency. Patterns: *we decided to liaise at midnight; they planned to liaise with the*

advance units at the border. See also ENTHUSE.

libel, slander *Libel* is usually written, printed, etc., while *slander* is spoken. There are, of course, various other legal ramifications that only an experienced lawyer can explain. Both words are either nouns or transitive verbs.

liberal, radical In reference to politics: a *liberal* is in favor of gradual reforms that provide greater individual power and freedom; a *radical* wants rapid, far-reaching (or even extreme) change in society and/or the political structure of a state or nation.

Both words are used either as adjectives or nouns denoting persons. The philosophy: *liberalism, radicalism*.

libretto, *n.* For plural, see NOUN, 6L4.

lie, *v.* When to *lie* means *to tell an untruth*, the past tense or participle is, of course, *lied*. For forms of the other verb *lie*, see LIE, LAY below.

LIE, LAY, *v*

This is undoubtedly the most confusing and frustrating pair of verbs in the English language.

To gain complete control over these demons, and to be absolutely self-assured that you can use the correct form of the proper verb at all times, you must first learn thoroughly the distinction between *transitive*, *intransitive*, and *linking* verbs. (*Transitive*, *intransitive*, and *linking* verbs are covered completely under SENTENCE PATTERNS 1–6, and it is recommended, if you are not completely familiar with the distinction, that you study these pages before continuing with *lie* and *lay*.)

So, to start:

1. *Lie* is an *intransitive* or *linking* verb—that is, it is *not* followed by a direct object. The -ING form of *lie* is **lying**. For example:

   a. *The baby lies on its side.* There is no direct object—*on its side* is a P-GROUP (see PREPOSITION.)

   b. *The baby is **lying** quietly.* Again, no direct object—*quietly* is an adverb.

   c. *Please lie down. Down* is an adverb.

   d. *We lie on the beach every morning. Every morning* is an adverbial, not a direct object. (For adverbials, see ADVERB 4.)

   e. *The land lies barren and desolate for many miles. Barren* and *desolate* are adjectives, so in this sentence *lie* is a linking verb; *for many miles* is a P-GROUP. So there is no direct object.

   f. *Nevada lies east of California.* Again, no direct object.

2. *Lay* is a *transitive* verb—it is followed by a direct object. The -ING form is **laying**. For example:

   a. *Lay the book down. Book* is the direct object.

   b. *She lays a ten dollar chip on number 6, hoping that fortune will smile on her. Chip* is the direct object.

   c. *We are **laying** our lives down for the cause. Lives* is the direct object.

   d. *We are **laying** a stock of firewood in for the winter months ahead. Stock* is the direct object. *In* is an adverb that is movable to a position immediately after **laying**. (*Movability* is a characteristic of adverbs and adverbials.)

TEST YOURSELF

1. *(Lie, Lay)* still for a few minutes.
2. The dog was *(lying, laying)* behind the chair.
3. Please *(lie, lay)* your book down.
4. They are *(lying, laying)* the groundwork for the campaign.
5. I never saw so much junk *(lying, laying)* around!

KEY: 1. *Lie (linking v.)*; 2. **lying** *(intr.)*; 3. **lay** *(trans.)*; 4. **laying** *(trans.)*; 5. **lying** *(intr.)*.

So far, the distinction is simple enough: *lay* has a direct object—i.e., it is a *transitive* verb; *lie* has no direct object—i.e., it is an *intransitive* or *linking* verb.

But wait! The thorniest problem occurs in the *past tense*:

1. The past tense of *lie* is *lay*! (One can go slowly mad figuring out the ramifications of *lie* and *lay*.) For example:

　　a. *The baby lay* (past tense) *on its side all yesterday morning.* No direct object—*on its side* is a P-GROUP; *all yesterday morning* is a movable adverbial. We use the past tense of the *intransitive* verb *lie.*

　　b. *She lay asleep until the alarm rang.* No direct object— *asleep* is an adjective. We use the past tense of the *linking* verb *lie.*

2. The past tense of the *transitive* verb *lay* is *laid*—*layed* is a nonword, an incorrect spelling of *laid.* For example:

　　a. *They laid a trap for their opponents. Trap* is the direct object—the past tense of the *transitive* verb is required.

　　b. *She laid her cards down, claiming a grand slam in the bridge game. Cards* is the direct object.

Verbs have participles, the forms used after the auxiliary *has, have,* or *had.*

The participle of *lie* is *lain.* The participle of the transitive verb *lay* is *laid.* For example:

　　1. *They have laid our fears to rest.* Direct object: *fears.*

　　2. *The cat has lain in the sun all morning.* Intransitive verb—*in the sun* is a P-GROUP; *all morning* is a movable adverbial.

Two more points require consideration:

1. After the auxiliary *did,* the *present tense* of any verb is used: *did go, did eat,* etc. So: *They did not lie* (pres.) *awake for long; did you lay* (pres.) *the dishes away?*

2. *In the passive voice* (see VERB, 9), do not figure out whether the verb is transitive, intransitive, or linking.

The passive voice follows the pattern: N_1 + BE + PARTICIPLE.

N_1 is the *subject,* and any form of BE may occur (i.e., *am, is, are, was, were, being, been,* or *be*). Thus, *he was seen; it will be done; it has been taken;* etc.

When the verb in a sentence is in the passive voice, choose the participle of *lay*—namely: *laid.* (*Lain* is rarely used in the passive construction, except in a structure like *that couch has not been lain on all week.*)

Let us now look at this material in chart form, repeating the two special points above:

VERB *lie* *(intransitive* *or linking)*	-ING FORM *lying*	PAST TENSE *lay*	PARTICIPLE *lain*
lay *(transitive)*	*laying*	*laid*	*laid*

Point 1: Use the present tense after the auxiliary *did*.
Point 2: In a passive construction, use the participle *laid*.
Additional point: The -ING form of a verb has no tense.
Use *lying* for an *intransitive* or *linking* verb, *laying* for a
transitive verb, no matter what form of BE precedes the -ING
form: *is lying, was lying; are laying, were laying;* etc.

If the distinction between *lie* and *lay* is now clear (though
still complicated), you will be able to decide on the correct
verb to use in each sentence of the following test.

TEST YOURSELF

1. Smog *(lay, laid)* over Whittier like a blanket.
2. Have you *(lain, laid)* away your books?
3. He has *(lain, laid)* asleep all morning.
4. Why did you *(lie, lay)* awake so long?
5. The packages have been *(lain, laid)* under the Christmas tree.
6. Were they *(lying, laying)* in wait for the enemy to attack?
7. *(Lie, Lay)* down, Fido!
8. She *(lay, laid)* the table with her best silverware.
9. Dust was *(lying, laying)* all over the furniture.
10. The doctor *(lies, lays)* the infant on the examining
    table.

KEY: 1. *lay*—past tense of *lie*, intransitive verb *(v.i.)*; 2.
laid—participle of *lay*, transitive verb *(v.t.)*—*books* is the
direct object; *away* is an adverb; 3. *lain (v.i.)*—*asleep* is an
adjective; *all morning* is a movable adverbial; 4. *lie (v.i.)*
—present tense after *did*; 5. *laid*—use the participle of the
transitive verb in most passive constructions; 6. *lying*
(v.i.)—no direct object; 7. *lie (v.i.)*—*down* is an adverb; 8.
laid (v.t.)—past tense of *lay*; the direct object is *table*; 9.
lying (v.i.); 10. *lays (v.t.)*—*infant* is the direct object.
Incidentally, the correct expression is *the lie of the land,*

not *the lay of the land; lie* is the noun form of the intransitive verb *lie*, and the expression means "how the land *lies*."

---

lie, lay *(of the land)*, n. See FINAL PARAGRAPH OF LIE, LAY.

lift, *v.* See THIEVERY.

lighted, lit, *v.* Use either form as the past tense or participle of *light (v.)*: *We lighted* (or *lit*) *the lamp; the room was lighted* (or *lit*) *by a kerosene lamp.*

lightening, lightning. *Lightening* is the -ING form of the verb *to lighten*—i.e., make or become lighter; *lightning* is the weather phenomenon, as in *flash of lightning. Lightning* is also a verb: *it was lightning all night; it lightninged all night.* (The latter example may sound strange, but is neverthless correct.)

like, *prep.* A preposition is followed by the *objective* form of a personal pronoun: *talks like you and me.* See also PRONOUN, 8, 8B.

like, as, as if See AS/LIKE, AS IF/LIKE.

LIKELY (TO), LIABLE (TO), APT (TO), PRONE (TO)

To show probability, *likely (to)* is preferable in formal usage to *liable (to)* or *apt (to)*: *they are very likely to be late.* (Some authorities demand a qualifier such as *very, most, quite,* or *rather,* preceding *likely* when *likely* is used in the sense indicated, but there is no hard and fast rule for this.)

In formal English, *liable (to)* indicates the probability of something unpleasant or undesirable: *liable to hurt himself; liable to lose the race; liable to punishment;* etc.

Apt (to), in formal usage, implies a habitual tendency: *he is apt to lose courage whenever he senses danger.*

Prone (to) is synonymous with *apt (to)* in the sense indicated above, but is more often used to show a natural disposition to do something regrettable, unacceptable, unpleasant, or not in one's best interests: *he is prone to making errors (getting involved in questionable activities, driving too fast, losing his balance, etc.); prone to anger, temper tantrums,* etc.

See also PRONE, SUPINE, PROSTRATE.

---

linage, lineage, *n. Linage* designates lines of print or writing on a page. A variant spelling is *lineage,* but however spelled, the word is pronounced LĪN'-əj.

Lineage, pronounced LIN'-ee-əj, is *ancestry, line of descent,* etc.

lineal, linear, *adj. Lineal* refers to the line of descent or heredity—i.e., to *lineage* (see LINAGE, LINEAGE).

Linear refers to lines in general, and therefore also means *straight. Lineal* is used in this context, too, but less frequently than *linear*.

linguist, linguistician, polyglot, *n.* A *linguist* is fluent in several languages or is an expert in linguistics. Thomas H. Middleton, a popular writer on matters linguistic, prefers the term *linguistician* for such an expert, as do some other linguistic authorities.

Polyglot is another, less common, term for one who is fluent in several languages.

linguistics, philology, semantics, *n. Linguistics* is the science of language.

Philology is the earlier term for this science, now generally replaced by *linguistics*.

Semantics is the science of meaning as expressed in language. A less frequently used term for this science is *semasiology*.

See also -ICS.

linking verbs See SENTENCE PATTERNS, 3, 3A.

lion's share, the The term is now popularly used to mean *the largest portion or part*, though in the Aesop fable from which the phrase derives, *the lion's share* was, of course, the whole thing—i.e., all of it.

liquefy, rarefy, putrefy, stupefy, torrefy, *v.* These are the only five nontechnical verbs ending in the suffix *-efy* instead of the usual *-ify*. The noun derivatives are also unusual: *liquefaction, rarefaction, putrefaction, stupefaction, torrefaction.* (The normal noun derivative of a verb ending in the suffix *-ify* is *-ification: simplify (v.), simplification (n.).* The noun form of *petrify (v.),* however, is *petrifaction; petrification* is an alternate form.

liquid See FLUID, LIQUID.

lit, *v.* See LIGHTED, LIT.

literally, figuratively, *adv. He literally died of shame*— does this mean that he *actually* died, that his life was in fact ended? If we follow the strict meaning of *literally,* the sentence in question means exactly that. If the speaker or writer intended us to understand that he *virtually* (or *seemingly*) died of shame, he or she is using *literally* loosely and incorrectly. *Die of shame* is a figure of speech and therefore not to be taken *literally*—i.e., in a factual, real, or exact sense.

So when you do not wish your words to be taken in their *exact* (or *literal*) meaning, use *figuratively, virtually,* etc., *not literally*.

See also DENOTATION, CONNOTATION.

llama, *n.* See LAMA, LLAMA.

loan, *v.* See LEND, LOAN.

loath, loathe *Loath* (LŌTH) is an *adjective*, generally followed by an infinitive, meaning *unwilling, very reluctant. She is loath to end the marriage.* (*Loth* is a variant spelling of *loath*.)

Loathe (LŌTH) is a *verb;* meaning *to hate and be disgusted by.* He *loathes* traitors. In *loath*, the *th* is pronounced as in *thing;* in *loathe*, the *th* is pronounced as in *this*.

loathsome, *adj.* Oddly enough, the verb *loathe* (see LOATH, LOATHE) has a derivative adjective *loathsome* (the *th* pronounced as in *this*), not *loathesome*.

locomote, *v.* See ENTHUSE.

locus, *n.* For plural, see NOUN, 6P.

lodgings, *n. pl.* Though singular in concept *(a rented room or apartment, often in a private house)*, the noun is construed as a plural: *his lodgings were expensive.*

logistics, *n.* See -ICS.

lonely, lonesome, *adj.* As applied to persons and their feelings, the two words are pretty much interchangeable.

Lonesome, however, more strongly suggests a desire for companionship, an acute feeling of unhappiness over lacking such companionship, or sadness because another has left one alone: *felt lonesome for his wife.*

longshoreman, stevedore, *n.* Either term refers to the person who works at docks loading and unloading ships.

looker-on, *n.* The plural is *lookers-on*. In formal style, *onlooker* is the preferable term. See also NOUN, 6U.

loose, loosen, lose *Loose* (LŌŌS) is an adjective *(a very loose knot);* it is also a verb synonymous with *loosen* *(v.).*

Loose (v.) also means *let fly* or *to discharge: loose a volley of shots.*

With the meaning of *make or become loose* or *untie*, *loosen* is the more commonly used verb.

Lose (LŌŌZ) is a verb only: *lose one's money; lose sight of.* Past tense and participle are *lost*.

Unloose (v.) and *unloosen* (v.) are, oddly enough, synonyms of the verbs *loose* and *loosen* and are interchangeable with them.

LOT, *n.*

A lot of may mean *several* or *many*, in which case it is treated as a plural: *a lot of my best friends were at the party.*

A lot of may also mean *a large part* or *portion*, in which case it is considered singular: *a lot of the work is finished.*

A lot, without the prepositional phrase, follows the same rule. Do you mean *several* or *many* (individuals, items, etc.)? *A lot* is plural: *a lot are missing* (i.e., many people, items, etc.). Do you mean *much*? *A lot* is singular: *a lot has been accomplished* (i.e., much).

Lot may refer to a unit, and is then usually preceded by *one, this, that,* or *the: One lot is ready for shipping; this (that, the) lot was sold at auction for a record price.*

Lot is also a piece of land, and is then of course singular: *a lot in the north area of the city is very expensive.*

See also NUMBER, NOUN, 1.

---

loth, *adj.* See LOATH, LOATHE.

low, *adj.* See NOMINAL, LOW.

lubricious, lubricous, *adj.* Two equally acceptable spellings for the same word. The pronunciations, of course, differ: lōō-BRISH'-əs for the first, LŌŌ'-brə-kəs for the second. *Noun: lubricity.*

lucid, pellucid, *adj. Lucid* may mean *clear,* in the sense of *easily understood* (*lucid explanation*) or *rational, unconfused, clearheaded* (*lucid moments*). In poetry, the word is sometimes used to mean *bright or shining.*

Pellucid may, on the one hand, be a much stronger descriptive than *lucid* in reference to clarity of style or meaning; or, on the other hand, may describe the physical clearness of an object, and would then be a synonym of *translucent* or *transparent: pellucid waters of the lake.*

See also TRANSPARENT, TRANSLUCENT, OPAQUE.

lunch, luncheon, *n.* The words are more or less interchangeable, but a *luncheon* is usually more formal and eaten with another or others. *Luncheon* may, in addition, be a party or function at which a midday meal is served.

Only *lunch,* of course, may be used also as a verb.

luxurious, luxuriant, *adj. Luxurious* describes that which is expensive, sumptuous, pleasure-producing, and, of course, not necessary to health or life: *luxurious yachts; luxurious mink coats; luxurious dining on an expense account;* etc. Noun: *luxury, luxuriousness.*

Luxuriant describes that which grows naturally and is thickly and lushly abundant: *luxuriant vegetation; luxuriant golden tresses; luxuriant coat of fur.*

Luxuriant may less frequently also characterize that which is richly, wildly, or excessively ornate or extravagant, as in design: *luxuriant architecture; a* **luxuriant** *and fevered imagination* or *inventiveness.* Noun: **luxuriance**.

M

mad, *adj.* See ANGRY, MAD.

magnate, potentate, *n.* A *magnate* is a powerful and important person, usually in the business world.

A *potentate* is either one who has the power to rule over, or dominate, others in the same field of endeavor; or a politically powerful ruler, especially in a nation, state, or other large group not founded on democratic principles.

maid of honor, *n.* For plural, see NOUN, 6U.

maidservant, *n.* For plural, see NOUN, 6U.

majority, plurality, *n.* In reference to voting, a *majority* of votes signifies at least one more than half the votes cast; a *plurality* of votes signifies a greater number of votes for one of three or more candidates or issues, but less than a *majority*.

See also NOUN, 1.

maladroit, *adj.* See CLUMSY, MALADROIT, GAUCHE.

malfeasance, misfeasance, nonfeasance, *n.* Public officials who violate the laws or regulations of their office are guilty of *malfeasance*.

If such officials commit an act that in itself is lawful, but do so in an illegal manner, with the result that the rights of others are violated, they are guilty of *misfeasance*.

And if they fail to fulfill the legal responsibilities and requirements of their office, they are guilty of *nonfeasance*.

This somewhat complicated distinction makes etymological sense, for the Latin prefix *mal-* means *bad*, *mis-* means *wrong*, and *non-*, of course, means *not*.

mania, phobia, *n.* The two words, as here contrasted, are more or less opposed in meaning.

A *mania* is a morbid and obsessive need, desire, or craving, or an irresistible compulsion (to do or act). A *phobia*, on the contrary, is a morbid and irrational dread (of something). Thus, *pyromania* is an irresistible need to set fires, *pyrophobia* a morbid dread of fire.

manifesto, *n.* For plural form, see NOUN, 6L1.

manipulable, manipulatable, *adj.* The former word is preferable; both are correct.

121

manipulative, manipulatory, *adj.* The first form is more commonly used; both are correct.

manly, mannish, *adj.* **Manly,** a complimentary term, refers to a male and describes the qualities, characteristics, attributes, and/or appearance traditionally expected of a man.

Mannish refers to a female, and is not necessarily derogatory. The adjective describes characteristics, clothing, hair style, appearance, etc. that usually would be found in a male.

See also WOMANISH, WOMANLY.

man-of-war, *n.* For the plural form, see NOUN, 6U.

manservant, *n.* For the plural form, see NOUN, 6U.

manslaughter, *n.* See HOMICIDE, MANSLAUGHTER, MURDER, ASSASSINATION.

mantel, mantle, *n.* The shelf over, and/or the facing around, a fireplace is preferably spelled **mantel. Mantle** is a variant spelling. Similarly, **mantelpiece** is the preferable, **mantlepiece** the variant, spelling.

For other meanings, and, of course, for the verb, **mantle** is the correct spelling.

mare, *n.* See NOUN, 2D.

marchioness, *n.* See MARQUEE, MARQUIS, MARQUISE, MARCHIONESS.

marina, *n.* See PIER, DOCK, MARINA, QUAY, WHARF.

marine, maritime, nautical, naval, *adj.* These adjectives are partially synonymous, with minor distinctions as noted:

Marine is the all-inclusive adjective referring to the sea, ocean, navigation, ships, navies, sailors, etc.

Maritime especially describes people or areas that are on, bordering, or near a sea or ocean; but this word, though less commonly, may also refer to ships, shipping, navigation, or sailors.

Nautical refers to ships, sailors, or navigation.

Naval refers to a navy, including both the ships and their personnel.

marital, martial, *adj.* Though similar in appearance, and containing the same letters in different order, these adjectives are pronounced differently and are totally unrelated.

Marital (MÂR'-ə-təl): *referring to marriage.*

Martial (MAHR'-shəl): *referring to war, the armed forces, or a warrior.*

(Although some **marital** relations may at times be **martial,** such cases have no application to the meanings of the words.)

See also MARSHAL, MARTIAL.

maritime, *adj.* See MARINE, MARITIME, NAUTICAL, NAVAL.

marquee, marquis, marquise, marchioness, *n.* A *marquee* is the structure or awning over the entrance to a theater, hotel, etc. Occasionally, though rarely, such a structure is also called a *marquise*.

Marquis is the title of a European nobleman; the wife, widow, or female counterpart of a *marquis* is a *marquise* or a *marchioness*.

marriageable, nubile, *adj.* Both words mean *ready or suited for marriage*, but *nubile* refers only to a female, and suggests sexual maturity or development: *of marriageable age; nubile young women.*

marshal, martial *Marshal* is a noun designating European military rank, a police or court officer, or other official. *Martial* is an adjective. (See MARITAL, MARTIAL.)

The two words are pronounced identically.

marten, martin, *n.* A *marten* is a mammal; a *martin* is a bird.

martial, *adj.* See MARITAL, MARTIAL; MARSHAL, MARTIAL.

mask, masque, *n.* See MASQUE, MASK.

masochist, sadist, *n.* *Masochists* derive pleasure, usually on an unconscious level, from being hurt, humiliated, mistreated, etc. Such pleasure may, but need not be, sexual in nature.

The *sadist*, on the other hand, enjoys hurting, humiliating, or mistreating another or others—again the pleasure may, but need not be, sexual in nature.

masque, mask, *n.* *Masque* usually designates a type of drama popular in England in the sixteenth and seventeenth centuries. (*Mask* is a variant spelling for this meaning.)

Mask, of course, designates the facial covering worn to disguise one's identity. (*Masque* is a variant spelling for this meaning.)

massacre The *-re* ending is required so that the preceding *c-* is pronounced like a *k*, not like an *s*. Other forms of the noun or verb may look strange, but are in fact correct: *massacred, massacring, massacrer.* See also -ER, -RE.

masseur, masseuse, *n.* A *masseur* is a man, a *masseuse* a woman, who gives professional massages.

See also NOUN, 2C.

masterful, masterly, *adj.* *Masterful* may mean either *acting the master* (i.e., domineering, dictatorial, powerful, or in command), or *like a master* (i.e., unusually competent, brilliant, etc.).

Masterly, however, means only *like a master* (i.e., competent, etc.).

Both words may describe either people or their actions, performances, etc.

material, materiel, matériel, n. *Materiel*, written with or without the French accent, and pronounced mə-teer'-ee-EL', is the "*material*," or equipment and supplies, of the armed forces (as opposed to the personnel), or, less commonly, of any other organization.

materialize, occur, v. To use *materialize* as a synonym of *occur* is considered unacceptable in formal usage. *A day in which nothing significant materialized*, meaning *an uneventful day*, sounds like an abortive attempt to achieve elegance at the expense of good usage.

mathematics, n. See -ICS.

matricide, n. See PARRICIDE, PATRICIDE, MATRICIDE.

matrix, n. For plural, see NOUN, 6O.

matron of honor, n. For plural, see NOUN, 6U.

maudlin, mawkish, adj. See SENTIMENTAL, MAUDLIN, MAWKISH.

mausoleum, n. For plural, see NOUN, 6Q.

mawkish, maudlin, adj. See SENTIMENTAL.

maximum, n. For plural, see NOUN, 6Q.

maximum, optimum, adj. In a context like *maximum (optimum) class size* (*capacity, number,* etc.), *maximum* means *the most possible* while *optimum* means *the best possible.*

may, can, aux. See CAN, MAY.

may, might, aux. Both auxiliaries indicate either present or future time. *May* shows greater probability, however, than *might. I may go* indicates a stronger likelihood of going than *I might go.*

As the auxiliary of one of two or more clauses in a sentence, *might* is required if the verb or verbs in the other clause or clauses indicate past time: *if he were to ask me politely, I might* (not *may*) *do it; if he had asked me politely, I might* (not *may*) *have done it.*

For *may* indicating permission, see CAN, MAY.

may of See COULD HAVE, COULD OF.

maybe, may be If you mean *perhaps,* write the word solid. Otherwise, write as separate words: *it may be true.*

meager, meagre, adj. *Meagre* is the British spelling. See also -ER, -RE.

MEANS, *n.*

In the sense of *resources*, **means** is a plural noun. *The* **means** *are available to fund the project.*

In the sense of *method* or *methods*, **means** is treated as either a singular or plural noun, depending on whether the word signifies one method, or a plurality of methods. For example:

> *Every* **means** *was* taken to assure success.
> *This* **means** *has* always worked.
> *One* **means** to make him behave *is* to bribe him.
> *A* **means** to an end *is* all I'm searching for.
> There *are several* **means** to a desired goal.
> *Such* **means** *are* not working; we will have to think of other methods.
> *All* possible **means** *were* used.

---

measles, *n.* Certain diseases or afflictions end in the letter *s*; since a *single* disease or affliction is indicated in each instance, the term is treated as a singular noun. Examples are: *AIDS, herpes, hives, measles, mumps, rickets, shingles.* So: *AIDS is often fatal; hives is an uncomfortable condition to have; measles is contagious; mumps is usually a childhood disease; shingles is generally a painful affliction;* etc.

media, *n.* Like *candelabra, data,* and *insignia, media* is, strictly, a *plural* noun—i.e., several forms of mass communication; for example the press, radio, television, etc. One such form, again strictly, is a *medium* of communication.

And, like *candelabra, data,* and *insignia, media* is

so often used as a *singular* noun, that one has no choice but to consider such usage acceptable.

It is therefore unrealistic to call the *media was present* or *television is a powerful media* incorrect English.

In very formal English, on the other hand, *the* **media** *were present* or *television is a powerful* **medium** is considered preferable.

As is so often mentioned in these pages, one cannot hold out against changes in language. General and popular usage will ultimately prevail.

See also CANDELABRA, CANDELABRUM; DATA; INSIGNIA; NOUN, 6Q.

mediaeval, *adj.* See MEDIEVAL, MEDIAEVAL.

medical examiner, *n.*   See PA-THOLOGIST, MEDICAL EXAM-INER, CORONER.

medicament, medication, *n.* Meaning *a medicine* or *any agent that is intended to heal, cure, relieve pain,* etc., the words are interchangeable. In lay language, **medication** is the more popular term.

medieval, mediaeval, *adj.* The former is the preferable spelling, the latter now some-what old-fashioned or pedantic.

mediocracy, *n.*   A nonword, used in error for the noun **mediocrity.** Too bad there is no such word—if there were, it might mean *rule by inept and incompetent people.*

mediocre, *adj.*   The noun form is **mediocrity.** (See MEDIOCRACY.)

medium, *n.*   See MEDIA.

meet, meet with   You *meet with* a person or group for purposes of discussion, etc.; a person or thing *meets with* one's approval, hostility, etc. If things or people come to-gether, see one another, etc., they simply *meet*: *I'll meet* (not *meet with*) *you at ten o'clock.*

megaphone, microphone, bull-horn, *n.*   A **megaphone** is a funnel-shaped, portable de-vice that amplifies the voice; a **microphone** amplifies the voice electrically, as on the stage of a theater, auditorium, etc. (A **megaphone** that is elec-trical is called a **bullhorn.**)

(If you are interested in et-ymology, you will be amused by the fact that *mega-* comes from a Greek word meaning "large," while *micro-* derives from a Greek word meaning "small.")

melancholy, melancholic *Melancholy* can be used as both a noun and an adjective; as an adjective it is in more common use than *melan-cholic,* which has a distinct literary flavor.

mellifluous, mellifluent; mel-liferous, mellific, *adj.*   The first two words are completely synonymous and interchange-able, describing sounds, voices, tones, etc. that are sweet and smooth—i.e., like honey. *Mellifluous* is the more com-monly used adjective.

The final two words are also interchangeable, describ-ing literally that which pro-duces or bears honey. *Mel-liferous* is the more com-mon of the two adjectives.

melodic, melodious, *adj.* *Melodic* means *pertaining to, using,* or *containing a mel-ody or melodies. Melodious,* on the other hand, describes that which is pleasing in sound, tuneful, etc.

The words are occasionally used interchangeably, but the distinction avoids ambiguity.

memento, *n.*   For plural, see NOUN, 6L2.

memorabilia, *n.* This is a plural noun: *the **memorabilia** of the Roosevelt era were kept in a special room in the museum.*

The singular form is ***memorabile*** {mem'-ə-RAB'-ə-lee}, and designates *one* such token, memento, etc.

memorandum, *n.* The plural is ***memoranda*** or ***memorandums,*** the latter occurring infrequently.

It is incorrect to use ***memoranda*** as a *singular: The **memoranda** are* {not *is*} *on your desk; these* or *those* {not *this* or *that*} ***memoranda** are . . .*

See also NOUN, 6Q.

meretricious, meritorious, *adj.* Though similar in appearance, these words are totally unrelated.

Meretricious*: insincere; tawdry; specious; attractive in a vulgar or flashy manner.* {Obviously not a complimentary adjective.}

Meritorious*: worthy of merit* {*praise, reward,* etc.}. {Certainly a complimentary term.}

mesmerism; mesmerize See HYPNOTISM, HYPNOSIS, MESMERISM.

metal, mettle, *n.* Something tests your ***mettle***; you are on your ***mettle***; etc. Iron or lead is a ***metal***.

metamorphosis, *n.* For plural, see NOUN, 6N.

metaphor, *n.* See SIMILE, METAPHOR.

metastasis, *n.* For plural, see NOUN, 6N.

meter, metre, *n.* *Metre* is the British spelling. See also -ER, -RE.

methods, methodology, *n.* To use *methodology* as a synonym of *methods,* meaning *ways of getting things done,* is not standard English.

Methodology is a system of *methods,* as in a science; it is also a branch of logic dealing with principles of reasoning.

mettle, *n.* See METAL, METTLE.

microphone, *n.* See MEGAPHONE, MICROPHONE, BULLHORN.

midget, *n.* See DWARF, MIDGET.

midst, *n. Midst* is chiefly used in a phrase like *in the midst of* or *in our (your, their) midst.*

might, may, *aux.* See MAY, MIGHT.

might of See COULD HAVE, COULD OF.

militate, *v.* Followed by the preposition *against: his shabby way of dressing will militate against his getting a position that requires a well-groomed appearance.*

Do not confuse this word with *mitigate,* discussed

in the entry EXTENUATE, MITIGATE.

millennium, *n.* For plural, see NOUN, 6Q.

mimic, mime, *n.* A *mimic* is a person who imitates, or an actor skilled in imitations or mimicry.

A *mime* is an actor or actress skilled in pantomime— i.e., communication through gestures instead of speech; also, the performance of a pantomime.

Less commonly, a *mime* is an actor or actress specializing in comic mimicry, or any comic or buffoonish character.

mineralogy, *n.* Note the *a* before the *l*—this is the science of minerals. Oddly enough, however, the science of crime and criminals is criminology. (The study of family descent is genealogy, not geneology.)

minimum, *n.* For plural, see NOUN, 6Q.

minus In the sense of *lacking* or *without, minus* is colloquial or informal English: *I would like to pay you, but I'm* **minus** *five dollars.*

It is incorrect to use *minus* as a verb. *Minus the smaller number from the larger number* is nonstandard English. Correct substitution: *subtract.*

minutia, *n.* This is *one* small or unimportant detail

or *item; the plural is* **minutiae,** pronounced mə-NOO'-shee-ee. See also NOUN, M1.

misanthrope, misogynist, misogamist, misandrist, *n.* The *misanthrope* hates everyone, the whole world. (*Misanthropist* is an equally acceptable form of the word.)

The *misogynist* hates women.

The *misogamist* hates marriage.

The *misandrist* is a woman who hates men.

miscellanea, miscellany, *n.* Both words may designate a miscellaneous collection of literary works. Both words are treated as singular nouns; the first is more impressive and shows one's erudition. *Miscellany,* of course, may also be a varied collection of anything else.

misdemeanor, *n.* See FELONY, MISDEMEANOR.

misfeasance, *n.* See MALFEASANCE, MISFEASANCE, NONFEASANCE.

mislead, *v.* The past tense or participle is *misled.*

misogamist *n.* See MISANTHROPE, MISOGYNIST, MISOGAMIST, MISANDRIST.

misogynist, *n.* See MISANTHROPE, MISOGYNIST, MISOGAMIST, MISANDRIST.

misremember, disremember, *v. To misremember* is *to remember incorrectly.*

To disremember is to be unable to remember, or to forget—but this word is at best a regional or colloquial usage.

missal, *n.* See MISSIVE, MISSILE, MISSAL.

missile, *n.* See MISSIVE, MISSILE, MISSAL.

missive, missile, missal, *n.* A *missive* is a letter or other message sent or received; a *missile* is a weapon fired or hurled through the air at a target; a *missal* is a prayer book.

mistrust, *v.* See DISTRUST, MISTRUST.

mitigate, *v.* See EXTENUATE, MITIGATE.

mnemonics, *n.* See -ICS.

moat, mote, *n.* A protective ditch around a castle or fortress is a *moat*; a speck of dust is a *mote*.

moist, *adj.* See HUMID, MOIST.

mol-, moul- Certain words spelled *mol-* in the U.S. are written *moul-* in Britain—e.g., *mold, molder, molding, moldy, molt.* The British forms are *mould, moulder, moulding, mouldy, moult.*

moneyed, monied, *adj.* The first spelling is preferable; the second is also correct. Similarly, *honeyed* is the preferable spelling; *honied* is also acceptable.

moneys, monies, *n. pl.*

Moneys is preferable, but *monies* is so often used that it is correct and fully acceptable. However, the plural of *honey* is *honeys* only. See also NOUN, 6F.

mongoose, *n.* Though the plural of *goose* (the bird) is *geese*, the plural of *mongoose* is *mongooses*.

monied, *adj.* See MONEYED, MONIED.

monkey, *n.* For plural see NOUN, 6F.

monotheism, *n.* See THEISM, MONOTHEISM, POLYTHEISM, PANTHEISM, DEISM.

monster, monstrous, *adj.* The adjective *monster* means *very large; huge: a monster rally was held.*

Monstrous may also mean *very large,* though some authorities object to such usage.

Preferably, *monstrous* signifies *abnormally large; abnormal in shape, size, or type* (i.e., *like a monster*); *evil, wicked, outrageous, shocking, hideous,* etc.: *a monstrous and infamous crime.*

See also ENORMITY, ENORMOUSNESS.

moose, *n.* For plural, see NOUN, 6H.

moral, morale, *n.* The lesson taught by a fable, anecdote, or story is a *moral.*

Confidence, courage, enthusiasm, etc., especially in reference to a group, is one's

morale; the **morale** of the faculty, etc.

morals, mores, n. pl. **Morals** are the generally accepted principles of good, ethical, honest, right, etc. behavior (often sexual behavior).

Mores (pronounced MÔR'-eez or MÔR'-ayz) are the traditional customs or folkways of a group, tribe, nation, etc. that are considered essential to the welfare of society and that thus often have the power of law.

morass, quagmire, slough, n. All three words designate literally a marsh, a swamp, or bog of one sort or another.

Figuratively, a **morass** is a difficult and confusing state or condition: found himself in a **morass** of indecision; a **quagmire** is a position of difficulty from which one cannot easily escape: beset by a **quagmire** of peril, (fear, debt, etc.); and **slough** is a feeling, or feelings, of deep despair, depression, discouragement, etc.: pull yourself out of your **slough**.

Meaning a swamp, **slough** is pronounced SLOO; in its figurative connotation, it is pronounced SLOU.

An entirely different **slough**, pronounced SLUF, refers as a noun to whatever is shed or cast off (as a snake's skin, for example), and as a verb to shedding or casting off. The verb also means to make light of, shrug off, in which sense

it is followed by the preposition off or over.

moratorium, n. For plural see NOUN, 6Q.

more important, more importantly In a structure such as working enabled her to earn some extra money; **more important,** it made her feel needed and useful, some authorities insist that **more important** is the correct usage, claiming that it is a shortened form of what is more important. Many people, however, see an adverbial construction in such a sentence, and prefer **more importantly.** The choice is yours—either way you are using standard English.

more preferable Preferable says it all; more preferable is redundant.

more than See BETTER THAN, MORE THAN; PREFER TO, MORE THAN, RATHER THAN.

more than one In a construction such as **more than one** person has remarked on that, we consider the subject singular, even though **more than one** signifies two, three, four, or more. Hence, we use the -S FORM of the present tense of the verb or auxiliary. See also SUBJECT, VERB AGREEMENT.

moreover, conj. For correct punctuation when this conjunction introduces a clause, see HOWEVER.

mores, *n. pl.* See MORALS, MORES.

moron, moronic See FEEBLE-MINDED, CRETINOUS, MORONIC, IMBECILIC, IDIOTIC.

mortality, *n.* See CASUALTY, FATALITY, MORTALITY.

mortgagor, mortgagee, *n.* The *mortgagor* has borrowed money, using real property as collateral; the *mortgagee* has lent the money—i.e., holds the mortgage.

Mortgager is a variant spelling of *mortgagor*—in either form, the second *g* is pronounced like a *j.*

mosaic, *n.;* **Mosaic,** *adj.* With a lowercase *m,* a *mosaic* is the design. With a capital *M,* the adjective refers to the Moses of the Ten Commandments. An alternate adjective form of *Mosaic* is *Mosaical.*

mosquito, *n.* For plural, see NOUN, 6L2.

most, 'most See ALMOST, MOST, 'MOST.

mote, *n.* See MOAT, MOTE.

mother-in-law, *n.* See IN-LAWS.

motif, motive, *n.* As a theme, etc. in art, including literature, music, and architecture. *motif* (mō-TEEF') is the preferable spelling, *motive* (MŌ'-tәv or mō-TEEV') the variant spelling.

motor, *v.* In the sense of drive or ride in a motor vehicle, this verb is standard English, despite some pedantic quibbling to the contrary.

motto, *n.* For plural, see NOUN, 6L2.

moul- See MOL-, MOUL-.

moustache, *n.* See MUSTACHE, MOUSTACHE, MUSTACHIO.

muchly A nonword, used by those misguided souls who like to have an adverb end in *-ly.*

mucous, mucus *Mucous* is the adjective (variant form: *mucose*); *mucus* is the noun.

mulatto, *n.* For plural, see NOUN, 6L2.

multilingual, polyglot, *adj.* These adjectives are synonymous, but *multilingual* usually describes a person (*she is multilingual*), *polyglot* a group or place (*Los Angeles has a polyglot population; Switzerland, a polyglot nation, . . .*).

See also LINGUISTICS, PHILOLOGY, SEMANTICS; LINGUIST, LINGUISTICIAN, POLYGLOT.

mumps, *n.* See MEASLES.

murder, *n.* See HOMICIDE, MANSLAUGHTER, MURDER, ASSASSINATION.

muscle, mussel, *n.* The edible bivalve is spelled *mussel.*

must *Must* may be a noun (*this is a must*), meaning *a requirement,* etc.; it is used as an adjective (this is a **must** assignment) only in colloquial or informal English.

must of See COULD HAVE, COULD OF.

mustache, moustache, mustachio, n. *Mustache* is the common American spelling, *moustache* is chiefly the British spelling (the two words are pronounced identically—MUS'-tash or mə-STASH'), and *mustachio* is generally used humorously. (The plural of *mustachio* is **mustachios**.)

My dear ... See DEAR ..., MY DEAR ...

myriad Most commonly found in formal usage as an adjective: *myriad treasures; myriad ethnic groups.* Since *myriad (adj.)* describes a very large, but indefinite, number, the noun following should be in the plural form.

Also used as a noun: *myriads of treasure; a myriad of ethnic groups.*

myself, pron. It is not good usage to substitute *myself* for

I or *me,* as in *my husband and myself appreciate* ... (correct usage: *my husband and I appreciate . . .*), or as in *she invited my husband and myself* ... (correct usage: *she invited my husband and me . . .*).

The same principle applies to **ourselves** as an incorrect substitution for *we* or *us.*

Myself and *ourselves* should be used only as reflexive pronouns—i.e., *I hurt myself; we found ourselves; I myself did it; we ourselves finished it; I did it by myself; we did it by ourselves.*

See also OURSELF, OURSELVES.

mysterious, mystical, adj. These words are not synonyms. *Mystical* (or the variant *mystic*) describes something beyond rational explanation in a religious rite or spiritual experience.

The noun form of *mystical* is *mysticism,* and the person who believes in, or practices, *mysticism* is a *mystic.*

myth, n. See LEGEND, MYTH, FOLKLORE.

N

nadir, *n.* See ZENITH, NADIR.

NAIVE, INGENUOUS, INGENIOUS, *adj.*

Call persons *naive* who are lacking in worldly experience, who are unsophisticated and almost childlike in their innocence and trust. *Naive* is also spelled with the dieresis (¨)—*naïve*; the noun, too, is spelled with or without the dieresis—*naiveté* or *naïveté*—and is pronounced nah-eev-TAY'. Variant noun forms are *naivety* (nah-EEV'-ə-tee) and *naiveness*. A variant adjective form is spelled *naif* or *naïf* (nah-EEF').

Call persons *ingenuous* who are childlike in their directness and frankness, not sophisticated enough to disguise or hide their feelings or thoughts when tact would suggest they do so. *Noun: ingenuousness.*

Ingenious (in-JEEN'-yəs), on the other hand, has no relationship in meaning to *ingenuous* or *naive.* An *ingenious* person, act, plan, mind, etc. is clever, inventive, cunning, etc. *Nouns: ingenuity* (in-jə-NOO'-ə-tee) or *ingeniousness.*

---

natatorium, *n.* For plural, see NOUN, 6Q.

naught, *n.* See ZERO, AUGHT, OUGHT, NAUGHT, NOUGHT.

nauseous, nauseated, *adj.* Strictly, *nauseous* means *causing nausea* (a *nauseous* concoction), and *nauseated* signifies *feeling nausea.*

However, colloquially and informally, *nauseous* is widely used with the same meaning as *nauseated.*

nautical, *adj.* See MARINE, MARITIME, NAUTICAL, NAVAL.

naval, *adj.* See MARINE, MARITIME, NAUTICAL, NAVAL.

navel, *n.* The umbilicus (or "bellybutton") is a *navel.* So the orange containing an indentation resembling the umbilicus is, of course, a *navel* orange.

nebula, *n.* For plural, see NOUN, 6M.

necessaries, necessities, *n. pl.* These words are interchangeable, but the latter is more frequently used. *Necessaries* may specifically refer to supplies and/or money required for an endeavor, journey, etc.

neglect, negligence, *n.* As here compared, the words are interchangeable. *Negligence,* however, is often used to mean *habitual neglect.*

Negress, *n.* Now considered a derogatory, offensive, or patronizing term. See also BLACK; JEWESS; NOUN, 2B.

Negro, *n.* See BLACK; NOUN, 6L1.

neither . . . nor, *conj.* If you use the conjunction *neither,* the correlative conjunction that follows is properly *nor,* not *or: neither one nor the other.*

For the correct form of the verb to use in such constructions, see EITHER . . . OR, NEITHER . . . NOR.

neither of See EITHER OF, NEITHER OF.

nemesis, *n.* For plural, see NOUN, 6N.

nerve-racking, nerve-wracking, *adj.* The first spelling is preferable; the second is also correct. See also RACK, WRACK.

NEUROSIS, PSYCHONEUROSIS, PSYCHOSIS, *n.*

A *neurosis* is a functional emotional disorder involving one or more of the following: excessive anxiety or tension, depression, phobias, obsessions, compulsions, behavior built on fantasy, etc.

Psychoneurosis is simply a longer form of the same word—it does not imply any greater degree of the condition or conditions of a *neurosis.*

Psychosis is the medical term for what is commonly or legally called *insanity*—briefly, a serious mental derangement the victim of which has lost contact with reality.

Neurotic, psychoneurotic, and *psychotic* are the adjective forms and also the nouns for the persons afflicted.

A simplistic and so-called humorous distinction puts it this way: The *neurotic* builds castles in the air, the *psychotic* lives in them—and the psychiatrist collects the rent.

See also PSYCHOPATH, SOCIOPATH; PSYCHOPATHIC.

---

nevertheless, *conj.* For correct punctuation when this conjunction introduces a clause, see HOWEVER.

new innovation An obvious

redundancy, since an *innovation is* new. (Omit *new.*)

nice, *adj.* It is not true that *nice* is an inappropriate word for showing approval—*a nice person, a nice time,* etc. are fully acceptable usages.

Another charge leveled against the word is that it is overused—as it indeed may be by those people who are addicted to it. Everything they like is *nice,* when, perhaps, they mean *kind, pleasant, enjoyable, good,* etc.

There is the story of the executive who said to his assistant, "I wish you would stop overusing two words in your reports. One is *nice;* the other is *lousy.*"

"O.K.," said the assistant. "What are the two words?"

So, the fact that *nice* may, for some, be a catchall adjective does not make the word disreputable.

nice and *Nice and cold, nice and hot,* etc. are colloquialisms, not acceptable in formal English.

nickle, nickel, *n.* Both the metal and the U.S. coin are spelled *nickel*—*nickle* is a misspelling despite words like *tickle, pickle, fickle, sickle,* etc.

night, nite, *n.* The second spelling is incorrect. It is often used, nevertheless, in ads, signs in store windows, friendly letters, etc.

nighttime, *n.* Written as a solid word only.

Nipponese, *n.* See JAPANESE, NIPPONESE.

nite, *n.* See NIGHT, NITE.

no, *n.* For plural, see NOUN, 6L1.

no body When *no body* is written as two separate words, *body* refers to an actual *body: no body* (i.e., no corpse) was found; *no body can stand the abuse you are giving your body.*

no doubt See DOUBTLESS, NO DOUBT.

no one Always written as separate words, whether a pronoun (*no one is here*) or *no* plus the numeral *one* (*no one* of his answers i.e., not a single one.) See also ANYBODY.

no one else's See ELSE.

no place Always written as two words, whether an adverbial (meaning *nowhere*) or a noun: *she's going no place; there is no place for any more books.* See also ANYPLACE, ANY PLACE; SOMEPLACE, SOME PLACE.

no sooner than . . . no sooner when . . . The conjunction that follows *no sooner* is *than,* not *when: She had no sooner left than* (not *when*) *her husband arrived.* (Comparatives are followed by *than: better than, later than, sooner than.*)

nobody, *pron.* See ANYBODY.

nod one's head, shake one's head   One *nods one's head* (i.e., up and down) to mean *yes* or to show approval; one *shakes one's head* to mean *no* or to show disapproval.

nohow, *adv.*   This word is not acceptable in standard English. At best, it is dialectical.

noisome, noisy, *adj.*   Despite the similarity in appearance, the two words are unrelated. *Noisome* means *foul-smelling; injurious to health. See also* FULSOME, FULL.

nom de plume, *n.*   See ALIAS, PSEUDONYM, PEN NAME, NOM DE PLUME, INCOGNITO.

nominal, *n.*   A term in Structural Grammar identifying a part of speech other than a noun used in a sentence as a noun or in the noun position. In the sentence To *is a preposition, and* happy *is an adjective,* to and *happy* are, in such a construction, *nominals.* See also NOUN.

nominal, low, *adj.*   When the charge, price, or cost is *nominal*, it is, of course, very low in comparison to value, but the word signifies more than just low: *nominal* indicates that the charge, price, or cost is a mere token, so that the object or service will not be free of all charge.

NOMINALLY, PRACTICALLY, VIRTUALLY, *adv.*

Nominally the *chief* signifies that *chief* is only the name or title given to the person, without the actual power that usually accompanies such an office.

Practically the *chief* indicates that the person is the chief for all practical purposes, but without having the actual title.

Virtually the *chief* means that the person is indeed the chief in effect or power, but without, again, the actual title. In these examples, *practically* and *virtually* are close synonyms.

In formal English, *practically* and *virtually* should not be used as substitutes for *nearly* or *almost: I'm* **practically** *(virtually)*—i.e., *nearly—penniless* is acceptable only on a colloquial level.

As here compared, the *adjective* **nominal** means *in name only;* **practical** *and* **virtual** mean *in practice or effect, though not in name: the* **practical** *(virtual) head of the house.*

---

nominative case   See PRONOUN, 8, 8A.

non, non-   In compounds, with this prefix, use a hyphen only if the root word starts with a capital letter: *non-American, non-Chinese,* *non-English-speaking,* etc. But: *nonverbal, nonaddictive,* etc.

NONE, *pron.*

None is construed as either singular or plural, depending on meaning. For example:

None is ready (i.e., not a single one).

None were finished (i.e., not any of the several things, items, people, etc.)

None of your work *is* acceptable (i.e., no portion, no part).

None of her friends *have* arrived (i.e., not any of several).

None of these voters is a Republican (i.e., not a single one).

None of these voters *are* Democrats (i.e., not any of them).

(Some stylebooks insist that *none* is always a singular pronoun; such invariable usage can result in awkwardness.)

nonetheless, *conj.* For correct punctuation when this conjunction introduces a clause, *see* HOWEVER.

nonfeasance, *n.* See MALFEASANCE, MISFEASANCE, NONFEASANCE.

nonflammable, noninflammable, *adj.* See FLAMMABLE, INFLAMMABLE, NONFLAMMABLE.

nonmoral, *adj.* See AMORAL, NONMORAL, UNMORAL, IMMORAL.

nonreligious, *adj.* See IMPIOUS, SACRILEGIOUS, IRRELIGIOUS, NONRELIGIOUS.

nonrestrictive clause See RESTRICTIVE CLAUSE, NONRESTRICTIVE CLAUSE.

nonsexual, *adj.* See ASEXUAL, NONSEXUAL, SEXLESS.

nonsocial, *adj.* See ANTISOCIAL, ASOCIAL, UNSOCIAL, UNSOCIABLE, NONSOCIAL.

NOR, OR, *conj.*

Use *nor* as a correlative conjunction with *neither: neither rain **nor** snow.*

In other negative constructions, *nor* is the preferable

conjunction: *He will not let us accompany him nor even say where he is going.*

It is not strictly incorrect, however, to use *or* after some negatives, as witness these examples from the columns of a single issue of the *Los Angeles Times*:

"*Never flamboyant or interested in personal acclaim, he . . .*" (President Reagan describing Senator John P. East, on the death of the latter in 1986.)

"*The defendant chose not to testify or to call any witnesses. . . .*" (Harry Anderson, assistant business editor of the *Times*, writing on the "op-ed" page.)

Nevertheless, in formal English, *nor* would be preferable in the excerpts above.

See also EITHER . . . OR, NEITHER . . . NOR.

---

normalcy, normality, *n.* *Normality* is preferable. Nouns are generally formed from adjectives ending in *-al* by adding the noun suffix *-ity*: *banality, technicality, actuality*, etc. *Normalcy* was supposedly first used by President Warren G. Harding, and though it has since caught on to a great extent, this noun form is generally avoided by careful writers. (No one uses *abnormalcy* as the noun form of the adjective *abnormal*.)

-Cy is the suffix used to derive nouns from adjectives ending in *-nt: hesitant, hesitancy; potent, potency;* etc.

North, north; Northern, northern Capitalize *N* if *North* or *Northern* is part of the official name: *North Dakota, North America, North Carolina,* etc.; *Northern Hemisphere; Northern Ireland.*

If the northern part of a region is meant, capitalize *N*:

the North (i.e., of the U.S., the world, etc.); *the Northeast* (of the U.S.).

Otherwise, use a lowercase *n*; *going north, the northern part of town, the north coast,* etc.

See also EAST, EAST, EASTERN, EASTERN; SOUTH, SOUTH, SOUTHERN, SOUTHERN; WEST, WEST, WESTERN, WESTERN.

northward, northwards See -WARD, -WARDS.

not only . . . but also These correlative conjunctions belong together. *She's not only rich but also famous* is preferable to *she's not only rich but famous, too.* In *he not only refused to speak to me, but also pretended that I was not in the room, but also* is preferable to *but* or *but even.*

notary public, *n.* For plural see NOUN, 6U.

notorious, *adj.* See FAMOUS, NOTORIOUS.

nought, *n.*   See ZERO, AUGHT,
OUGHT, NAUGHT, NOUGHT.

NOUN

In Structural Grammar, parts of speech are identified by
position in a sentence pattern, or structure; such position is
usually called a *slot*.

The *noun slot* is the blank in the following *noun pattern*:

(DET) _____ is good, etc. . . .

DET is the symbol for *determiner* (see DETERMINER), and
the parentheses indicate that a determiner is optional—i.e., it
may but need not occur, depending on the noun. (The symbol
for a noun is N.)

Etc. after *good* means that any word that makes sense can
be used after *is: bad, important, running*, etc.

And the three dots (. . .) tell you that you may complete the
sentence, if necessary, with any additional words.

Note first how a noun (N) fits into the noun slot without
the optional determiner (DET).

       N
_____Food_____ is good for you.
      N
___Grammar___ is easy to understand.
     N
___Health___ is important.

Now note how a noun (N) fits into the noun slot *following
a determiner* (DET).

DET   N
My ____food____ is cold.
DET   N
His ___grammar___ is poor.
DET   N
Your___health___ is important.
DET   N
That _development_ is surprising.

In typical sentence patterns, nouns also precede and/or
follow verbs. (The symbol for verb is V; see VERB for a
complete discussion.) For example:

DET N　V　DET　N
The dog found　a　bone.

DET N　　V
The rain started early.

1. noun, collective: Certain nouns indicate a group of persons, things, animals, items, etc. For example:

class	majority
collection	number
couple	pair
family	party
fleet	plurality
group	variety
lot	

A collective noun is treated as a *singular* if the concept is that of a *single group* or *single entity*. For example:

> The *class was* attentive.
> The newly-married *couple was booked on flight 18.*
> The stamp *collection was* sold at auction.
> The *family was* seated at the dinner table.
> The *fleet was* in the harbor.
> The *group was* becoming restless.
> That *lot* of books *is* to be sold as a unit.
> A *majority* of voters *is* required to pass the proposition.
> The *number* of students attending class *is* always lower on rainy days.
> That *pair* of trousers *has* been reduced in price.
> There *is* a *party* of five people waiting for you.
> The *variety* of goods in a large department store *is* astonishing.

A collective noun is treated as a *plural* if the concept stresses the individual or separate members or items. For example:

> A *collection* of different letters *are* ready for your signature.
> The *couple* decided to go to Hawaii on *their* honeymoon.
> A *lot* of farmers *are* suffering.
> The *majority* of voters *were* waiting until evening to go to the polls.
> A *number* of her relatives *are* very rich.
> A *pair* of my friends *were* waiting for me.

A *party* of petitioners *were* occupying all the chairs in the senator's office.

A *variety* of dresses *were* offered for her choice.

See also LOT; NUMBER; PAIR; PERCENT, PER CENT, PERCENTAGE.

2. **noun, feminine:** a. Our language is becoming less and less gender-oriented, and some nouns indicating a female, as opposed to a male, have become archaic or fallen into disuse. For example:

ambassadress	instructress
authoress	poetess
editress	

b. *Jewess* and *Negress* may be considered condescending or offensive terms.

c. The following feminine nouns, among others, are still in common use (the masculine form, if there is one, follows in parentheses):

actress	(actor)
administratrix	(administrator)
	(of wills, estates, etc.)
alumna	(alumnus)
ancestress	(ancestor)
aviatrix	(aviator)
benefactress	(benefactor)
cantatrice	
chairwoman, chairlady	(chairman)
chanteuse	
coiffeuse	(coiffeur)
comedienne	(comedian)
confidante	(confidant)
(confidant, however, can designate either sex)	
diseuse	
divorcée or divorcee	(divorcé)
(divorcee, however, can designate either sex)	
enchantress	
equestrienne	(equestrian)
executrix	(executor)
	(of wills, estates, etc.)
fiancée	(fiancé)
heiress	(heir)
heroine	(hero)
hostess	(host)
masseuse	(masseur)
ogress	(ogre)

patroness   (patron)
                (of the arts, etc.)
postmistress   (postmaster)
                (of a branch post office)
protegée   (protegé)
        (Protegé, however, can designate either sex)
sorceress   (sorcerer)
waitress   (waiter)
                (in a restaurant, etc.)
witch   (wizard, warlock)
(i.e., one having supernatural powers, practicing black magic,
                        etc.)

   d. some animals, usually for necessary reasons of identification, have special terms for the female. For example (again,
the male counterpart, if there is one, is in parentheses):

cow   (bull)
(for cattle; also for elephant, moose, buffalo, etc. The cas-
    trated bull, in domestic cattle, is called a steer.)
doe   (buck)
                (deer, rabbit, antelope, etc.)
duck   (drake)
            (but duck can also designate the male)
ewe
                (female sheep)
filly   (colt)
                (young horse, donkey, etc.)
goose   (gander)
            (but goose can also designate the male)
lioness   (lion)
                (but lion can be male or female)
mare   (stallion)
(adult horse—the stallion is uncastrated. If castrated, the
                male is a gelding.)
tigress   (tiger)
                (but tiger can be male or female)
vixen   (fox)
        (female fox; but fox can be male or female.)

3. noun, inflections: A noun has four inflections: singular (n.
sing.); plural (n. pl.); singular possessive (n. sing. pos.); and
plural possessive (n. pl. pos.).
   For example:

n. sing. child girl	*n. pl.* children girls	*n. sing. pos.* child's girl's	*n. pl. pos.* children's girls'

Only a noun, of the four parts of speech, (i.e., noun, verb, adjective, adverb) has a plural or possessive inflection.

(Many pronouns, which are substitute nouns, also have plural and possesive inflections.)

See also NOUN, 6; NOUN, 7; PRONOUN.

4. **noun pattern:** The *noun pattern* is:

(DET) _____ N _____ is good, etc. . . .

For an explanation of the *noun pattern*, see the beginning of this entry.

5. **noun phrase:** A *noun phrase*, in Structural Grammar, consists of one or more determiners plus one or more adjectives plus the noun or nouns:

DET	ADJ	N
some	early	risers
many	unusual	people
one	interesting	fact
a	strange	man and woman

A *noun phrase* may also consist of one or more determiners plus a noun or one or more adjectives plus a noun or nouns.

Determiner or determiners plus a noun or nouns:

```
┌──DET──┐  N
my many other sisters
┌DET┐    N
her few possessions
DET  N        N
these plants and animals
```

Adjective or adjectives plus one or more nouns:

```
ADJ      ADJ    N
wild and ferocious beasts
ADJ  N        N
rich women and men
```

6. **noun, plural:** a. The plural of a noun is typically formed by adding *-s: occurrence, occurrences.*

b. If a noun ends in *-ch, -s, -ss, -sh, -x,* or *-zz,* add *-es* to form the plural: *pouch, pouches; yes, yeses; kiss, kisses; tax, taxes; buzz, buzzes.*

c. The plurals of some nouns are derived by an internal vowel change: *mouse, mice; foot, feet; tooth, teeth; goose, geese;* etc.

d. Some few nouns have plural inflections ending in *-en: men, women, children, oxen,* etc.

e. If a word ends in *y* preceded by a *consonant* or in *-quy,* the plural inflection generally ends in *-ies: army, armies; beauty, beauties; obloquy, obloquies; colloquy, colloquies; soliloquy, soliloquies; worry, worries; spy, spies;* etc.

f. If a word ends in *-y* preceded by a *vowel,* simply add *-s* to form the plural inflection: *day, days; alley, alleys; attorney, attorneys; donkey, donkeys; honey, honeys; monkey, monkeys;* etc. (However, *monies* is an acceptable, though not preferable, plural form of *money.*)
   f1. If a proper name ends in *-y,* add *-s* directly: *Mary, Marys; Murphy, Murphys; Billy, Billys;* etc.
   f2. But the Allegheny Mountains and the Rocky Mountains are pluralized, in short form, as the *Alleghenies* and the *Rockies.*

g. If a noun ends in *-f, -lf,* or *-fe,* the usual plural ending is *-ves:*

calf	calves
half	halves
knife	knives
life	lives
loaf	loaves
self	selves
sheaf	sheaves
shelf	shelves
wife	wives

However, *still lifes* is the plural of *still life* (i.e., a picture or painting of inanimate objects); and *low-lifes* is the plural of the slang term *low-life.*
   g1. Note the plurals of the following nouns ending in *-f, -lf, -ff,* or *-fe:*

beef	beeves *or* beefs

(but the slang beef—*i.e.,* complaint—*is only* beefs)

belief	beliefs
brief	briefs
chef	chefs
chief	chiefs
dwarf	dwarfs *or* dwarves
fife	fifes
gulf	gulfs
hoof	hoofs *or* hooves
oaf	oafs
proof	proofs
roof	roofs
ruff	ruffs
scarf	scarfs *or* scarves
scruff	scruffs
serf	serfs
staff	staffs

(but if staff *is a rod, pole, or the musical symbol,* staves *is an alternate plural)*

turf	turfs
waif	waifs
wharf	wharves *or* wharfs

(Where alternate plurals are given, the first form is usually more common.)

h. Mammals, birds, fish, marine life, etc., especially as prey to be hunted or fished for, are usually singular in form even though the plural is meant: hunt for *bear, buffalo, elk, moose,* or *quail;* fish for *haddock, salmon, trout;* etc.

i. *Fish* is the plural of *fish,* unless two or more species are involved, in which instances *fishes* may be used.

j. The plural of *deer* is preferably *deer; deers* is also correct, though seldom used. But the plural of *sheep* is *sheep,* only.

k. If a word ends in *o* preceded by a *vowel* add *-s* to form the plural: *duo, duos; embryo, embryos; pistachio, pistachios; ratio, ratios; rodeo, rodeos; studio, studios; trio, trios;* etc.

l. If a word ends in *-o* preceded by a *consonant* the plural may end in *-os* or *-oes,* depending on the word.
  11. For example, the following nouns are pluralized only by adding *-es:*

echo	echoes
embargo	embargoes
hero	heroes
manifesto	manifestoes
Negro	Negroes
no	noes
potato	potatoes
tomato	tomatoes
torpedo	torpedoes
veto	vetoes

12. The following nouns, among others, have alternate plural forms as indicated. Generally, the first form is the more common.

banjo	banjos *or* banjoes
buffalo	buffaloes *or* buffalos
commando	commandos *or* commandoes
dido	didoes *or* didos
domino	dominoes *or* dominos
innuendo	innuendoes *or* innuendos
lasso	lassos *or* lassoes
memento	mementos *or* mementoes
mosquito	mosquitoes *or* mosquitos
motto	mottoes *or* mottos
mulatto	mulattoes *or* mulattos
peccadillo	peccadilloes *or* peccadillos
proviso	provisos *or* provisoes
salvo	salvos *or* salvoes
stiletto	stilettos *or* stilettoes
tornado	tornadoes *or* tornados
virago	viragoes *or* viragos
volcano	volcanoes *or* volcanos
zero	zeros *or* zeroes

13. Most other nouns ending in o preceded by a *consonant* have plural forms ending in *os*. A few examples:

alto	altos
bongo	bongos
Eskimo	Eskimos
Filipino	Filipinos
piano	pianos
piccolo	piccolos
tyro	tyros

14. To pluralize nouns that come from Italian, especially

musical terms, and end in *o* you may either add *s* (the Anglicized version) or change final *-o* to *-i* (Italian version). In musical circles, the Italian version is often more popular. (The final *-i* of the Italian form is pronounced *-ee*.)

For example (and note that a few nouns have only one plural form):

cello	cellos *or* celli
concerto	concertos *or* concerti
contralto	contraltos *or* contralti
divertimento	divertimentos *or* divertimenti
duo	duos *or* dui
fortissimo	fortissimos *or* fortissimi
libretto	librettos *or* libretti
pianissimo	pianissimos *or* pianissimi
pizzicato	pizzicati *only*
presto	prestos *only*
scherzo	scherzos *or* scherzi
soprano	sopranos *or* soprani
tempo	tempos *or* tempi
timpano	timpani *only*
violoncello	violoncellos *or* violoncelli
virtuoso	virtuosos *or* virtuosi

l5. Some nonmusical terms from the Italian also have alternate plurals; the Anglicized versions are more popular. Two examples are:

bandit	bandits *or* banditti
dilettante	dilettantes *or* dilettanti

m. The plurals of Latin-derived singular nouns that terminate in the letter *a* may end, with exceptions, either in *-s* (Anglicized version) or in *-ae* (Latin version). Generally the Anglicized version is more common, except in scientific writing. (When the Latin form is given first, it is more common, even in nonscientific usage.)

If the Latin version is used in speech, final *-ae* is pronounced *-ee*.

Some examples:

amoeba	amoebas *or* amoebae
antenna	antennas *(for electronic transmission);*
	antennae *or* antennas *(for the term in biology meaning* feelers)
cicada	cicadas *or* cicadae

corona	coronas or coronae
formula	formulas or formulae
lacuna	lacunas or lacunae
larva	larvae or larvas
nebula	nebulae or nebulas
penumbra	penumbras or penumbrae
uvula	uvulas or uvulae
vagina	vaginas or vaginae
vertebra	vertebrae or vertebras

m1. The following nouns, among a few others, have only the Latin-derived plural forms:

alga	algae
alumna	alumnae
minutia	minutiae
succuba	succubae
vita	vitae

n. If a singular noun ends in *-is*, the plural form generally ends in *-es*. Some examples are:

amanuensis	amanuenses
analysis	analyses
antithesis	antitheses
axis	axes
basis	bases
crisis	crises
dialysis	dialyses
dieresis	diereses
ellipsis	ellipses
hypothesis	hypotheses
metamorphosis	metamorphoses
metastasis	metastases
nemesis	nemeses
oasis	oases
parenthesis	parentheses
synopsis	synopses
synthesis	syntheses
thesis	theses

(Incidentally, the final *-es* of each plural noun is pronounced *-eez*.)

o. Some nouns ending in *ex* or *ix* have alternate plural forms. For example:

administratrix	administratrixes or administratrices
apex	apexes or apices
appendix	appendixes or appendices
executrix	executrixes or executrices
index	indexes or indices
matrix	matrices or matrixes
radix	radices or radixes
vertex	vertexes or vertices
vortex	vortexes or vortices

(The *ces* plural is more common in scientific or technical usage; the ending *ces* is pronounced *seez*.)

o1. The plural form of *cicatrix*, a medical or botanical term, is *cicatrices* only.

o2. The plural form of *aviatrix* is *aviatrixes* only.

p. If a singular noun ends in *-us*, it is often of Latin or Greek derivation. The plural may be formed by adding *-es*, by substituting final *-i* for *-us*, by either method, or in some other way—all depending on the specific word. Some examples (the first of two or more forms is usually preferable):

abacus	abacuses or abaci (AB'-ə-sī')
alumnus	alumni (ə-LUM'-nī')
anthropophagus	anthropophagi (-POF'-ə-jī')
apparatus	apparatus or apparatuses
cactus	cacti (KAK'-tī') or cactuses
caduceus	caducei (kə-DOO'-see-ī')
corpus	corpora
cumulus	cumuli (KYOOM'-yə-lī')
esophagus	esophagi (ə-SOF'-ə-jī')
focus	focuses or foci (FO'-sī')
fungus	fungi (FUN'-jī') or funguses
genus	genera
gladiolus	gladioluses or gladioli (-ō-lī')
hiatus	hiatuses or hiatus
hippopotamus	hippopotamuses, hippopotamus, or hippopotami (POT'-ə-mī')
incubus	incubuses or incubi (IN'-kyə-bī')
locus	loci (LO'-sī')
nucleus	nuclei (NOO'-klee-ī') or nucleuses
octopus	octopuses, octopi (OK'-tə-pī'), or octopodes (ok-TOP'-ə-deez)
opus	opera (*pronounced* O'-pə-rə, *except as in an* opera, Grand Opera, *etc.*) or opuses

platypus	platypuses *or* platypi (PLAT'-ə-pī')
radius	radii (RAY'-dee-ī') *or* radiuses
sarcophagus	sarcophagi (sahr-KOF'-ə-jī') *or* sarcophaguses
status	statuses
stimulus	stimuli (STIM'-yə-lī')
succubus	succubi (SUK'-yə-bī')
syllabus	syllabuses *or* syllabi (SIL'-ə-bī')
talus *(ankle bone)*	taluses *or* tali (TAY'-lī')
terminus	terminī' (TUR'-mə-nī) *or* terminuses
uterus	uteri (YOO'-tə-rī')

q. Singular nouns ending in *-um* often come from Latin or Greek. Such words, as in the case of other classical derivatives, may have an Anglicized plural ending *(-s)*; only a classical plural ending (-um changing to -a); or either of the two endings. In the list below, when alternates are given, the first form is generally preferable. Scientific usage often prefers the classical endings.

addendum	addenda
agendum	agenda *or* agendums
arcanum	arcana
auditorium	auditoriums *or* auditoria
bacterium	bacteria
candelabrum	candelabra *or* candelabrums
cilium	cilia
colloquium	colloquia *or* colloquiums
corrigendum	corrigenda
crematorium	crematoriums *or* crematoria
curriculum	curricula *or* curriculums
datum	data
delirium	deliriums *or* deliria
desideratum	desiderata
dictum	dictums *or* dicta
effluvium	effluvia *or* effluviums
emporium	emporiums *or* emporia
encomium	encomiums *or* encomia
equilibrium	equilibriums *or* equilibria
erratum	errata
gymnasium	gymnasiums *or* gymnasia
indicium	indicia
mausoleum	mausoleums *or* mausolea
maximum	maximums *or* maxima

medium *(of communication)*	media
memorandum	memoranda *or* memorandums
millennium	millenniums *or* millennia
minimum	minimums *or* minima
modicum	modicums
moratorium	moratoriums *or* moratoria
natatorium	natatoriums *or* natatoria
odeum	odeums *or* odea
optimum	optimums *or* optima
paramecium	paramecia
pericardium	pericardia
perineum	perinea
peritoneum	peritonea *or* peritoneums
phylum	phyla
planetarium	planetariums *or* planetaria
podium *(platform)*	podiums *or* podia
referendum	referendums *or* referenda
residuum	residua
sanatorium	sanatoriums *or* sanatoria
sanitarium	sanitariums *or* sanitaria
serum	serums *or* sera
solarium	solaria *or* solariums
spectrum	spectra *or* spectrums
speculum	specula *or* speculums
stadium	stadiums *or* stadia
stratum	strata *or* stratums
symposium	symposiums *or* symposia
tympanum	tympanums *or* tympana
ultimatum	ultimatums *or* ultimata
vacuum	vacuums *or* vacua
viaticum	viatica *or* viaticums

r. Singular nouns that derive from Greek and that end in -*on* are pluralized by substituting -*a* for -*on* (classical form) or by simply adding -*s* (Anglicized version). Of the alternate plurals given, the first is more commonly used and therefore preferable. Examples:

automaton	automatons *or* automata
criterion	criteria *or* criterions
encephalon	encephela
ganglion	ganglia *or* ganglions
phenomenon	phenomena *or* phenomenons

s. Some singular nouns of French origin may add -*x* to form the plural. Often, the Anglicized -*s* ending is an alternate. In the examples below, the first of two optional forms is more commonly used.

bandeau	bandeaux
beau	beaus *or* beaux
bijou	bijoux
bureau	bureaus *or* bureaux
chateau	chateaux *or* chateaus
	(*also spelled* château, châteaus, châteaux)
Esquimau	Esquimaux
	(*a variant and flossy spelling of* Eskimo)
nouveau riche	nouveaux riches
plateau	plateaus *or* plateaux
portmanteau	portmanteaus *or* portmanteaux
rondeau	rondeaux
tableau	tableaux *or* tableaus
trousseau	trousseaux *or* trousseaus

t. To pluralize a symbol, numeral, letter, combination of letters, etc., you may add *'s*, or simply *s*. The choice is personal, or may depend on the style sheet of a publishing house; however, the modern trend is to omit the apostrophe. Thus: *5s* or *5's*; *Qs* or *Q's*; *#s* or *#'s*; *IOUs* or *IOU's*; *UFOs* or *UFO's* (or *U.F.O.s* or *U.F.O.'s*); etc.

If a word is used not as a meaningful part of a sentence, but to indicate the word itself, as in *There are too many "ands" in that sentence*, the word may be pluralized with or without the apostrophe (i.e., *ands* or *and's* in the example given), but it is preferable to omit the apostrophe. (To emphasize such use of a word, you may simply pluralize it and either underline it, italicize it, or surround it with quotation marks.)

u. To pluralize a compound noun, whether or not it is hyphenated, add *-s* to the principal part. Examples:

> aides-de-camp
> ambassadors-at-large
> attorneys at law
> attorneys general (*perferable to* attorney generals)
> brothers-in-law
> carryings-on
> chiefs of staff
> commanders in chief
> consuls general (*preferable to* consul generals)
> counselors-at-law
> courts-martial (*preferable to* court-martials)

delegates-at-large
editors in chief
goings-on
hangers-on
ladies in waiting
lookers-on *(but* onlookers *is the preferable term)*
maids of honor
maidservants
matrons of honor
men of the world
men-of-war *(i.e., warships)*
menservants *(note that both* man *and* servant *are pluralized)*
notaries public *(preferable to* notary publics*)*
passers-by *or* passersby
poets laureate *(preferable to* poet laureates*)*
postmasters general *(preferable to* postmaster generals*)*
secretaries-general
sergeants at arms
surgeons general

See also -FUL, -FULS for the plurals of *cupful, spoonful,* etc.; IN-LAWS for the plural of *mother-in-law,* etc.

7. **noun, possessive: a.** To derive the *singular possessive* inflection of a noun, add *'s: man's, woman's, car's, horse's,* etc.

b. If a singular noun ends in -*s,* you may either add *'s* or just an apostrophe to form the *possessive* inflection; *Thomas's* arm or *Thomas' arm; Moses's Ten Commandments* or *Moses' Ten Commandments; the kiss's flavor* or *the kiss' flavor.* (Apostrophe plus *s* is the more popular form.)

c. To derive the *plural possessive* form of a noun, *add 's if the plural noun does not end in* -*s: men's, women's, children's, oxen's, alumni's, alumnae's,* etc.

d. *If the plural noun ends in* -*s, add only an apostrophe: boys', girls', teachers',* etc.

e. After the preposition *of,* a possessive noun or pronoun is often used, even though *of* implies possession: *a friend of* **John's;** *a friend of* **ours.**

8. **noun suffixes:** There are many *suffixes (endings)* common to nouns. The following are only a few:

-*acy:* fallacy, accuracy
-*ance;* resistance, reluctance
-*or:* actor, tutor, doctor

-*er:* worker, feeler, user
-*ist:* typist, gynecologist, orthodontist
-*th:* length, strength, width, health

9. **noun vs. adverbial:** A *noun* or *noun phrase* that tells *when* or *where* or *how much* is called, in Structural Grammar, an *adverbial*. Note the distinctions:

> *Home* is where the heart is. (*Home* is a *noun*.)
>
> You can't go *home* again. (*Home*, by itself, is a *noun*. In this section *home* tells *where*, and is called an *adverbial*.)
>
> *Today* is Sunday. (*Today* is a *noun*, subject of the verb.)
>
> *Today*, he looks better. (*Today* tells *when* and can be moved to the end of the sentence; it is an *adverbial*.)
>
> He spent *his early years* in jail. (The italicized *noun phrase* consists of a *determiner*, an *adjective*, and the plural *noun years*, direct object of the verb *spent*.)
>
> He was in jail *last year*. (The italicized *noun phrase* tells *when* and can be moved to the beginning of the sentence; *last year* is an *adverbial*.)

See also ADJECTIVE; ADVERB, 4; DETERMINER; NOUN 5.

10. **noun vs. verb:** A word can be a *noun* or a *verb*, depending on the structure of a sentence. Note these distinctions:

> *a.* A modern *dance* was seen on TV. *(noun)*
> *b.* Mary will *dance* a waltz. *(verb)*
> *c.* The *play* was most enjoyable. *(noun)*
> *d.* They will *play* for us. *(verb)*

You can recognize a *noun* by its *position* in a sentence—i.e., preceding and/or following a *verb*; or following a *determiner* and/or an *adjective* in a *noun phrase*; or by its convertibility to a plural form.

In sentence *(a.)* above, *dance* can be pluralized: (*modern dances were seen*); *dance* is in a *noun phrase*, following the determiner *a* and the adjective *modern*; *dance* precedes the **verb phrase** *was seen*.

In sentence *(b.)* above, *dance* follows the auxiliary *will* and the subject noun *Mary*; it also precedes the noun *waltz*. (**Verbs** precede and/or follow **nouns** or **pronouns**.) Additionally, the sentence can be restructured so that *dance* is in the past tense: Mary **danced** a waltz.

The same criteria can be used to distinguish the noun *play* in sentence *(c.)*, above, from the verb *play* in sentence *(d.)*.

If you can distinguish a noun from a verb (and vice versa) in a sentence, you will be able to conquer one of the most formidable problems in correct usage, namely, when to spell the word *affect*, when to spell it *effect*.

So try this test. Decide, by looking for the clues discussed above, whether the italicized word in each sentence is a **noun** or a **verb**.

1. What strange *effects* have you noticed N? V?
2. The experience *affected* him deeply. N? V?
3. What (a) *affects* some people may not (b) *affect* others. (a) N? V? (b) N? V?
4. The *effects* of the earthquake were still apparent. N? V?
5. The medication will cause no ill *effects*. N? V?
6. His appearance may *affect* you strangely. N? V?
7. He *affects* different people in different ways. N? V?
8. It was an *effect* we had not expected. N? V?
9. She is still getting over the *effects* of her illness. N? V?
10. He *affects* a British accent even though he was born in California. N? V?

KEY: 1. **N** (a DET [*what*] and an ADJ [*strange*] precede a N to form a typical *noun phrase*); 2. **V** (past tense, ending in -*ed*); 3. (a) **V** (between a PRON. [*what*] and a N. [*people*]); (b) **V** (follows AUX [*may*]); 4. **N** (follows a DET [*the*] and precedes a V. [*were*] as subject); 5. **N** (follows a DET [*no*] and an ADJ [*ill*]—another typical *noun phrase*—and follows the verb phrase [*will cause*]); 6. **V** (follows an AUX [*may*] and also occurs between a N. [*appearance*] and a PRON. [*you*]); 7. **V** (occurs between a PRON. [*he*] and a N. [*people*]); 8. **N** (preceded by a DET [*an*] and follows a V. [*was*]); 9. **N** (follows a DET [*the*]); 10. **V** (between a PRON. [*he*] and a N. [*accent*]).

See also AFFECT, EFFECT; DETERMINER; NOUN; VERB.

---

nouveau riche, *n.* For plural, See NOUN, 6S.

nowhere, nowheres, *adv.* See -WHERE -WHERES.

nubile, *adj.* See MARRIAGE-ABLE, NUBILE.

nucleus, *n.* For plural form, see NOUN, 6P.

NUMBER, *n.*

When **number** (as in *a number of . . .*) is the subject of a verb, and means *many*, it is a collective noun treated as a plural. (In such a case, the preceding determiner is usually *a*.)

A number of the reports *have* been written.
A large number of people *are* waiting for you.
A number of my friends *spend their* evenings watching television.

When *number* is the subject of a verb and actually means *number* (not *many*), it is treated as a singular noun. (In such a case, the preceding determiner is usually *the*, *this*, or *that*.)

The number of absentees *is* usually larger in rainy weather.
This (That) number of votes *was* smaller than we had expected.

See also LOT; NOUN, 1; SUBJECT, VERB AGREEMENT.

---

number of, amount of See AMOUNT OF, NUMBER OF.

numbers SEE ORDINAL NUMBERS, CARDINAL NUMBERS; FOR PLURALS OF NUMBERS AS FIGURES, SEE NOUN, 6T.

numismatist, philatelist, *n.* A *numismatist* collects coins and medals. The hobby or specialty is *numismatics*.
Numismatics, like other studies or specialties ending in -*ics*, is treated as a singular noun: *numismatics* is an expensive hobby.
A *philatelist* collects postage stamps, postmarks, etc. The hobby or specialty is *philately*.

See also -ICS.

numskull, numbskull, *n.* Illogical as it may be (and spelling is nothing if not illogical), *numskull* is the preferable spelling; *numbskull* is a variant spelling.
See also DUMFOUND, DUMBFOUND.

nutcracker, *n.* Write as a solid word. One such instrument is *a nutcracker, not nutcrackers*.

nymphomania, satyromania, satyriasis, *n.* Morbid and uncontrollable sexual desire in the *female* is *nymphomania*; in the *male*, *satyromania* or *satyriasis*.

O

o, oh   See OH, O. For plural, see NOUN, 6T.

-o, -ough   See -OUGH, -O, -U.

oaf, *n.*   For plural, see NOUN, 6G1.

oasis, *n.*   For plural, see NOUN, 6N.

object, *n.*   For the grammatical terms *object, direct object, indirect object,* and *object complement,* see SENTENCE PATTERNS.

object complement   See SENTENCE PATTERNS, 5.

object, objective, *n.*   In the sense of *purpose, aim, goal,* etc., these words are largely interchangeable. If a distinction exists, it is that *objective* may refer to a specific goal or aim that one is striving, or will strive, to attain.

objective, subjective, *adj.*   When you are *objective,* take an *objective* point of view, etc., you are neutral, unbiased, impartial—i.e., you are not influenced by your personal feelings, selfish interests, etc.

Subjective is quite the opposite—i.e., involving one's feelings, state of mind, personal needs, desires, etc.

objective case   See PRONOUN, 8B.

objective pronoun   See PRONOUN, 8B.

obligate, oblige, *v.*   In the sense of *require* (to act, etc.) the words are interchangeable.

Oblige, however, has the added sense of *do a favor for,* or *kindness to: Please oblige me by . . .; I'm much obliged to you for seeing me today.*

Obligated and *obliged* both have the further sense of *being in debt,* but *obligated* is the much less ambiguous, much stronger, word: *I don't wish to feel obligated to him.*

oblivious of, oblivious to   Meaning *unmindful* or *inattentive, oblivious* may be followed by either preposition: *oblivious of (to) the child's needs.*

obloquy, *n.*   For plural, see NOUN, 6E.

OBSERVANCE, OBSERVATION, *n.*

Generally, *observance* is used in the sense of *obeying or staying in conformity with*—in *observance* of traffic laws; in *observance* of the Protestant ethic—or of *celebrating* (an event or holiday): in *observance* of Independence Day.

However, this noun is also used, though infrequently, to signify a watching, and is thus synonymous with one of the meanings of *observation.*

Observation refers to seeing, watching, noticing, being watched: *under observation.*

An *observation* is also a statement about something seen, noticed, etc., or a statement of considered opinion; and it is loosely used as a synonym of *comment* or *remark.*

The verb form of both *observance* and *observation*, in any of the meanings of these nouns, is *observe: observed* the holiday; *observed* the traffic laws; *observed* what was going on; "You look tired," *observed* his friend.

observant, *adj.* As the adjective form of *observance* in its primary meanings, this word is followed by the preposition *of: observant of all laws and customs; observant of family traditions.* See OBSERVANCE, OBSERVATION.

Observant is also the adjective form of *observation: you are very observant* (i.e., *attentive, watchful*).

Observant may also mean *perceptive; alert.*

observation, *n.* See OBSERVANCE, OBSERVATION.

obsession, *n.* See COMPULSION, OBSESSION, FIXATION.

obsolescent, obsolete, *adj.* Something *obsolescent* is in the process of going out of use or out of date. Something *obsolete* is already completely out of use or out of date.

The noun form of *obsolescent* is *obsolescence;* the intransitive verb is *obsolesce.*

The noun form of *obsolete* is *obsoleteness;* the transitive verb is *obsolete*—i.e., *render no longer useful, fashionable, etc., by replacing with something new: computers have obsoleted many forms of record-keeping.*

For **transitive, intransitive** verbs, see SENTENCE PATTERNS.

obstetrics, *n.* See GYNECOLOGY, OBSTETRICS; -ICS.

obverse, reverse The *obverse* side of a coin, medal, etc. contains the principal design. (The *obverse* side of a U.S.

coin is the side imprinted with the date of issue.) In this sense, *obverse* is the opposite of *reverse*.

The *obverse* side of a building, statue, monument, etc. is the side meant to be seen by the observer—i.e., the front.

The *reverse* side is either the back, as opposed to the front, or simply the side that is visible when you turn something over.

The *adjective obverse* is pronounced ob-VURS' or OB'-vurs; the *noun* is pronounced OB'-vurs. *Reverse, adjective, noun,* or *verb,* is pronounced rə-VURS'.

occupancy, occupation, *n.* As here contrasted, *occupancy* is the occupying of a house, office, apartment, etc. by one or more persons living or working there.

Occupation, on the other hand, is the forcible taking possession and keeping control of a place (fort, hill, city, nation, etc.) by an army or other militant group. *Occupation* as one's business, career, way of earning a living, etc. is rarely, if ever, confused with *occupancy.*

occupied by, occupied with One is *occupied* (i.e., busy) *with* reading, studying, cleaning house, etc.

A place (office, home, etc.) is *occupied by* the people in the office, home, etc.; or a city is *occupied by* enemy troops.

See also OCCUPANCY, OCCUPATION.

occur, *v.* See MATERIALIZE, OCCUR.

ocher, ochre, *n., v.* *Ocher* is the preferable spelling. For *ocher (v.)* other forms are *ochers, ochered, ochering;* the adjective is *ocherous.* Other forms of *ochre (v.)* are *ochres, ochred, ochring.* The adjective form of *ochre* is *ochreous.*

octet, octette, *n.* The shorter spelling is preferrable.

octopus, *n.* For plural, see NOUN, 6P.

ocular, ophthalmic, optic, optical, *adj.* Strictly, *ocular* and *ophthalmic* refer to the eye or eyes; *optic* and *optical* refer to either vision or sight, or to the eye or eyes. An illusion, of course, is *optical,* only.

oculist, *n.* See OPHTHALMOLOGIST, OCULIST, OPTOMETRIST, OPTICIAN.

odeum, *n.* For plural, SEE NOUN, 6Q.

odor, odour, *n.* *Odour* is the British spelling. See also -OR, -OUR.

Oedipus complex, Electra complex *Oedipus complex* strictly refers to the male child's attachment to his mother and (perhaps unconscious) hostility to his father.

Electra complex refers to the female child's attachment

to her father and (perhaps unconscious) hostility to her mother.

Oedipus complex is often loosely used in reference also to the female child, but *Electra complex* is the more precise term.

of which, of whose See WHOSE, OF WHICH.

off-, *prefix* Words with this prefix are generally written solid: *offbeat*, *offhand*, *offshore*, etc.

These adjectives, however, are hyphenated, especially, preceding a noun: *off-Broadway*, *off-color*, *off-key*, *off-limits*, *off-line*, *off-putting*, *off-season*, *off-the-shelf*, *off-track*, *off-white*, *off-year*, *off-the-record*; *off-Broadway production*, *off-year election*, etc.

off, *suffix* Most words with this suffix are written solid: *cutoff*, *sendoff*, *standoff*, etc.

off, off of, off from *Off* is not followed by *of* or *from* in good usage: *stepped off* (not *off of* nor *off from*) *the sidewalk*.

I borrowed a dollar off my friend is also unacceptable. Use *from* in place of *off*.

offhand, offhanded, offhandly *Offhand*, as an adverb, means *without previous thought*: *answered offhand that*; *refused offhand to* . . .

Offhand is also an adjective with similar meaning:

an offhand answer (*refusal*, etc.).

Offhanded is an adjective only and is generally used in the sense of *brusque*, *curt*, *inconsiderate*, or *unfeeling*: *offhanded treatment of his subordinates*. (*Offhanded* is also, however, occasionally used as a synonym of the adjective *offhand*.)

Offhandly is a nonword, used, probably, in the mistaken notion that *offhand* is not by itself an adverb. The adverb derived from *offhanded* (*adj.*) is *offhandedly*.

official, officious, *adj.* The words are not synonymous. An *officious* person gives gratuitous advice or acts in a meddlesome and haughty manner, especially in offering services or instructions that are not needed nor desired.

offspring, progeny, *n.* Both words designate the children or descendants, collectively, or a person or animal.

Offspring may also refer to one such child or descendant, but *progeny* is used only in the collective sense: *their progeny were numerous*; *an offpsring of a wealthy family*; *her first offspring was Charles*; *her offspring were all fairhaired*.

oftentimes, ofttimes, *adv.* The words are identical in meaning (i.e., *frequently*), but *ofttimes* is chiefly found in poetry.

-og See -OGUE, -OG.

ogre, *n.* The adjective is **ogreish**, the feminine form **ogress**. See also -ER, -RE; NOUN, 2C.

-ogue, -og Words like *demagogue, dialogue, epilogue, monologue, pedagogue, prologue, synagogue, and travelogue* are preferably spelled with the **-ogue** ending; *demagog, dialog,* etc., are variant spellings.

In the case of *catalogue,* the spelling for the card collection in a library is, indeed, only **catalog.** And the person responsible for such a collection is a *cataloger, cataloguer, catalogist,* or *cataloguist.* The -*ed* and -*ing* forms of the verb may be spelled **cataloged** or **catalogued, cataloging** or **cataloguing.** In every form of the word, the *g* is hard, as in *game.*

oh, o *O* is rare, except in poetry; *oh* is the preferable spelling. In referring to the actual word *as a word,* you may pluralize it as *oh's* (or *o's*) or, to follow the modern trend, **ohs** (or *os*).

See also NOUN, 6T.

old, *prefix* Adjective compounds are hyphenated: *oldfashioned, old-line, old-style, old-time, old-world.* The noun *old-timer* is also hyphenated.

old, *adj.* See ELDERLY, OLD, AGED.

old, olden, *adj.* *Olden* is chiefly used in poetry.

old adage Since an *adage,* by definition, is an *old* saying, *old* is redundant—there are no new adages!

old maid, spinster, *n.* Both words designate a woman who has never married, and both words are considered, by feminists, to be in bad taste. The neutral *unmarried* (or *single*) *woman* is, accordingly, more acceptable if it is necessary to describe a woman's marital status.

older, oldest See COMPARISON; ELDER, ELDEST, OLDER, OLDEST.

omelet, omelette, *n.* The shorter form is the preferable spelling.

omen, augury, *n.* The words are synonymous as a sign or indication of a future occurrence, but *augury* has additional meanings; namely; *the art of foretelling the future;* and *the rite performed by one*—i.e., an *augur*—*who foretells the future. Verb form of augury:* **augur.** See also OMINOUS.

ominous, *adj.* *Ominous* suggests that something unpleasant will happen (*ominous quiet before the storm*), although an *omen* is neutral—i.e., a sign of either a pleasant or an unpleasant future occurrence. See also OMEN, AUGURY.

omnifarious, omnipotent, om-nipresent, omniscient, *adj.*
Omnifarious: *of all varieties, kinds, types, forms, etc.*
Omnipotent: *all-powerful.*
Omnipresent: *present, or found, everywhere.*

Omniscient: *all-knowing.*

omnivorous, *adj.* See CAR-NIVOROUS, HERBIVOROUS, VO-RACIOUS, OMNIVOROUS.

on account of See DUE TO.

ON, UPON, UP ON, ON TO, ONTO

He jumped on the bed may mean that he was already on the bed and then started jumping. To indicate, unambiguously, a jump from one place to another, **upon** is the clearer preposition. **On** and **upon** are often interchangeable *(sat on* [or *upon*] *the throne)*, but **on** more definitely shows position or state of rest, while **upon** stresses direction or movement. When **up** is used adverbially, the words **up** and **on** are written as two words: *the horse rose up on its haunches* (i.e., the upward direction is emphasized); *the dog stood up on its hind legs.*

Onto, as a preposition, suggests, like **upon**, movement or direction: *he jumped onto the roof. He jumped on the roof* is also correct in this context, but again the ambiguity exists that he was already on the roof and started jumping up and down.

When **on** is used adverbially, separate it from the preposition **to**: *let us move on to the next topic; go on to Paris; danced on to the late hours of the night.*

on behalf of See BEHALF.

on line See IN LINE, ON LINE.

on purpose See PURPOSELY,

PURPOSEFULLY, ADVISEDLY.

one another See EACH OTHER, ONE ANOTHER.

ONE IN, ONE OUT OF *(plus plural noun)*

In constructions like **one in** ten people (plus verb or auxiliary), or **one out** of five answers (plus verb or auxiliary), the subject is **one**, not *people* nor *answers*. The verb therefore agrees with the singular pronoun **one**. For example:

One in ten people *is* likely to be a victim of crime.
One in every ten men *has* been called to active duty.

One out of five answers *is* incorrect.
One out of eight women *has* married in *her* teens.

---

one, one's, oneself In strict or formal style, the pronoun *one* is preferably followed by *one's* or *oneself*: *One should guard one's language; one must learn to take care of oneself.*

One should guard his (her) language, or *one must learn to take care of himself (herself)* is closer to informal or colloquial usage.

(Additionally, from a practical point of view, the use of *one's* instead of *his (her)* and *oneself* instead of *himself (herself)* avoids the problem of gender reference.)

See also ONESELF, ONE'S SELF.

ONE OF (*plus plural noun*)

In constructions like *one of my friends, one of my uncles,* etc. (i.e., *one of* plus a plural noun followed by a verb or auxiliary), the subject is *one,* a singular pronoun; use a form of the verb or auxiliary that agrees with a singular subject. For example:

> *One of* my friends *is* ready to help.
> *One of* my uncles *has* just remarried.
> *One of* the best results *was* obtained by ...
> If *one of* the applicants *comes* early ...

(Prepositional phrases [called P-GROUPS in Structural Grammar], such as *of my friends, of my uncles,* etc., do not contain the subject of a verb.)

See also SUBJECT, VERB AGREEMENT, 5.

ONE OF THOSE ... WHO

In a sentence like *She is one of those women who* (is? are?) *always well dressed,* the question arises, "Is the word *who,* as the subject of the verb, singular or plural?"

The rule is clear:

Who has the same number as its immediate antecedent—i.e., the word that *who* refers to: in this instance, *women (plural),* not *one (singular).* Since *women are* is the correct structure, *are* is the strictly correct verb form in the sentence above.

This rule is so often violated in print that one cannot get too fussy about it.

Nevertheless, in the construction *one of those ... who*, strict usage dictates a verb or auxiliary that agrees with *who* as a plural pronoun. For example:

> He is *one of those* men who never *take* "no" for an answer.
> She is *one of those* people who *are* always changing *their* minds.

See also SUBJECT, VERB AGREEMENT; WHO (PLUS VERB)

ONE OR TWO

When two or more subjects of a verb are connected by the conjunction *or*, the subject *closer* (or *closest*) to the verb or auxiliary governs the verb or auxiliary form. For example:

> One or *two* of my friends *were* always with me. (*Two* is closer to the verb.)
> My brother or my *sisters are* usually at home in the evening. (*Sisters* is the closer subject.)
> My sisters or my *brother is* usually at home. (*Brother* is closer to the verb.)
> *Has* your *sister* or your brothers telephoned lately? (*Sister* is closer to the auxiliary *has*.)
> *Have* your *brothers* or your sister telephoned lately? (*Brothers* is closer to the auxiliary *have*.)
> *Is* Pat or I invited to the party? (*Pat* is closer to the auxiliary *is*.)
> *Am* I or Pat invited? (*I* is closer to the auxiliary *am*.)

Some of these examples, though correct, may sound awkward. If so, reword to obviate the problem: *Am I invited, or is Pat invited? Is Pat invited, or am I:*; etc.

See also EITHER ... OR, NEITHER ... NOR; OR; SUBJECT, VERB, AGREEMENT, 4.

one out of See ONE IN, ONE OUT OF.

oneself, one's self The reflexive pronoun is *oneself*, as in *one can hurt oneself; one's self* is a variant form rarely used. See also HIMSELF, HIS SELF, HISSELF; ONE, ONE'S, ONESELF.

one-time, onetime, one time As an *adjective* the hyphenated form is preferable: *a one-time* stage star. (The adjective *onetime*, written solid, as a variant form.)

As an *adverbial*, the words are separated: *One time, he lost all his money in a swindle.*

only In strict, formal usage, *only* is placed as close as possible to the word or phrase that it modifies. Thus, *she works on only one job at a time* is preferable to *she only works on one job at a time.* Similarly, *she lived there only for two months* (or *for two months only*) is preferable to *she only lived there for two months. She has only one sister* is preferable to *she only has one sister.*

In colloquial and informal usage, of course, the second of each pair of sentences above is frequently found, and it would be unrealistic to label such constructions incorrect.

Sometimes, ambiguity is avoided by the proper placement of *only. I only work here* means, obviously, *I don't own the business. I work only here* means *I work here only, nowhere else.*

ontogeny, phylogeny, *n.* As terms in biology, *ontogeny* signifies the development of the *individual,* *phylogeny* the development of the *species.*

opaque, *adj.* See TRANSPARENT, TRANSLUCENT, OPAQUE.

open-, *prefix* Adjective com-

pounds, especially if they precede a noun, are hyphenated: *open-air, open-and-shut, open-door, open-ended, open-eyed, open-heart* (surgery), *open-minded, open-mouthed.* But the adjectives *openhanded* and *openhearted* are written solid.

ophthalmic, *adj.* See OCULAR, OPHTHALMIC, OPTIC, OPTICAL.

ophthalmologist, oculist, optometrist, optician, *n.* The *ophthalmologist* and the *oculist* are medical doctors specializing in diseases and other problems of the eye. *Ophthalmologist* is the standard professional term; *oculist* is an earlier word for *ophthalmologist,* no longer in frequent use.

The *optometrist* is not a physician, but a doctor of *optometry* who treats vision disorders, usually by prescribing eyeglasses with corrective lenses, and sometimes by other means (eye exercises, etc.).

The *optician* grinds these corrective lenses, according to a prescription from an *optometrist* or *ophthalmologist,* and makes and sells eyeglasses and other optical equipment and instruments.

opine, *v.* See ENTHUSE.

optic, optical, *adj.* See OCULAR, OPHTHALMIC, OPTIC, OPTICAL.

optician, *n.* See OPHTHAL-

MOLOGIST, OCULIST, OPTOME-
TRIST, OPTICIAN.

optimum, *adj.* See MAXI-
MUM, OPTIMUM.

optimum, *n.* For plural, see
NOUN, 6Q.

optometrist, *n.* See OPTHAL-
MOLOGIST, OCULIST, OPTOME-
TRIST, OPTICIAN.

opulence, *n.* See AFFLUENCE,
OPULENCE.

opus, *n.* For plural form, see
NOUN, 6P.

OR, *conj.*

When **or** joins two or more *singular* subjects, the verb or
auxiliary is in the form that follows a singular subject. For
example:

> The manager, his assistant, **or** his secretary *is* al-
> ways in the office.
> A nurse **or** a doctor *is* always present.
> Rella **or** her sister *has* already taken care of the
> problem.

When **or** connects *plural* subjects, the verb or auxiliary is
in the form that follows a plural subject. For example:

> Carrots **or** peas *are* served at every lunch.

When **or** connects subjects one of which is *singular* and the
other *plural*, the verb agrees with the *nearer* subject. For
examples of such constructions, see ONE OR TWO.
See also SUBJECT, VERB, AGREEMENT, 4.

Or *(to start a sentence)* Even
in formal writing, a sentence
may start with *Or*—also with
And or *But*.

or, nor, *conj.* See NOR, OR.

-or, -our The ending *-our* is
the British spelling in words
like *behaviour, neighbour,
odour, valour, honour, parlour,* etc. The American spelling for such words uses *-or:
behavior, neighbor,* etc.

However, *glamour* is preferable to *glamor* in American spelling, even though
other forms of the word *(glamorous, glamorize)* omit the *u*
preceding *r*.

oral, aural, *adj.* See AURAL,
ORAL, AUDITORY, AURICULAR.

oral, verbal, *adj.* See VERBAL,
ORAL.

**ordinal numbers, cardinal
members** *Ordinal numbers*
are *first, second, third,* etc.

(or *1st, 2nd, 3rd,* etc.)— *cardinal numbers* are *1, 2, 3, 4,* etc. (or *one, two, three, four,* etc.)

To pluralize a number in the form of a figure, you may, or need not, use an apostrophe before adding *s: 5's* or *5s, 12's* or *12s.* Modern trends lean to the omission of the apostrophe.

See also NOUN, 6T.

ordinance, ordnance, *n.* In it most common meaning, an *ordinance* is a law, regulation, etc., usually of a municipal government.

Ordnance, on the other hand, designates military weapons and equipment collectively, or the branch of the military in charge of such weapons and equipment.

orgasmic, orgastic, orgiastic, *adj.* The first two adjectives derive from the noun *orgasm. Orgiastic* refers to orgies, and is pronounced ôr'-jee-AS'-tik.

orient, orientate, *v. Orient* is the preferable verb form, *orientate* a variant. The noun is *orientation.* See also DISORIENT, DISORIENTATE.

orotund, rotund, *adj.* A voice or sound that is rich and full in quality may be described as either *orotund* or *rotund,* but the former adjective is more frequently used in this sense.

An *orotund* style of expressing oneself in speaking or writing, on the other hand, is

overelegant, pompous, etc.

Rotund more often refers to bodily shape—i.e., well-rounded. Hence, the word is sometimes used as a euphemism for *fat, chubby, stout,* etc.

orphan, *n.* Strictly, an *orphan* is a child both of whose parents have died. In loose usage, *orphan* may designate a child who has lost only one parent.

oscillation, vacillation, *n.* As the words are generally used, *oscillation* refers to physical swaying, swinging back and forth, etc., and *vacillation* to mental swinging from one decision to another. *Verbs: oscillate, vacillate.*

osculate, oscillate, *v.* To *osculate* is an elegant way of saying *to kiss.* (It also has a technical meaning in biology.)

Oscillate is defined in OSCILLATION, VACILLATION.

otologist, otolaryngologist, audiologist, *n.* An *otologist* is a medical specialist in the pathology of the ear and of hearing. If the specialty includes the nose and throat as well as the ear, the physician is an *otolaryngologist,* or, less frequently, an *otorhinolaryngologist.*

An *audiologist* is not a physican, but a specialist in alleviating hearing problems, as by fitting hearing aids, etc.

-ough, -o, -u Words like *although, though, thorough,*

and *through*, may be spelled *altho, tho, thoro, thru* only in very informal and chatty styles of writing.

Thruway, however, is the correct spelling for a type of superhighway; *no thorofare* is often seen on traffic signs, perhaps to save space.

ought, aught, naught See ZERO, AUGHT, OUGHT, NAUGHT, NOUGHT.

ought to of See COULD HAVE, COULD OF.

-our, -or See -OR, -OUR.

ours, our's *Ours* is a possessive personal pronoun. *Our's* is a misspelling.
See also PRONOUN, 8.

ourself, ourselves—*Ourself*, referring to one person, is acceptable only in royal or formal proclamations, or in editorials. It is the reflexive pronoun corresponding to the so-called royal or editorial "we." See also MYSELF.

out-, *prefix* As a prefix, *out* is usually written solid with its compound: *outdate, outdistance, outrun, outboard, outbuilding, outpatient,* etc.

Adjective compounds of three or more words starting with *out-* and preceding their nouns are generally hyphenated: *out-and-out, out-of-date, out-of-door, out-of-doors, out-of-print, out-of-the-way, out-of-work; an out-of-print book; an out-of-the-way place.*

(The) *out*-group and (the) *in*-group are hyphenated words.

Out is hyphenated in a compound before a capital letter: *out-Herod Herod*, etc.

out, out of *Out* is used to mean *through (he walked out the door), out of* to mean *from the inside to the outside (she walked out of the room; sent him out of the room).*

outdoor, out-of-door, outdoors, out-of-doors *Outdoor* (variant form: *out-of-door*) is an *adjective: an outdoor ceremony.*

Outdoors (variant form: *out-of-doors*) is an *adverb* or *noun: let us step outdoors* (adv.) *Outdoors* (n.) *is where you should be.*

outside, outside of In formal usage, *outside* is preferable to *outside of* as a preposition: *stood outside the house; the problem was outside her scope of authority.*

Informally and colloquially, *outside of* is often used to mean *other than: outside of your classroom teaching, what other school duties do you have?*

over-, *prefix* Compounds with this prefix are written solid, except for the adjective *over-the-counter* (stocks). The adjective *overall* is preferably a solid word, but may also be hyphenated: *an overall* (or *over-all*) *view.*

overage This word is both a *noun* (pronounced Ō'-vər-aj) and an *adjective* (pronounced ō'-vər-AYJ'): *an* **overage** (n.) *of ten dollars; he was* **overage** (adj.) *for the class he was in.*

overalls, n. Though singular in concept (i.e., one garment), this noun is treated as a plural: *the* **overalls** *were washed.*

On the other hand, the pair of **overalls** (still one garment, but the subject, *pair*, is singular) *is threadbare.*

See also PAIR.

overlay, n. *A layer over, or covering, something.* (See OVERLIE, OVERLAY for the distinction between the *verbs* **overlay** *and* **overlie.**

OVERLIE, OVERLAY, v.

These verbs have the same forms of the corresponding verbs *lie* and *lay*:

PRESENT	PAST	PARTICIPLES
overlie	overlay	(has, was) overlain
overlay	overlaid	(has, was) overlaid

But, unlike *lie* and *lay*, both **overlie** and **overlay** are *transitive* verbs (see SENTENCE PATTERNS 1–6). The distinction in use, then, depends on meaning.

Overlie (v.) means *to be or lie over or upon.* Thus:

The carpet **overlies** *(pres. tense)* a very thick padding.
The carpet **overlay** *(past tense)* a very thick padding.
The carpet *had* **overlain** *(part.)* a very thick padding.
The padding *was* **overlain** *(part.)* by a velvet carpeting.

(*Note:* **overlie** is not used as a *noun.*)

Overlay (v.) means *to place, put, or superimpose* (something) *over or upon* (something else).
Thus (and note the use of the preposition *with*):

He often **overlays** *(pres.)* his words with a sarcastic tone.
He often **overlaid** *(past)* his words with a sarcastic tone.
He *has* often **overlaid** *(part.)* his words with a sarcastic tone.
His words were **overlaid** *(part.)* with a sarcastic tone.

See also LIE, LAY; OVERLAY; UNDERLAY, UNDERLIE.

overly In the sense of *excessively; to a great degree*, this word is in standard usage, despite the objection of some writers. Thus, **overly** *cautious*, **overly** *concerned*, etc. are completely accepted even in formal style.

oviparous, ovoviviparous, *adj.* See VIVIPAROUS, OVIPAROUS, OVOVIVIPAROUS.

owing to See DUE TO.

P

paid See PAYED, PAID.

painless, *adj*. See HOPELESS, MORE HOPELESS.

PAIR, *n*.

Pair or *pairs* may be used as a plural after a cardinal number: *two **pair*** (or ***pairs***) *of socks*. *Pairs* is the more commonly used form.

Pair as a subject of a verb may be either singular or plural, depending on the concept. For example:

A *pair* of scissors (pants, trousers, etc.—i.e., one implement, garment, etc.) *is* on the table.

That *pair* of shoes (i.e., taken together as a unit) *was* reduced in price.

A *pair* of shoes (i.e., *two* shoes) *were* under the bed.

The *pair* (i.e., *two* people) *were* being watched by the police.

See also COUPLE; DOZEN, DOZENS; DUO, DUET, DUAD, DYAD; NOUN. 1.

pajamas, pyjamas, *n*. *Pyjamas* is the British spelling.

Although the word is singular in concept (i.e., one garment, though it may have a top and a bottom part), *pajamas* is construed as a plural: *her **pajamas** were ready for washing*. (Other words that are singular in concept, but construed as plurals, are *lodgings, overalls, premises, scissors, pants, trousers*, etc.) See also PAIR.

pandemic See ENDEMIC, EPIDEMIC, PANDEMIC.

pander, panderer, *n*. Both forms are used to designate a person who panders; *pander* is also the intransitive verb, followed by the preposition to: *to **pander** to the lowest tastes*.

pantheism, *n*. See THEISM, MONOTHEISM, POLYTHEISM, PANTHEISM, DEISM.

panties, *n*. This word is generally considered informal usage; it is construed as a plural even though it is singular (i.e., one garment) in concept: *the panties were made of nylon.* See also PAIR.

pants, *n.* Meaning *trousers,* this word is construed as a plural form: *his pants were too loose.* On the other hand, *a pair* of pants was on the bed.

See also PAIR.

paper, paper-, *prefix* Compounds used as *adjectives* are hyphenated: *paper-covered book; paper-thin material; paper-wrapped chicken.* But *paperbound* (adj.) is a solid word.

Noun compounds are written solid: *paperback, paperboard, paperboy, paperhanger, paperweight.*

The nouns *paperknife* and *paperwork* may be solid or separated.—i.e., *paper knife, paper work.*

Paper clip, *paper* cutter, *paper* money, and *paper* tiger are written as separate words.

paper-mâché, papier-mâché Although the word is pronounced PAY'-pər-mə-SHAY', only the second spelling is correct.

paralyze, analyze, psychoanalyze, *v.* These are the only three nontechnical verbs ending in *-yze.* Hence, other forms of these words are spelled with a *y* after the *l: paralysis, paralytic; analysis, ana-*

lyst, analytic; psychoanalysis, psychoanalyst; psychoanalytic.

(*Dialyze, electrolyze,* and some other technical verbs also end in *-yze.*)

paramecium, *n.* For plural, see NOUN, 6Q.

parameter, *n.* See PERIMETER, PARAMETER.

paranoid, paranoiac These words are interchangeable, and may be adjectives that characterize the victims of *paranoia* or nouns to designate the victims. The first of the two forms is more commonly used.

paranormal, *adj.* See ABNORMAL, PARANORMAL.

parenthesis, *n.* This is a singular noun, but may refer to either or both of the curved symbols: (). It is, however, more precise to use the plural form, *parentheses,* to designate the two symbols: *the word was enclosed in parentheses.*

Explanatory material enclosed in *parentheses,* or separated in writing by dashes or commas within a sentence, is called a *parenthesis.*

The *verb* is *parenthesize,* the *adjective* either *parenthetical* or *parenthetic.*

See also NOUN, 6N.

parlour, parlor, *n.* See -OR, -OUR.

parole, probation, *n.* In reference to persons convicted of legal offenses:

Parole is the release of a person from imprisonment before the expiration of his (her) sentence on condition of future legal behavior.

Probation is the suspension of a prison sentence before the convicted person has been imprisoned, again on condition of future legal behavior, plus, sometimes, other conditions imposed by the sentencing judge.

The person on *parole* is a *parolee*; the person on *probation* is a *probationer*.

parricide, partricide, matricide, *n.* *Parricide* is the killing of either parent or of both parents; *patricide*, of one's father; *matricide*, of one's mother.

The same word in each instance also designates the person who has committed the killing. *Adjectives: parricidal; patricidal; matricidal*.

partake, participate, *v.* As here contrasted, you *partake of* (food, drink, etc.); you *participate in*, or less popularly, *partake in* (an experience, activity, etc.). In either instance, you are sharing (in the experience, activity, food, etc.) with another or others.

One who *partakes* is a *partaker*; one who *participates* is a *participant*, or, less frequently, a *participator*.

Partake, of course, incorporates the past tense and participle of the verb *take*: *partook, partaken*.

partial, *adj.*, **partiality**, *n. Partial (adj.)* is followed by the preposition *to. Partiality (n.)* is followed by *to, toward*, or, if the word means *fondness*, by the preposition *for: partiality to* (or *toward*) *the defense; partiality for* spicy foods.

partially, partly, *adv. Partially*—to some degree or extent: *partially* convinced, useful, cooked, developed.

Partly—in part (i.e., *as one part of*), as opposed to completely: *consisting partly of whole wheat; built partly of stone.*

This is a precise distinction, not universally observed in current usage.

participate, partake, *v.* See PARTAKE, PARTICIPATE.

participle In Structural Grammar, the term *participle* refers only to the form of the verb called, in traditional grammar, *the past participle*, and is the form that follows *has, have*, or *had*—i.e., *given, taken, spoken, used*, etc. In traditional grammar, there is also a *present participle*, which is the -ING form of a verb: *working, talking, running*.

See also: VERB, 3, 9.

partly, partially, *adv.* See PARTIALLY, PARTLY.

parts of speech Structural Grammar lists four parts of speech: NOUN (N); VERB (V); ADJECTIVE (ADJ); ADVERB (ADV).

A PRONOUN (PRON) is a substitute NOUN; auxiliaries, determiners, prepositions, connectors, and qualifiers are called *function words*.

Traditional grammar lists eight parts of speech: *noun, verb, adjective, adverb, pronoun, preposition, conjunction,* and *interjection.*

party, *n.* This word is used informally or colloquially to refer to one person *(he's a strange party)*—in formal English, *person, individual,* etc. is a better choice.

In "telephonese" *(your party is on the line)* and "legalese" *(party of the first part), party* meaning *person* is current usage.

See also NOUN, 1.

pass-, *prefix.* Compounds are usually written solid: *passbook,   passkey, passport, password.*

pass, *v.* See PASSED, PAST.

passable, passible, *adj.* **Passable**—*able to be passed, passed through,* etc.; *good enough, but not excellent.*

Passible—*able to feel, suffer, react emotionally,* etc.

The negative forms *(impassable, impassible)* have a similar distinction.

passed, past *Passed* is the past tense or participle of the verb *pass,* and may also be used in the adjective position: *we passed the house; the time has passed; a passed hand in bridge.*

Past is a noun, adjective, adverb, or preposition: *the past* (n.) *is history; her past* (adj.) *performances; walk past* (adv.) *quickly; rode past* (prep.) *the house; past* (adj.) *tense of a verb.*

passer-by, passerby, *n.* **Passerby** is the variant form. The plural form is **passers-by** or **passersby.**

See also NOUN, 6U.

passible, *adj.* See PASSABLE, PASSIBLE.

passive voice See VERB, 9.

passtime, *n.* See PASTIME, PASSTIME.

past, passed See PASSED, PAST.

past history An obvious redundancy, for history *is* the past. (Omit *past.)*

pastime, passtime, *n.* Though a *pastime* provides a pleasant way to pass time, only the first spelling is correct.

past participle See PARTICIPLE.

paternal, paternalistic, *adj.* **Paternal:** *fatherly; like, pertaining to, derived from,* etc. *a* (or one's) *father.*

Paternalistic: *treating one's subordinates, followers, servants, workers, constituents,* etc., *as if one were their father and they were one's young children*—i.e., in a kindly, indulgent manner but allowing them little or no power or responsibility. This adjective is used to characterize rulers, supervisors, administrators, managers, people holding political or other office, etc. *Noun: paternalism.*

pathologist, medical examiner, coroner, *n.* A *pathologist* is a physician whose specialty is the causes, nature, process, etc. of disease. A *pathologist* may do a biopsy on live tissue, or perform an autopsy on a corpse to discover the cause of death.

The *medical examiner* or *coroner* (the title varies according to locality) holds an inquest before a jury to determine the cause of death of someone who did not die of obviously natural causes.

See also AUTOPSY, BIOPSY.

pathos, bathos, *n.* As here contrasted, *bathos* is insincere, overdone *pathos*—i.e., *pathos* carried to a ridiculous or absurd degree.

patricide, *n.* See PARRICIDE, PATRICIDE, MATRICIDE.

patron, *n.* For feminine form, see NOUN, 2C.

payed, paid The past tense or participle of *pay* is *payed* in the nautical expression *payed out the line* (rope, etc.); or with the meaning, in nautical usage, of *coat, as with tar,* etc., *to make waterproof: the hull of the vessel was payed with a special paint.* Otherwise, of course, the past tense or participle of *pay* is *paid.*

peaceable, peaceful, *adj.* The words are interchangeable synonyms, except that *peaceable* has the additional meaning of *tending to promote or foster peace: peaceable attitudes. Peaceful* is otherwise the more commonly used word.

peccadillo, *n.* For plural, see NOUN, 6L2.

peculiar to See CHARACTERISTIC OF, PECULIAR TO.

pedagog, pedagogue, *n.* See -OGUE, OG; PEDANTIC, DIDACTIC, PURISTIC, PEDAGOGICAL, PEDAGOGUISH.

pedagoguish, *adj.* See PEDANTIC, DIDACTIC, PURISTIC, PEDAGOGICAL, PEDAGOGUISH.

pedagogy, pedagogical See PEDANTIC, DIDACTIC, PURISTIC, PEDAGOGICAL, PEDAGOGUISH.

pedal, peddle A *pedal* (*n.*) is a foot-operated lever. *Pedal* is also a verb: *pedal a bicycle.*

Peddle is a verb, as in *peddle merchandise; peddle gossip; peddle one's book to various publishers;* etc. The verb also means *to waste time on unimportant matters,* but *piddle* is more often used in this sense.

One who *peddles* is a *peddler* or, in the variant and infrequently used spellings, a *pedlar* or *pedler.*

The business of a *peddler,* or the merchandise sold by *peddling,* is *peddlery.* (*Pedlary* and *pedlery* are variant spellings of *peddlery.*)

PEDANTIC, DIDACTIC, PURISTIC, PEDAGOGICAL, PEDAGOGUISH, *adj.*

Pedantic: *insisting on excessively strict adherence to formal, sometimes unimportant, rules, especially in language, art, etc; or ostenstatiously displaying one's knowledge or learning.* The person: *pedant*. The attitude: *pedantry*.

Didactic: sometimes a neutral adjective, synonymous with *instructive;* more often, *giving (perhaps unwanted) instruction in moral behavior,* or *instructing in a pedantic manner.* Alternate adjective: *didactical*. The attitude or behavior: *didacticism*.

Puristic: a synonym of *pedantic* in its first-mentioned meaning above. This adjective, however, does not have quite the derogatory connotation of *pedantic*. Alternate adjective: *puristical*. The person: *purist*. The attitude of adherence to strict rules, or an instance of such: *purism*.

Pedagogical: a nonjudgmental, neutral adjective deriving from the noun *pedagogy*, which is *the profession, practice, science, art,* or *principles of teaching.* Alternate adjective: *pedagogic*. Alternate noun: *pedagogics*.

Then what is a *pedagogue*? This is now most frequently a derogatory term for a narrow-minded, stuffy, dull, *pedantic*, and often dogmatic teacher. Adjective: *pedagoguish*.

---

peddle, *v.*   See PEDAL, PEDDLE.

peeve, *n., v.   Peeve,* as a verb or noun, is a back-formation of the adjective *peevish,* and is more suitable to colloquial or informal, than to formal, English. *Felt peeved; you peeve me; my pet peeve*—these are all considered informal usage.

See also ENTHUSE.

pell-mell, pellmell   As adverb, adjective, or noun, the word may be written hyphenated or solid. The hyphenated form is more frequently found.

pellucid, *adj.*   See LUCID, PELLUCID.

penitentiary, *n.*   See JAIL, PRISON, PENITENTIARY.

pen name   See ALIAS, PSEUDONYM, PEN NAME, NOM DE PLUME, INCOGNITO.

penumbra, *n.*   For plural, see NOUN, 6M.

people, peoples, *n. pl.*   The plural *peoples* may be used to refer to different national, ethnic, religious, etc., groups: *the diverse peoples that inhabit our planet.*

PERCENT, PER CENT, PERCENTAGE

Percent may be written solid or as two words, and should be preceded by a numeral: *five percent (per cent) of the population. Percent (per cent)* without a numeral is acceptable on a colloquial or informal level; *percentage* is preferable in such instances: *a large percentage of the population; what percentage of the applicants.*

Percent (per cent) and *percentage* are construed as either singular or plural depending on whether the concept is a unified group or a single part or entity (in which case, the words are used as singular nouns), or a number of separate individuals or items (in which instance, the words are used as plural nouns). For example:

Ten *percent* of the students *are* not reading at grade level (i.e., a certain number of students).

Twenty *percent* of the book *is* sheer nonsense (i.e., a portion making up one-fifth).

A large *percentage* of the voters (i.e., a number of the voters) *do* not really understand the issues on which *they* are voting.

Only a small *percentage* of the report (i.e., a small part or portion) *deals* with crime in the streets.

Percentage is most often preceded by some qualifying modifier, other than a numeral *(a tiny percentage; a great percentage; a certain percentage)*, except in an expression like *the value has risen by ten percentage points.*

(Incidentally, *per centum* and *per cent.* [a supposed abbreviation of *per centum*] are now rarely used.)

See also LOT; NUMBER; NOUN, 1.

---

perfect, more perfect See EQUAL, MORE EQUAL.

pericardium, *n.* For plural, see NOUN, 6Q.

perigee, *n.* See APOGEE, PERIGEE.

perimeter, parameter, *n.* A *perimeter* is the outside boundary, or length of such a boundary, around a plane figure, a place, or an area.

A *parameter* is a mathematical term dealing with constants and variables; in recent years, however, the word has been used in the plural form to designate *bounds, boundaries, limits,* etc. Some authorities and writers object to such usage, but, as in so many other instances, if the new meaning becomes sufficiently prevalent, it will be accepted as standard English, if it has not already been so accepted. (Any coinage that gains popularity usually irritates those who want to keep language constant or precise.)

perineum, *n.* For plural, see NOUN, 6Q.

peritoneum, *n.* For plural, see NOUN, 6Q.

pernickety, *adj.* A variant of *persnickety*—either word may be used.

persecute, prosecute, *v.* The legal term is *prosecute*. The district attorney is a *prosecutor* (not, one hopes, a *persecutor*), and calls witnesses for the *prosecution*.

persevere, *v.* Followed by the preposition *in*: *persevere in one's efforts*. The noun form is *perseverance*.

persist, *v.* This verb is followed by the preposition *in*: *persist in their search*. The noun form is *persistence* or *persistency*.

persnickety, *adj.* See PERNICKETY.

PERSON, *n.*

A singular noun, *person* is therefore followed by singular forms. Examples:

> If any *person* objects, let *him/her* (not *them*) speak up.
> A *person* must watch *his/her* (not *their*) step.
> Is this the *person* who lost *his/her* (not *their*) watch?

See also ANYBODY.

Person *(grammatical term)* Personal pronouns are said to be in the first, second, or third *person*. The pronoun *I* or *me* is in the first *person*, singular; *we* or *us* is in the first *person*, plural. The pronoun *you* is in the second *person*, singular or plural. *She, he, her, him,*, and *it* are in the third *person* singular; *they* and *them* are in the third *person* plural.

persona, *n.* As a term in psychology, the plural is usually *personas*.

Persona is also a character in a drama, novel, etc., and is then generally used in the plural: *personae* (pər-SŌ'-nee) —i.e., cast of characters.

See also NOUN, 6M.

personal pronouns See PRONOUN, 7–8B.

personnel, *n.* *Personnel*

(pur'-sə-NEL')designates the working members of an organization— committee, corporation, faculty and other staff of an educational institution, army or navy group, etc. It is a collective noun that is construed as either singular or plural, depending on concept—i.e., a single entity (singular) or a number of individuals (plural): *the personnel of the English department is excellent; the personnel of the ship were all busily engaged in their respective duties.* See also NOUN, 1.

perspicacious, perspicuous, *adj.* A person of keen mind, judgment, or discernment is *perspicacious*.

Analysis, reasoning, questions, reports, etc. can also be called *perspicacious* if they show the sharpness of intellect, judgment, etc. of the person or persons responsible for them. *Nouns: perspicacity, perspicaciousness.*

Perspicuous describes only style or language, spoken or written, that is immediately clear and understandable. *Nouns: perspicuity* (pur'-spə-KYOO'-ə-tee), *perspicuousness.* See also LUCID, PELLUCID.

persuade, *v.* See CONVINCE, PERSUADE.

pertinacious, tenacious, *adj.* A *pertinacious* person is excessively, stubbornly, obstinately, even perversely *tenacious* or persistent. While *tenacious* may be a neutral or complimentary term, *pertinacious* is generally used derogatively.

petrify, *v.* The noun form is *petrifaction. Petrification* is a variant noun. Most verbs ending in *-ify* have derived noun forms ending in *-ification: simplification, purification*, etc. See also LIQUEFY, RAREFY, PUTREFY, STUPEFY, TORREFY.

phalanx, *n.* The plural is *phalanxes*, unless, as a term in anatomy, *a bone of the toe* or *finger* is meant, in which case *phalanges* (fə-LAN'-jeez) is the plural form. Such a bone, by the way, is also called a *phalange* (fə-LANJ').

phantasm, phantasy See FANTASM, PHANTASM, PHANTASY.

phantom, fantom, *n. Phantom* is the popular spelling: *fantom* is a variant form.

pharmaceuticals, *n. pl.* See DRUGS, PHARMACEUTICALS.

pharmacist, *n.* See DRUGGIST, PHARMACIST.

phenix, *n.* See PHOENIX, PHENIX.

PHENOMENA, n. pl.

This is the *plural* form of *phenomenon* (a variant plural is *phenomenons*), and should not be construed as a singular. Therefore:

> *These* or *those* (not *this* or *that*) *phenomena* are (not *is*) visible in the nighttime during June and July.

See also CRITERIA; NOUN, 6R.

---

philatelist, n. See NUMISMATIST, PHILATELIST.

Philippine Islands, Philippines, n. Either form is current and correct; also called the *Republic of the Philippines*. A resident or native, however, is a *Filipino*, of which the plural is *Filipinos*. See also NOUN, 6L3.

philology, n. See LINGUISTICS, PHILOLOGY, SEMANTICS.

philter, philtre, n. *Philtre* is the British spelling. See also -ER, -RE.

phobia, n. See MANIA, PHOBIA.

phoenix, phenix, n. *Phenix* is a variant spelling, not frequently encountered. The constellation and the city in Arizona are both spelled with a capital *P*, and *Phoenix* only.

phone, telephone, n. *Phone, auto,* and *photo,* as shortened forms of *telephone, automobile,* and *photograph,* are considered informal or colloquial by some authorities. However, all three short forms are in such wide use that one has no choice but to accept them as standard.

Of these words, only *phone* may also be used as a verb.

phonetics, phonics, n. *Phonetics* is the science of speech sounds.

Phonics is either a method of teaching reading, usually in elementary school, by having students learn to sound out syllables or words—usually distinguished from *sight-reading;* or the science of sound, hence a synonym of *acoustics*.

Like so many words ending in -ics, both words are *singular* nouns: *phonetics is a branch of linguistics; phonics is the method used in . . .*

See also -ICS.

phonograph, gramophone, record player, turntable, Victrola, n. These words all refer to the same device; the distinction is in the dating.

In these days of high-fidelity sound systems, the current

photo [181] Pidjin English

terms are **turntable** and **record player**—these are components of a system that includes tuners, amplifiers, and speakers as part of a radio–record player combination. (With compact discs replacing records in many such systems, the device is called a **disc player**. And, of course, eight-track tapes and cassettes have for some time competed with records, so there are also **tape players** and **cassette players**.)

Phonograph is still somewhat in current use, especially among older people. **Gramophone**, originally a trademark name, and **Victrola** (also a trademark) are no longer in the modern vocabulary, unless the speaker or writer needs to date the devices to much earlier times.

photo, photograph, *n*. See PHONE, TELEPHONE.

phrenetic, *adj*. See FRENETIC, PHRENETIC.

phrensy, *n*. See FRENZY, PHRENSY.

phylogeny, *n*. See ONTOGENY, PHYLOGENY.

phylum, *n*. For plural, see NOUN, 6Q.

physics, *n*. **Physic** is an earlier word for *laxative* or *cathartic*: *physics were once routinely prescribed for many illnesses*. (The term **physic** with this meaning is a dated word; **physic** meaning *medi-* *cal practice* is, of course, an archaic word, but the modern term **physician** is derived from it.)

Physics, the science of matter, energy, etc., like other sciences ending in -*ics*, is construed as a singular noun: *Physics was her hardest subject.*

The scientist involved in **physics** is a **physicist**. See also -ICS.

pianissimo, *n*. For plural, see NOUN, 6L4.

piano, *n*. For plural, see NOUN, 6L3.

piccolo, *n*. For plural, see NOUN, 6L3.

piddle, peddle, *v*. See PEDAL, PEDDLE.

Pidjin (or *pidjin*) **English, pigeon English** The correct spelling is **Pidjin** (or *pidjin*) **English**; those who spell it **pigeon English** cause great distress to some authorities. It is understandable that a familiar word (*pigeon*) would be substituted for an unfamiliar one, especially if the dialect of the South Pacific islands sounds like "pigeon talk" to someone unacquainted with it.

(The word *pidjin* is supposedly an attempt to spell the Chinese pronunciation of "business"—hence "business English." Such derivation may or may not have a basis in fact.)

PIER, DOCK, MARINA, QUAY, WHARF, *n.*

Referring to structures that abut, or project into, an ocean, bay, lake, etc., the slight distinctions, if any, are as follows:

Pier—extending over the water, used for landing of vessels; may contain a boardwalk, amusement devices, shops, etc.

Dock—structure for the landing, tying up, etc. of watercraft.

Marina—small boat basin where pleasure boats may dock, moor, be serviced, etc.

Quay—concrete or stone *wharf*, where vessels may load and unload. (Pronounced KEE.)

Wharf—may be roofed, built of wood, stone, etc., and provides facilities for loading, unloading, and temporary berthing of vessels. (Plural is *wharves* or *wharfs*.) *Wharf* is usually interchangeable with *pier* or *dock*.

The term applied is generally a matter of what such a structure is called in the area in which it exists.

---

pigeon English see PIDJIN (OR PIDJIN) ENGLISH, PIGEON ENGLISH.

Pigmy, Pygmy, *n.* See PYGMY, PIGMY.

pilfer, pilferage See THIEVERY.

pinch, steal, *v.* See THIEVERY.

pious, *adj.* See DEVOUT, PIOUS.

pistachio, *n.* For plural, see NOUN, 6K.

pitiful, pitiable, piteous, *adj.* These adjectives are closely synonymous. The distinctions are fine:

Pitiful—*causing one to feel pity.* This word is also used to describe a person or thing so low, insignificant, worthless, inferior, etc. as to arouse one's scorn: *offered what we considered a pitiful price; a pitiful attempt to . . .*

Pitiable—*arousing one's pity;* implies a greater degree of contempt than *pitiful.*

Piteous—refers to that which calls for or demands pity, in contrast with *pitiful* and *pitiable*, words that indicate the feeling of the person in whom pity is aroused: *piteous cries of the deserted cub; piteous squeals of the frightened child.*

pity, sympathy, *n.* As here contrasted, both nouns indicate sorrow or sadness over the misfortune, troubles, or suffering of another.

Pity, however, generally suggests some slight contempt.

Sympathy implies a positive understanding and perhaps even a sharing, of another's problems, grief, troubles, suffering, etc.

See also COMMISERATION, CONDOLENCE; EMPATHIZE, SYMPATHIZE.

pizzicato, *n.* For plural, see NOUN, 6L4.

planetarium, *n.* For plural, see NOUN, 6Q.

plateau, *n.* For plural, see NOUN, 6S.

platitude, *n.* See CLICHÉ, BROMIDE, ANODYNE, PLATITUDE.

platypus, *n.* For plural, see NOUN, 6P.

plausible, *adj.* See CREDIBLE, PLAUSIBLE, CREDITABLE.

plead, *v.* The past tense or participle is *pleaded* or, as a variant, *pled*. The noun form is *plea*.

pleasantness, pleasantry, *n.* *Pleasantness* is the noun derived from the adjective *pleasant.*

A *pleasantry* is a humorous or joking remark in conversation. The plural form, *pleasantries*, may also mean *small talk* or *polite conversation*: engage in *pleasantries*; spent some time exchanging *pleasantries* ("How are you? How's the family?" etc.).

Only *pleasantness* has a negative form, **unpleasantness**, though no doubt some people, when they meet, immediately start exchanging "unpleasantries" (a nonword,

unfortunately, but one that ought to have a place in the English vocabulary.)

plenitude, plentitude, *n.* One would certainly expect a *t* after the *n*, but only *plenitude* is a word, and is perhaps an elegant way of saying *plenty*, *plentifulness*, *abundance*, *completeness*, *fullness*, etc. *Adjective:* **plenitudinous.**

plenty *That's* **plenty** *good*; *we have* **plenty** *money*; etc. —such use of *plenty* as a qualifier or adjective is not standard English, though acceptable on a colloquial or informal level.

pleonastic, *adj.* See WORDY, VERBOSE, PROLIX, PLEONASTIC, REDUNDANT, TAUTOLOGICAL.

plethora, *n.* A *plethora* (PLETH'-ə-rə) is too much— i.e., it is an overabundance, more than needed, excessive fullness, etc. *Plethora* is not a synonym of *plenty* or *abundance*. *Adjective:* **plethoric** (plee-THÔR'-ik, preferably; also plə-THAHR'-ik, PLETH'-ər-ik).

pliable, pliant, *adj.* The words are interchangeable and may describe either a substance easily bent or shaped, or, figuratively, a person who is receptive to change or who adapts easily to new conditions, demands, influences, etc. *Pliable* is somewhat more frequently used than *pliant* in the figurative sense. *Nouns:*

pliability, pliableness; pliancy, pliantness.

pliers, *n.* Though singular in concept, this noun is construed as a plural: *the pliers are in the toolbox.* Hence, not *a pliers*, but *the pliers* or *a pair of pliers.*

plough, plow *Plough* is the British spelling.

plunge, *v.* To indicate downward movement from a higher to a lower place or position, or movement to a new situation, use the preposition *into* rather than *in: plunged into* the pool; *plunged* his family into debt; *plunged* his hands into the water; *plunged* the nation into war.

When *plunge* is used as a noun, it is generally followed by *in: a plunge in the lake; a plunge in the market.*

When the participle is used as an *adjective* and has a figurative meaning, *in* is the preposition of choice: *she was plunged in despondency (despair, etc.).*

plural nouns See NOUN, 6.

plurality, *n.* See MAJORITY, PLURALITY; NOUN, 1.

PLUS, *prep.*

To express addition, one may say:

Three *plus* three *equals* (or *is*) six (i.e., the concept of *three,* hence a singular noun).

X *plus* Y *equals* 12 (i.e., the concept of X).

Three *plus* three *equal* (or *are*) six (the subject is a plural number, *three,* rather than the concept of *three*).

In other, nonmathematical concepts, the word after *plus* is not part of the subject, but rather the object of the preposition *plus.* Hence:

Her sense of humor *plus* her friendliness *makes* her a very popular person. (The subject is the singular noun *sense.*)

His negative reactions *plus* his shyness *have* made him unpopular. (The subject is the plural noun *reactions.*)

See also PREPOSITION; SUBJECT-VERB AGREEMENT.

---

podiatrist, chiropodist, *n.* Both words designate the practitioner who deals with problems of the feet. *Podiatrist* is the term in more frequent use today, as well as the formal professional title.

podium, n. See DAIS, PODIUM, LECTERN. For plural, see NOUN, 6Q.

poesy, posy, n. *Poesy* is the archaic word for *poetry*; *posy* is a flower or bouquet of flowers.

poetess, n. see NOUN, 2A.

poet laureate, n. For plural, see NOUN, 6U.

police, n. This noun is construed as a plural as the subject of a verb and in reference to any number of police officers: *the police are here; the police were guarding all exits.*

politesse, politeness, n. *Politesse* is formal *politeness*. It is largely a literary word, but does give an interesting Gallic flavor to one's writing.

political, politic, adj. *Political* is the adjective that derives from the noun *politics*; *politic* has a number of different meanings: *judicious; prudent; cunning; artful; shrewd; diplomatic;* etc. The correct term is the *body politic*.

politics, n. See -ICS.

pollute, v. See CONTAMINATE, POLLUTE.

polyandry, n. See BIGAMY, POLYGAMY, POLYGYNY, POLYANDRY.

polygamy, n. See BIGAMY, POLYGAMY, POLYGYNY, POLYANDRY.

polyglot See LINGUIST, LINGUISTICIAN, POLYGLOT; MULTILINGUAL, POLYGLOT.

polygyny, n. See BIGAMY, POLYGAMY, POLYGYNY, POLYANDRY.

polytheism, n. See THEISM, MONOTHEISM, POLYTHEISM, PANTHEISM, DEISM.

pompon, pompom, n. The decoration is a *pompon; pompom* is a variant spelling. *Pompom* may also designate a military weapon.

poorly, adj. *To feel poorly* is a regional expression meaning *to feel ill, in poor health,* etc. The usage is not considered standard English.

populace, population, n. While *populace*, like *population*, can designate all the people (of a city, state, nation, area, etc.), it more commonly refers to "the common people," "the masses," the *hoi polloi.* See also HOI POLLOI.

pore, pour, v. See POUR, PORE.

port, starboard, n. The *port* is the *left-hand* side of watercraft or aircraft; *starboard* is the *right-hand* side.

portmanteau, n. For plural, see NOUN, 6S.

position, n. See JOB, POSITION.

possessed of, possessed by, possessed with You are *possessed of* any thing or quality that you own or have: *possessed of great wealth; possessed of rare beauty;*

possessed of *aristocratic ancestry;* etc.

You are **possessed by** or **with** some compulsion or some emotion or need that has irresistible control over you: *possessed by (with) a desire for revenge; possessed by (with) a reckless and self-destructive urge to gamble (to drink oneself into an alcoholic stupor;* etc.).

One is, of course, **possessed by** the devil, by spirits, etc.

possessive forms　See NOUN, 7; PRONOUN, 6, 8.

postmaster general　For plural, see NOUN, 6U.

postmistress, *n.*　See NOUN, 2C.

posy, *n.*　See POESY, POSY.

potato, *n.*　For plural, see NOUN, 6L1.

potentate, *n.*　See MAGNATE, POTENTATE.

potential, *adj.*　See DORMANT, LATENT, POTENTIAL.

pour, pore, *v.*　You *pour* water from a bottle; the rain *pours* down; etc. When you read or study (something) with great care or rapt attention, or when you give very deep thought to (something), you *pore* over (the book, the material, the problem, the question, etc.).

practicable, practical, *adj.*　A *practicable* plan, invention, idea, or suggestion can be put into effect or practice—i.e., it will work.

Anything *practical* is sensible, useful, worthwhile. A *practical* person is realistic, able to manage everyday problems or affairs with competence. (A person, obviously, cannot be *practicable.*)

Practical, however, in reference to plans, etc., also may mean *workable* or *capable of being put into practice.* So the distinction, though fine, is as follows: we call a plan *practicable* if it has not yet been tried, but we believe it will work; we call a plan *practical* if we know from previous experience that such a plan has worked in the past, or is capable of working.

practically, virtually, *adv.*　See NOMINALLY, PRACTICALLY, VIRTUALLY.

practice, practise　Whether noun or verb, *practice* is the American spelling; *practise* is chiefly British.

pray, prey　See PREY, PRAY.

PRE-, *prefix*

When this prefix is used, the general rules are:

1. If the root word starts with the letter *e,* you may write the compound solid, hyphenated, or with a dieresis (¨) over

the initial *e* of the root. (These choices are given in descending order of frequency in current usage.) Thus:

preelection, pre-election, preëlection
preeminent, pre-eminent, preëminent
preempt, pre-empt, preëmpt
preestablish, pre-establish, preëstablish
preexist, pre-exist, preëxist

(How you write these words and their derivative forms is a matter of personal preference.)

2. If the root word starts with a capital letter, use a hyphen:

pre-Columbian
pre-Raphaelite
pre-Renaissance

3. Otherwise, write words solid:

predestine
preoccupy
preoperative

---

precept, example, *n.* In expressions such as *by example rather than precept*, the point is that it is more effective to set an *example* (i.e., by your own behavior) than to lay down a *precept* (i.e., a rule, principle, etc.).

precipitant, precipitate, precipitous, *adj.* In the sense of *rushing rapidly or suddenly, dropping steeply, flowing with speed*, etc., the words are interchangeable.

However, *precipitate* is the adjective of choice in describing a person's actions that are hasty and thoughtless—i.e., not only too fast, but without proper consideration: *precipitate purchases of stocks.*

Precipitant may also be used in the sense mentioned above, but emphasizes speed and suddenness: *precipitant departure.*

Precipitous generally is used when physical steepness is involved: *a precipitous drop in the sea level; the road winds precipitously down the cliff side.*

(Nevertheless, if you have a special fondness for one of these words, you may use it in any of the meanings cited.)

predacious, predatory, *adj.* Both words describe animals that live by preying on other animals. (A variant spelling of *predacious* is *predaceous*.)

To characterize people who victimize others, marauding armies, or groups or individuals that pillage, plunder, etc., *predatory* is the more frequently used term.

Either a *predacious* animal or a *predatory* person is a *predator (n.).*

predicament, *n.* See FIX, PREDICAMENT.

predicate, *n.* This grammatical term designates that part of a sentence or clause that starts with the verb and follows the subject and any modifiers of the subject. In this sentence, the *predicate* is printed in italics: A fat man wearing a red shirt *was waiting on the corner.*

predicate adjective, predicate nominative, or predicate noun Called *subject complement* in Structural Grammar. See SENTENCE PATTERNS, 3, 3A.

predominant, predominate, *adj.* These adjectives are interchangeable, but the former is more commonly used.

preferable, more preferable See MORE PREFERABLE, PREFERABLE.

prefer to, more than, rather than *To,* not *than,* follows *prefer: she prefers vanilla to chocolate, not she prefers vanilla more than* (or *rather than) chocolate.*

However, when two infinitives follow *prefer, rather than* may be used: *she prefers to eat alone rather than to join us.* A recasting of the idea as follows is better style: *she prefers eating alone to joining us, she prefers to eat alone instead of joining us,* or *she would rather eat alone than join us.*

prejudice, *n.* One can have a *prejudice* against, or be *prejudiced* against, in the negative sense. One can also have a *prejudice* in favor of, or be *prejudiced* in favor of, in a positive sense.

PREMISES, *n.*

Though singular in concept, this noun is plural in form and is so construed:

> *These premises are* ready for occupancy.
> The *premises have* been vacant for over a year.

---

prepare, *v.* See FIX, PREPARE.

PREPOSITION

1. A preposition, in grammar, combines with a noun or

pronoun to form what is called in traditional grammar a *prepositional phrase* or, in Structural Grammar, a *P-GROUP*. More than one noun or pronoun may follow the preposition, or a noun (or nouns) and a pronoun (pronouns) may follow the preposition. Some examples of P-GROUPS:

PREP   N
under the house

PREP   N   PRON
between John and me

PREP PRON PRON
except you and me

PREP   N   N
after the dinner and the speeches

2. A preposition may consist of one word *(above)*, or two or more words *(together with; on account of)*.

3. The noun or pronoun following the preposition is called the *object of the preposition* (OP).

4. Here is a list of commonly used prepositions. You can easily imagine a noun or pronoun following each preposition to form a P-GROUP.

about	beneath	in	since
above	beside	inside	through
across	between	into	throughout
after	betwixt	like (i.e., similar to)	till
against	beyond	near	to
along	but (*i.e.*, except)	of	toward
alongside	by	off	under
amid	concerning	on	unlike
amidst	despite	onto	until
among	down	opposite	unto
amongst	during	out	up
around	except	outside	upon
at	excepting	over	via
before	for	per	with
behind	from	plus	within
below		round	without

Multiple-Word Prepositions

according to	in addition to	instead of
alongside of	in back of	in view of
as well as	in accordance with	next to

back of	in front of	on account of
because of	in lieu of	owing to
by means of	inside of	together with
contrary to	in spite of	with respect to
		with the exception of

5. The word *to* preceding the noninflected form of a verb (*to run, to sprawl, to inhabit,* etc.) is called, in Structural Grammar, *the sign of the infinitive.* Such a combination (*to run,* etc.) is called an *infinitive.*

6. A P-GROUP may also consist of a preposition plus an adverb: *until later; from now to then; up to now.* The adverbs *later, now,* and *then* are in the noun position and, therefore, in Structural Grammar, are called *nominals.* See also NOMINAL.

7. The -ING form of a verb may follow a preposition to form a P-GROUP: *without waiting, after leaving, instead of running,* etc. Such verb forms in P-GROUPS are called *gerunds* in traditional grammar, *nominals* in Structural Grammar.

8. When a personal pronoun follows a preposition (OP), it is in the objective case: *to them and us; between you and her;* etc.

9. When a preposition is used without an object (i.e., sit *down;* stand *up;* walk *by*), such a preposition is called, in Structural Grammar, *an adverbial.*

See also SUBJECT, VERB AGREEMENT; ADVERB, 4; NOUN; PRONOUN 8, 8A, 8B.

---

prepositional phrase See PREPOSITION, 1.

preposition ending a sentence It is a myth that a preposition is a word you should not end a sentence *with.* In questions such as *Where are you living at?, Were are you going to?,* etc., *at* and *to* are certainly unnecessary and faintly illiterate; but there is no possible way to eliminate the terminal preposition in *When are you coming in?, They don't enjoy being laughed at; They* don't enjoy being made fun of. In very formal writing or speaking, it may be preferable to place the preposition before its object, if possible: *to whom you are referring; with which we are working;* and *of which we have enough* are more literary than *whom you are referring to; which we are working with;* and *which we have enough of—* more literary and formal, but not necessarily superior. See also PREPOSITION.

prerequisite When this word is used as an adjective, the preposition that follows is *to*: *English 10 is prerequisite to English 11.*

When the word is used as a noun, the preposition that follows is *of*: *English 10 is a prerequisite of English 11.*

prescribe, proscribe, *v.* As here contrasted, *to prescribe* is *to order or recommend*: *prescribed insulin for her diabetic patient*; *to proscribe* is *to forbid*: *sugar is often proscribed for diabetics.*

After the noun forms of these verbs, different prepositions are used: *wrote a prescription for insulin; consider this a prescription for wealth (happiness, success, etc.); issued a proscription against using obscene language in school.*

present-day, present-time, *adj.* These terms are hyphenated when used as adjectives: *present-day morals; present-time activities.* Otherwise, of course, the words are separated: *during the present day, we . . .; at the present time, I . . .*

presently, directly, soon, *adv. Presently* means *soon* (*he'll arrive presently*). It may also mean *now; at the present time* (*we are presently occupied with . . .*); however, for reasons hard to fathom, some writers and authorities object to such usage.

Directly, as contrasted with *presently* and *soon,* means *at once; immediately* (*directly after we receive the order, we will . . .*)

Directly as a syononym of *soon* is not considered acceptable in standard English. At best, it is a dialectal or regional usage. If you mean *soon,* say so!

present participle see PARTICIPLE.

pressure, *v.* This word is correctly used as a verb meaning *to put (emotional) pressure on* (someone): *don't pressure me to do something I do not wish to do.*

presto, *n.* For plural, see NOUN, 6L4.

presume, *v.* This verb may be used in a derogatory sense to mean *do without proper authority: how dare you presume to take money that does not belong to you!*

When followed by the preposition *on,* *presume* may mean *take liberties with: you are presuming on her good nature when you do that.*

For other uses, see ASSUME, PRESUME.

presumptive, presumptuous, *adj.* Only *presumptuous* (note the spelling: an *i* is sometimes incorrectly substituted for the second *u*) means *taking undue liberties; overstepping proper bounds; showing arrogance or excessive boldness: how presumptuous of you!*

Presumptive means *based on probability or reasonable belief*—i.e., describing what may be presumed or taken for granted: *presumptive indications; make a presumptive judgment.*

The noun form for both adjectives is *presumption*; an alternate and frequently used noun form of *presumptuous* is *presumptuousness*.

pretension, *n.*; **pretentious,** *adj.* Why is *pretension* spelled with an *s* following the *n,* and *pretentious* with a *t* in the same position? The first word is derived from a Latin root containing an *s,* the second from a French term containing a *t.* And yes, the words are, at least in part, related in meaning.

pretty, *qualifier* Pretty as a qualifier, as in *pretty tall, pretty good,* etc. is a correct and fully acceptable usage. See also QUALIFIER.

preventive, preventative As either an adjective or noun, the shorter form is preferable; the longer form is also correct.

prey, pray Prey is either a noun (*hunted for prey; fell prey to*) or a verb (*preyed on* [*or upon*] *innocent victims.*)

Pray is, of course, only a verb: *let us pray; prayed to God.* The noun form of *pray* is *prayer,* pronounced PRĀR, unless the word designates *one who prays,* in which case it is pronounced PRAY'-ər.

PRINCIPAL, PRINCIPLE

The words are pronounced identically, so the problem occurs only in writing.

Spell the ending *-le* when the word has some relationship to a r*ule* (also spelled *-le*), as in a science or art, or in behavior (i.e., an ethic), or a fundamental truth. Thus:

a *principle* in physics, mathematics, etc. *(rule)*
spelling *principles (rules)*
a person of *principle (ethical rules)*
an *unprincipled* villain *(without ethical rules)*
a highly *principled* person *(moral; follows ethical rules of conduct)*
a person of high *principles (moral rules)*
not the money, but the *principle (the rule, ethics, etc., of the situation)*

(*Principle* is used only as a *noun*, with the derivative adjective forms *principled* and *unprincipled*.)

For any meaning other than *rule*, etc., use the spelling *principal*. Thus:

> a *principal* in the play *(main actor)*
> the *principal* of the school *(supervisor)*
> ten percent interest on your *principal* *(money)*
> deals only with *principals*, not agents *(main people)*

In the sentences above, *principal* is used as a *noun*. It functions also as an *adjective*, and then means *main, most important*, etc. Thus:

> the *principal* city in the state
> his *principal* reason
> your *principal* error

The adverb *principally* is derived from the adjective *principal*: *principally* concerned with the welfare of . . .

---

prison, *n.* See JAIL, PRISON, PENITENTIARY.

probation, *n.* See PAROLE, PROBATION.

progeny, *n.* See OFFSPRING, PROGENY.

prognosis, *n.* See DIAGNOSIS, PROGNOSIS.

prohibit, *v.* See FORBID, PROHIBIT.

prolific, *adj.* See FERTILE, PROLIFIC.

prolix, *adj.* See WORDY, VERBOSE, PROLIX, PLEONASTIC, REDUNDANT, TAUTOLOGICAL.

prologue, *n.* See EPILOGUE, PROLOGUE; OGUE, -OG.

prone, supine, prostrate, *adj.* Strictly, **prone** is *lying flat and face down*; the word is loosely used, however, to mean *lying flat or horizontal*, face down or on one's back.

As here contrasted, **supine** is the precise word that means *lying flat on one's back*.

Prostrate is either **prone** or **supine**, but the word usually has one of the following implications: *lying face down to show complete submission, humility*, etc.; *fallen or thrown to the ground, and lying still, as from a blow; feeling exhausted, helpless, or defeated*, as in *prostrate with fear, grief, anxiety*, etc. (The final example usually indicates figurative, rather than literal, prostration.)

Prostrate is also a transitive *verb*, used in any of the senses indicated by the adjective: *grief will certainly prostrate him; prostrated*

himself at the feet of the
king; was *prostrated* by *fear*;
etc.

See also PROSTATE, PROS-
TRATE.

prone (to)   See LIKELY (TO), LI-
ABLE (TO), APT (TO), PRONE (TO).

PRONOUN

1. A pronoun (PRON) substitutes for a noun (N) and generally implies the noun. A pronoun (PRON) is a substitute noun.

PRON   N
Everything substitutes for *all the things*.

PRON   N   N   N   N
He substitutes for *a man, a male, a boy, Tom, a*
   N
   tomcat, etc.

PRON   N   N   N
She substitutes for *a woman, a female, Gloria*, etc.

2. A determiner (DET) not followed by a noun, but with the noun implied or understood, functions as a pronoun, For example:

    DET N
Do you have *any* food?

    PRON
Do you have *any*? (*Food* (N) is implied.)

     DET N
I'll take *these* books.

    PRON
I'll take *these*. (*Books* (N) implied.)

3. In addition to determiners without nouns, the following are commonly used pronouns. Note how each one substitutes for a noun.

anyone *(any person)*
someone *(some person)*
everyone *(every person)*
each one *(each person)*
anybody *(any person)*

no one *(no person)*
something *(some thing)*
nothing *(no thing)*
everybody *(every person)*
nobody *(no person)*

4. Since a pronoun is a *noun substitute*, it has many of the characteristics of the noun.

A pronoun (PRON) can fit into the noun pattern
    —— is good, etc. . . .
      PRON
    Everyone is good . . .

5. Some pronouns have plural inflections.

SING	PL
this	these
other	others
nobody	nobodies

6. Some pronouns have a singular possessive inflection.

SING	SING POS
everyone	everyone's
no one	no one's
another	another's
other	other's

(The pronoun *other* also has a plural possessive inflection: others'.)

7. Certain pronouns are called *personal pronouns*, even though two of these *(it, they)* need not refer to persons. The personal pronouns are:

I *(first person, singular)*   we *(first person, plural)*
you *(second person, singular)*   you* *(second person, plural)*
he, she, it *(third person, singular)*   they *(third person, plural)*

8. **Pronoun, case**: *Personal pronouns*, with the exception of *you* and *it*, change form according to their position in a sentence. These different forms are arbitrarily called *case*—the *nominative case* (NOM), the *objective case* (OBJ), and the *possessive case* (POS). (The *possessive case* is simply the possessive inflection of the pronoun.)

NOM	OBJ	POS
I	me	mine
you	you	yours
he	him	his
she	her	hers
it	it	its
we	us	ours
they	them	theirs

The relative pronoun *who* also changes its form according to case.

*Note that *you* may refer to one or more persons.

NOM	OBJ	POS
who	whom	whose

(Note: *His* and *its* are determiners when followed by a noun: *his hat, its paw*. See DETERMINER.)

(For more about the use of *who* and *whom*, see WHO, WHOM.)

SPECIAL NOTES: The possessive inflection of the personal pronoun and of the relative pronoun is not (not ever!) written with an apostrophe [']. It is incorrect to write *ours'* or *our's, their's* or *theirs', it's* or *its'*, or *who's* as possessive pronouns. In fact, *it's* means *it is (it's raining today)*, and *who's* means *who is (Who's there!).*

8A. Nominative case of the personal pronoun: A1. The *nominative personal pronoun* is used as *subject of the verb* and as *subject complement*. (If these terms are unfamiliar to you, refer to SENTENCE PATTERNS, 1–3A.)

A2. The subject of the verb is the personal pronoun *preceding* the verb (V) or verb phrase (VP):

     V   V   VP

I run; *he* runs; *she* was running.

     V   VP

We ran; *they* were running.

A3. A subject may be *compound*—i.e., have two or more pronouns; or one or more pronouns and one or more nouns. For example:

        VP

He and *I* are going.

            V

We and the other customers waited impatiently.

            V

Her husband and *she* have an interesting relationship.

A4. For our purposes in this section, let us consider any pronoun a *subject complement* if it follows a form of the verb *to be*.

(*To be* has eight forms, or inflections: *am, is, are, was, were, being, been, be*. This definition of *subject complement* involves the verb *to be* as a *verb*, not as an *auxiliary*. In *we are happy, are* is the verb; in *we are waiting, are* is an *auxiliary*. For further information on *verbs* and *auxiliaries*, see VERB.

Note that the *nominative personal pronouns* follow the verb *to be* in the following sentences:

It is *I*.
It was *he*.
It will be *she* who will meet you.
It was not *they*.
Is it *we* you are calling?

(This is very formal usage. In everyday conversation, many educated speakers prefer to use the objective pronouns after the verb *to be*—i.e., *it's me, it wasn't her*, etc.).

If a personal pronoun is part of a *compound subject complement*, the nominative case is, of course, still the strictly correct form. For example:

It was *she* and her husband at the door.
Is it you and *I* who are going?
Was it Bill and *I* they were waiting for?
It will be *he* and *I* who will have to work.

8B. Objective case of the personal pronoun: The *objective personal pronoun* is used:

    a. as direct object of the verb (DO);
    b. as indirect object of the verb (IO);
    c. as object of a preposition (OP); and
    d. as subject of an infinitive (SI).

(For a better understanding of these terms, see SENTENCE PATTERNS.)

Problems in usage occur chiefly when a personal pronoun is part of a compound object or of a compound subject of an infinitive. Here are examples of each of the four categories above:

    a. DIRECT OBJECT (DO)
They invited *my wife and me* to the party.
    b. INDIRECT OBJECT (IO)
We sent *you and him* a letter.
    c. OBJECT OF A PREPOSITION (OP)
1. This is a present for *you and her*.
2. I have nothing against *him or his friends*.
3. This can be settled between *you and me*.
4. No one knows about it but *you and her*.
5. Let us take a trip with *them and their parents*.

(In the sentences above, the prepositions are: 1. *for;* 2. *against;* 3. *between;* 4. *but* (meaning *except*); 5. *with*.)

    d. SUBJECT OF THE INFINITIVE (SI)
1. They want *you and me* to do the work.

2. He told *Harry and me* to attend the hearing.
3. I expect *you and her* to be more discreet.

(In the sentences above, the infinitives are: 1. *to do*; 2. *to attend*; 3. *to be*.)

A TEST ON PRONOUN USAGE

Check the correct pronoun in each sentence. Then indicate how the pronoun is used by circling S (for *subject*); SC (for *subject complement*); DO (for *direct object*); IO (for *indirect object*); OP (for *object of a preposition*); SI (for *subject of the infinitive*.)

1. No one came to the meeting except *(she, her)* and her brother. *[S, SC, DO, IO, OP, SI]*
2. We expect Ralph and *(she, her)* next week. *[S, SC, DO, IO, OP, SI]*
3. Let's keep this a secret between you and *(I, me)*. *[S, SC, DO, IO, OP, SI]*
4. Pam invited you and *(I, me)* to her party. *[S, SC, DO, IO, OP, SI]*
5. No one but my father or *(I, me)* can do this work. *[S, SC, DO, IO, OP, SI]*
6. My wife and *(I, me)* will be happy to see you. *[S, SC, DO, IO, OP, SI]*
7. They need you and *(we, us)* at the meeting. *[S, SC, DO, IO, OP, SI]*
8. We have nothing against Sam or *(they, them)*. *[S, SC, DO, IO, OP, SI]*
9. You told my sister and *(I, me)* a lie. *[S, SC, DO , IO, OP, SI]*
10. It was Paul and *(she, her)* who were responsible. *[S, SC, DO, IO, OP, SI]*
11. Do you want *(he and I, him and me)* to go with you? *[S, SC, DO, IO, OP, SI]*
12. Is it *(she, her)* you are waiting for? *[S, SC, DO, IO, OP, SI]*

KEY: 1. **her** *[OP]*; 2. **her** *[DO]*; 3. **me** *[OP]*; 4. **me** *[DO]*; 5. **me** *[OP]*: 6. **I** *[S]*; 7. **us** *[DO]*: 8. **them** *[OP]*; 9. **me** *[IO]*; 10. **she** *[SC]*; 11. **him and me** *[SI]*; 12. **she** *[SC]*.

See also PREPOSITION; SENTENCE PATTERNS.

pronouncement, pronunciation, pronunciamento, *n.* *Pronouncement* is the noun form of *pronounce (v.)* when the verb means *declare officially* as in *issued a pronouncement;* or *state officially* (that one is), as in *pronounced him dead (insane, guilty, innocent,* etc); *pronounce you husband and wife.*

The noun form of the verb that means *articulate* (a word or words, etc.) is **pronunciation,** sometimes misspelled and mispronounced **pronounciation.**

Pronunciamento has a marvelous Latino or Hispanic appearance and sound. It chiefly designated a statement of great importance, perhaps even an edict made by, for example, the leader of a revolutionary group, a dictator, or some other type of authoritarian or powerful personage. *Plural:* **pronunciamentos.**

proof, *n.* For plural, see NOUN, 6G1.

proof *suffix* Do not hyphenate words using this suffix: *heat**proof**, stain**proof**, waterproof,* etc.

prophecize, *v.* See PROPHECY, PROPHESY.

prophecy, prophesy The distinction is simple: *Prophecy* (PROF'-ə-see) is a noun, the plural form of which is **prophecies:** *made a prophecy; many of her prophecies came true.*

Prophesy (PROF'-ə-sī') is a verb; the past tense and participle are **prophesied** (PROF'-ə-sīd'); the ING form is **prophesying** (PROF'-ə-sī'-ing): *can she prophesy the future?; prophesied that we would soon be at war; consider her an expert at prophesying.*

When the ING form is used in the noun position (*accurate prophesying is impossible*), the verb form (i.e., with the letter *s*, not *c*) is used.

What about *prophecize* and *prophesize*? These are nonwords, misspellings and misuses of the verb *prophesy.* Since so many verbs do end in *-ize,* the error is understandable—but not permissible.

prophesize, *v.* See PROPHECY, PROPHESY.

proportional, proportionate, *adj.* Both adjectives derive from the noun *proportion* and are often used interchangeably. However, there is a distinction: *proportional* usually refers to a number of things that are related in some way (*proportional size of the armies*), while *proportionate* indicates a reciprocal relationship between two things (*his success was not proportionate to the effort he expended.*)

proposal, proposition, *n.* A *proposal* is an offer, suggestion, plan, etc.: *a marriage proposal; a proposal to join forces.*

A *proposition,* in colloquial or informal use, may designate a business or commercial offer (*made him a proposition he could not afford to refuse*), or an offer of illicit sexual relations (*if you're leading up to a proposition, the answer is No!*). Strictly, and formally, a *proposition* is a theory or statement set up to be debated, or the truth of which one intends to prove (*dedicated to the proposition that all men are created equal; will prove the proposition in geometry that the square of the hypotenuse....*)

propose, purpose, *v.* *Propose* means *offer, suggest,* etc. However, as in *I propose to use my vacation time,* it also means *plan, intend,* etc., in which sense it is synonymous with the verb *purpose,* pronounced PUR'-pəs.

proscribe, prescribe, *v.* See PRESCRIBE, PROSCRIBE.

prosecute, persecute, *v.* See PERSECUTE, PROSECUTE.

proselyte, proselytize, *v.* As verbs, these words are interchangeable.

Proselyte is also a *noun* designating the person who has been converted; the one who converts, or attempts to convert, another or others is a *proselyter* or *proselytizer.*

prostate, prostrate The *pros-*

tate, or *prostate gland,* is an internal organ of male mammals. (The word is also an adjective, referring to the gland; an alternate adjective form is *prostatic.*)

Prostrate,, adjective or verb, is totally unrelated to *prostate.* (For meanings and uses of *prostrate,* see PRONE, SUPINE, PROSTRATE.)

prostrate, prostrated see PRONE, SUPINE, PROSTRATE.

protegé, protegée *n.* See NOUN, 2C.

prototype, archetype, *n.* The words are synonymous and interchangeable.

protruberance, protuberance, *n.* *Protruberance* is a nonword, used mistakenly for *protuberance.* The error is understandable, for there *is* a verb *protrude; jut, thrust,* or *stick out.* The noun derived from *protrude* is *protrusion,* the adjective is *protrusive.*

Protuberance is a noun form of the verb *protuberate: bulge out;* an alternate noun form is *protuberation;* the adjective is *protuberant.*

protuberance, *n.* See PROTRUBERANCE, PROTUBERANCE.

prove, *v.* The past tense is *proved.* The participle is either *proved* or *proven.*

PROVIDED, PROVIDING, *conj.*

Both forms are acceptable in the sense of *on the condition* (that); *if*. These conjunctions may, or need not, be followed by *that*: *provided (providing) he pays the full fee*; *provided (providing) that he pays the full fee*. (Some authorities consider *provided [that]* preferable in formal English.)

proviso, *n.* For plural, see NOUN, 6L2.

prudent, prudential, *adj.* Although both words mean *exercising prudence*, **prudent** is more commonly used in such a sense. *Prudential* also, and most often, means *related to, arising from, or characterized by, prudence.*

pseudonym, *n.* See ALIAS, PSEUDONYM, PEN NAME, NOM DE PLUME, INCOGNITO.

PSYCHIATRIST, PSYCHOANALYST, PSYCHOLOGIST, PSYCHOTHERAPIST, COUNSELOR, ALIENIST, *n.*

The *psychiatrist* is a medical doctor whose specialty is treating mental and emotional disorders by whatever means appear to be effective—counseling sessions, drugs, institutionalization, etc.

The *psychoanalyst* may, or need not, be a physician. (Nonmedical *psychoanalysts* are sometimes called *lay analysts*). The *psychoanalyst* uses methods, or variations of methods, devised by Sigmund Freud and others, that help patients become aware of their "unconscious" through "free association"—i.e., reporting, during sessions, whatever comes to mind no matter how trivial, irrelevant, etc.

A *psychologist* (as the titles are here contrasted) is a student of human behavior. As a *clinical psychologist*, she/he may counsel patients who have emotional problems. *Clinical psychologists* generally have a master's degree or, often, a doctorate in psychology, but are not physicians.

Psychotherapist is the general term for any person who treats people's emotional or mental problems in any of the various ways that different schools of therapy use, or, if the *psychotherapist* is "eclectic," in a combination of such methods, according to a patient's needs.

(Short forms for *psychoanalyst* and *psychotherapist*—i.e., *analyst* and *therapist*—are in current and acceptable use.)

Counselor is a vague term for anyone who is helpful with advice. *Counseling* is loosely used as a synonym of *therapy*. (See also COUNCIL, COUNSEL, CONSUL.)

Alienist is an earlier term for *psychiatrist*. If used at all today, it designates a *psychiatrist* who testifies in court.

---

psychoanalyze, *v.* See PAR-ALYZE, ANALYZE, PSYCHOANA-LYZED.

PSYCHOGENIC, PSYCHOSOMATIC, *adj.*

In reference to illness, there is at best a fine distinction, if any distinction at all, between these words.

Call any illness *psychogenic* and you are saying that it is due not to organic changes or trauma, but rather is caused by emotional problems, conflicts, etc. (*Noun: psychogenesis.*)

Call an illness *psychosomatic* and you say that it arises from the interaction of mind and body (assuming, if you will, that the mind is separate from the body)—in short, the illness again is not truly organic but results from emotional conflicts, etc. Obviously, we have here a distinction without a difference. (*Psychosomatic* is the more commonly used term.)

Bear in mind that a *psychogenic* or *psychosomatic* ailment is not pretended or imagined. The headache is real, the tic or eye-blink or gut pain is actual—but the cause is psychic, not organic.

---

psychologist, *n.* See PSYCHI-ATRIST, PSYCHOANALYST, PSY-CHOLOGIST, PSYCHOTHERAPIST, COUNSELOR, ALIENIST.

psychoneurosis, *n.* See NEU-ROSIS, PSYCHONEUROSIS, PSY-CHOSIS.

psychopath, sociopath, *n.* Though at one time *psycho-path* referred to a person with a mental illness, the label today indicates one who com-mits aggressively antisocial and/or criminal acts and is entirely devoid of pangs of conscience, guilt, shame, re-morse, etc. (A *psychopath* is also called a *psychopathic personality.*) The *psychopath* is apparently amoral rather than immoral—she/he has no concept that her/his acts are wrong—and is by no means considered psychotic.

Because the Greek roots for "mind" and "disease" com-bine to form the word *psy-chopath,* and also because of confusion with the adjective

psychopathic (see PSYCHO-PATHIC), another term—*sociopath*—was coined some years ago. *Sociopath* more precisely defines the personality and behavior of the *psychopath* or *psychopathic personality*. (*Adjective*: *sociopathic*.)

psychopathic, *adj.* Describes someone who is mentally deranged, or an act, etc. resulting from mental derangement. *Psychopathic*, then, is synonymous with *psychotic*. (*Noun*: *psychopathology*.) See also NEUROSIS, PSYCHONEUROSIS, PSYCHOSIS.

psychosis, *n.* See NEUROSIS, PSYCHONEUROSIS, PSYCHOSIS.

psychosomatic, *adj.* See PSYCHOGENIC, PSYCHOSOMATIC.

psychotherapist, *n.* See PSYCHIATRIST, PSYCHOANALYST, PSYCHOLOGIST, PSYCHOTHERAPIST, COUNSELOR, ALIENIST.

puristic, *adj.* See PEDANTIC, DIDACTIC, PURISTIC, PEDAGOGICAL, PEDAGOGUISH.

purloin, *v.* See THIEVERY.

purpose, *v.* See PROPOSE, PURPOSE.

purposely, purposefully, advisedly, *adv.* *Purposely* is *deliberately, intentionally, not by accident.* (A synonymous phrase is *on purpose.*)

Purposefully is the adverb derived from the adjective *purposeful*, which means *clearly aiming at a particular*

goal (or purpose): *he spent many hours **purposefully** reviewing the entire text, for his goal was to make a high grade on the examination.*

Advisedly is *after due deliberation, thought, or consideration.*

So when you do something *purposely* (or *on purpose*), you mean to do it; when you do something *advisedly*, you have seriously thought about it and have then decided to do it; when you do something *purposefully*, you have a clear aim, or purpose, in mind.

purposively, *adv.* When you do something *purposively*, you have some purpose in mind; you are not engaging in random or aimless behavior. This adverb is less specific than *purposefully*; nevertheless, the two words are fairly synonymous, as are also the adjectives *purposive* and *purposeful*. See also PURPOSELY, PURPOSEFULLY, ADVISEDLY.

purser, *n.* See BURSAR, PURSER.

putrefy, *v.* See LIQUEFY, RAREFY, PUTREFY, STUPEFY, TORREFY.

putrescent, putrefied, putrid, *adj.* Something is *putrescent* when it is in the process of rotting; when the process is complete, it is *putrefied* or *putrid*.

For verbs ending in *-efy*, such as *putrefy*, see LIQUEFY,

RAREFY, PUTREFY, STUPEFY, TORREFY.

Pygmy, Pigmy, *n.* With a capital *P*, a Pygmy is a member of various African or Asiatic tribes that are genetically extremely short in stature.

With a lowercase *p*, a *pygmy* is any very small creature or thing.

Variant spellings: *Pigmy, pigmy.*

See also DWARF, MIDGET.

pyjamas, *n.* See PAJAMAS, PYJAMAS.

pyromaniac, *n.* See ARSONIST, INCENDIARY, PYROMANIAC, FIREBUG.

Q

quack, *n.* See CHARLATAN, QUACK, IMPOSTOR.

quagmire, *n.* See MORASS, QUAGMIRE, SLOUGH.

QUALIFIER, *n.*

In Structural Grammar, a *qualifier* is the term given to a word or words, such as an *adverb, noun phrase, determiner,* or *adjective,* that qualify an adjective or adverb. Examples (the italicized word or phrase is the *qualifier*):

She is *a great deal* taller than her husband.
They are *much* happier today.
We are *rather* uncomfortable.
Emeralds are *extremely* expensive.
You are *very* unusual.
She works *quite* happily with her colleagues.
That is *pretty* important.

quarrelsome, *adj.* See QUERULOUS, QUARRELSOME.

quay, *n.* See PIER, DOCK, MARINA, QUAY, WHARF.

querulous, quarrelsome, *adj.* Despite the similarity in appearance, these words are unrelated.

Querulous means *complaining, fretful, peevish, grumbling, fault-finding;* expressing, or expressive of, dissatisfaction or discontent.

Quarrelsome means tending to pick *angry arguments, enter into petty disputes,* etc.

quieten, quiet, *v.* The standard American form for the verb is **quiet** (**quiet** the child; to **quiet** your anxiety); **quieten** is British.

quite *Quite* may mean *completely,* but it is also correctly used to mean *very; fairly;* to a certain or considerable extent or degree: **quite** warm; **quite** satisfied; etc.

R

rack, wrack, *n.*, *v.* A place where things are kept or displayed is a *rack*. To torment is *to rack*: *rack with pain, guilt, fear.* (But *wrack* is an alternate and acceptable spelling for this sense of the verb.)

In *rack one's brains* (memory, etc.) or *on the rack* (i.e., an instrument of torture—the phrase is now used figuratively), *rack* is the correct spelling. In *wrack and ruin*, *wrack* is the preferred spelling; *rack* is also correct.

racket, racquet, *n.* Either spelling is acceptable for the paddle used in tennis, badminton, etc., but *racket* is preferable. The pronunciation for both words is identical—RAK'-ət. The game, however, is *racquets*. (*n. sing.*) or *racquet ball.*

radical See LIBERAL, RADICAL.

radio, *n.* For plural, see NOUN, 6K.

radius, *n.* For plural, see NOUN, 6P.

radix, *n.* For plural, see NOUN, 6O.

raise, rear, *v.* You *raise* or *rear* children—*rear* is somewhat more formal; *raise* is perfectly correct.

raise, rise, *n.* In the sense of an *increase in salary, price, cost,* etc., either word is correct. *Raise* and *rise* are equally common terms in the U.S.; *rise* is more frequently used in Britain.

raise, rise, *v.* *Raise* is a transitive verb— i.e., takes a direct object; *raise the window; raised the curtain.* Occasionally, *raise* is used intransitively: *the barrier raises when a car approaches;* however, *rise* is more acceptable in such a context.

Rise is intransitive: *the river will rise; prices rise; rise early in the morning.*

The past tense of *rise* is *rose,* the participle is *risen.*

See also ARISE, RISE; PARTICIPLE; for *transitive* and *intransitive verbs,* see SENTENCE PATTERNS, 1—5.

rarefy, *v.* See LIQUEFY, RAREFY, PUTREFY, STUPEFY, TORREFY.

rase, *v.* see RAZE, RASE.

rather than see PREFER TO, MORE THAN, RATHER THAN.

ratio, *n.* For plural, see NOUN, 6K.

ravel, unravel, *v.* In the sense of *untwisting* or *separating the weave or threads of* (something), these two words, which look like opposites, are in fact synonyms. These verbs are either transitive or intransitive.

See also LOOSE, LOOSEN, LOSE; for *transitive* and *in-* *transitive verbs*, see SENTENCE PATTERNS, 1—5.

raze, rase, *v.* These are two spellings of the same verb (i.e., *demolish, tear down, level,* etc.); *raze* is the American, *rase* the British, spelling.

RE, *prefix*

Authorities differ on whether a hyphen should separate the prefix *RE-* preceding a root word that starts with *e*. Modern style tends to omit the hyphen, even though its use makes misreading less likely. So you have a choice in the way you spell these and similar words.

> reecho, re-echo
> reeducate, re-educate
> reemerge, re-emerge
> reenforce, re-enforce
> reenter, re-enter
> reexamine, re-examine
> reexport, re-export

However, some words have different meanings depending on whether *re* is, or is not, followed by a hyphen. *To* *recollect*, for example, means *to remember*; to *re-collect* means *to collect again*. Use a hyphen, therefore, when the word without the hyphen has a different meaning. For example:

> re-act *(act again)*
> re-call *(call again)*
> re-cover *(cover again)*
> re-dress *(dress again)*
> re-form *(form again)*
> re-mark *(mark again)*

-re, -er See -ER, -RE.

reactionary, *n.* See CONSERVATIVE, REACTIONARY.

read, *n.* To call a book *a good read*, meaning that the book is *interesting, worth reading*, etc., is not only a cliché unworthy of reviewers or authors commenting on the words of others, but sounds very much as if one is damning with faint praise (to use another tired cliché).

real, really *That's real good; she was real happy,* or *he works real hard* (i.e., using *real* as a qualifier before an adjective or adverb) is at best colloquial or informal, if not close to illiterate, usage.

Substituting *really* for *real* would certainly improve the sentences; or one can express the idea more precisely by using *extremely, exceptionally, truly, very, unusually,* etc.

See also SURE, SURELY.

rear, *v.* See RAISE, REAR.

(the) reason is because, (the) reason is that The *reason is that* is far preferable in good usage. *The reason he failed is that* (not *because*) *he did not study.*

reason that, reason why *Reason* (n.) is preferably followed by *that* plus a clause: *the reason that I called you* ... However, *why* or *for which* is also acceptable in such a construction: *the reason why (for which) I called you* ...

Reason (v.) may be followed by *why:* "*theirs not to reason why*"; *can't reason why she acted that way.*

rebellion, revolt, revolution, *n.* In reference to armed opposition to authority, the words are almost, but not completely, synonymous. The distinctions are as follows:

Rebellion designates such opposition that is not successful in fully achieving its purpose.

Revolt is a concerted refusal to continue allegiance to, and an attempt to overthrow, constituted authority.

Revolution is a successful *rebellion* that not only completely overthrows a government but also replaces it with a new and usually quite different organization, as the French, Russian, or American *revolution*.

rebut, refute, *v.* To *rebut* is to *refute* formally, as in a debate, court case, etc. Both verbs are transitive. The direct object of *rebut* is a statement, evidence, etc., rather than a person; the direct object of *refute* may be a statement, etc. or a person.

Nouns: rebuttal; refutation or, less commonly, *refutal.*

For *transitive* and *intransitive verbs,* see SENTENCE PATTERNS, 1–5.

recant, retract, *v. Recant*—formally and/or publicly renounce (a previously held philosophy, or a religious or other strong belief): *he finally recanted; was unwilling to recant his belief that the earth revolved around the sun.*

Retract—withdraw (a written or oral statement), usually admitting, by doing so, that one was in error: *the newspaper retracted its accusation against the senator.*

Recant is either transitive or intransitive. *Noun: recantation.*

Retract is transitive only. *Noun: retraction.*

For *transitive* and *intransitive verbs,* see SENTENCE PATTERNS, 1–5.

receipt, recipe, *n.* As here compared, *receipt* is an old-fashioned, regional, or obsolescent (if not obsolete) word for *recipe.*

recital, *n.* See CONCERT, RECITAL.

reckon, *v.* Like *figure, reckon (that) . . .* or *reckon so* is used as a synonym of *suppose, think,* etc. only on a colloquial or informal level. See also FIGURE, SUPPOSE.

reconcile, *v.* **(with, to)** You *reconcile* one thing **with** another (i.e., make or see them as consistent or logical): *it is difficult to reconcile his statements with his actions.*

You *reconcile* someone **to** a situation, condition, etc. (i.e., make that person content with or accepting of the situation or condition: *finally reconciled her to working overtime; became reconciled to his increased responsibilities.* Nouns: *reconciliation, reconcilement*—the latter noun is preferable for the meanings of *reconcile* considered in this entry.

reconnoiter, reconnoitre The latter spelling is chiefly British. See also -ER, -RE.

record player, *n.* see PHONOGRAPH, GRAMOPHONE, RECORD PLAYER, TURNTABLE, VICTROLA.

recur, reoccur, *v.* Yes, there is such a word as *reoccur* in standard English, but the shorter form is in far more current use.

recur again Obviously redundant, unless, one might argue, you mean a third or subsequence occurrence— *recur* means *occur again.*

redundant, *adj.* See WORDY, VERBOSE, PROLIX, PLEONASTIC, REDUNDANT, TAUTOLOGICAL.

refer, allude, *v.* To *allude* is to *refer* indirectly, not clearly or explicitly. So an *allusion* (*n.*) is an indirect *reference* (*n.*). Either verb or noun is followed by the preposition *to.*

refer (back) Since one meaning of *refer* is *look or go back, refer back* is redundant. Omit *back.*

referee, *n.* See UMPIRE, REFEREE.

referendum, *n.* For plural, see NOUN, 6Q.

refute, *v.* See REBUT, REFUTE.

regard, regards, *n.* Correct usage is the singular form, *regard,* in the phrases *in regard to, with regard to,* and *without regard to.*

However, the plural form is used in the phrase *as regards,* meaning *concerning.*

The plural form is also used in such expressions as *give my regards to Broadway; sent her regards to you;* etc.

regimen, regime, *n.* As a system of exercise, diet, etc., *regimen* is the term more frequently used. *Regime* (also spelled *régime*) has, of course, other meanings unrelated to *regimen—rule; system of government;* etc.

regress, *v.* See RETROGRESS, REGRESS.

regretful, regrettable, *adj.* Though both adjectives derive from *regret (v.),* a person who feels sorry about an act of commission or omission is *regretful;* an occurrence, situation, act, etc. is *regrettable* if one feels sorry about it.

reign, rein *Reign* (n. or v.) refers to formal government, power, rule, etc.

Rein (n.) is the leather strap used to control or guide a horse; generally the word is used in the plural, *reins.* Hence, figuratively, if you hold the *reins,* you have the power to control, check, etc. If you *rein (v.)* in a person, you restrain or hold that person back, again figuratively, from free action. On the other hand, if you give free *rein* to someone, you give her/him full freedom and power to act.

reiterate, *v.* See REPEAT, ITERATE, REITERATE.

relation, relative, *n.* Your *relation* may be someone connected to you by blood or marriage, but *relative* is the better word to use in this sense. The plural *relatives* is far preferable to *relations.*

relaid, relayed *Relaid* is the past tense or participle of *relay*—i.e., *lay again: relaid the carpet.* (With this meaning, the verb is usually written *re-lay* to avoid confusion with the *relay* that means *pass on* [information, a message etc.])

The past tense or participle of the latter verb is *relayed.*

See also LIE, LAY; PARTICIPLE.

religiosity, religiousness, religionism, *n.* *Religiosity* is a term of disparagement suggesting excessive, ostentatious, or affected *religiousness.*

Religionism is similar in tone and meaning to *religiosity*—i.e., excessive, affected, ostentatious, etc. religious fervor or zeal.

See also DEVOUT, PIOUS.

remains, *n.* Though singular in concept (i.e., the portion left over, or a corpse), *remains* is treated as a plural noun: *the remains of the turkey are in the refrigerator; his remains were buried.*

remediable, remedial, *adj.* If something is *remediable,* it can be remedied, improved, cured, etc.

Remedial refers to *reme-*

*dies: take remedial action;
offers remedial courses in
reading and composition.*

remind, *v.* You *remind*
someone *of, to,* or *that: you
remind me of your uncle;
remind me to put away the
leftovers; remind me that I
have to call Alberta.*

renascence, renaissance, *n.*
Written with a lowercase *r,*
either word designates any
rebirth, revival, etc., but
renascence is the term generally used for this concept.
Adjective derived from *renascence: renascent.*

Written with a capital *R,*
either word designates the revival of art, literature, learning, etc. that occurred in
Europe in the fourteenth
through the sixteenth centuries—but *Renaissance* is the
term generally used for this
phenomenon.

rendezvous Whether noun
or verb, the word is written
solid. The plural form of the
noun is the same as the
singular.

reoccur, *v.* See RECUR, RE-
OCCUR.

repairable, reparable, *adj.*
These words are identical in
meaning and therefore interchangeable. However, in current usage, *repairable* more
frequently describes objects,
articles, machinery, etc. that
can be repaired; *reparable* is
usually applied figuratively
to mistakes, bad decisions,

unfortunate or unwise acts,
etc. that can be compensated
for, made right, changed, or
remedied.
Negative forms: **unrepairable;** *irreparable.*
Reparable is pronounced
REP′-ər-ə-bəl; *irreparable* is
pronounced ə-REP′-ər-ə-bəl.

repeat again A redundancy,
unless you mean *to say for
the third or fourth time,* in
which case *repeat once more*
(or *once again*) is more precise.

repeat, iterate, reiterate,
v. Repeat is the general
term.
Iterate may imply a
repeating either once or again
and again.
Reiterate emphasizes that
the repetition is insistent and
made many times. *She
reiterated* (or *kept reiterat-
ing) that she had not stolen
the money.*
Obviously, since *reiterate*
includes *again and again, reiterate again* is redundant.

repel, repulse, *v.* The verbs
are interchangeable in all their
various shades of meaning.
Repel is somewhat more commonly used, and *repulse* may
have the added implication
of *gruffness, coldness,* or
discourtesy when the verb
means *reject, refuse,* or *rebuff.*
The noun form of *repel* is
repellence or *repellency;* the
adjective is preferably spelled
repellent; repellant is a variant spelling.
The noun form of *repulse*

is either *repulse* or **repulsion**. The latter noun additionally may mean *strong distaste* or *aversion: causes* **repulsion** *in him whenever he even thinks of it; has a* **repulsion** *for overaggressive males.*

The adjective derived from *repulse* is **repulsive**, which often is used as a synonym of *disgusting, offensive, sickening*, etc.

repertory, repertoire, *n.* In the sense of theatrical works, or the special skills, stock of stories, etc. that a person has at her/his command, the words are interchangeable.

However, the theater with a permanent company of actors that puts on different presentations during a season, or the system of doing this, is called *repertory theater*.

And *repertory* has, of course, other meanings: *storehouse, collection*, etc.

repetitious, repetitive, *adj.* **Repetitious** is *repetitive to an annoying, boring, almost painful degree.* **Repetitious** has a derogatory connotation; *repetitive* may, but need not, be derogatory.

See also WORDY, VERBOSE, PROLIX, PLEONASTIC, REDUNDANT, TAUTOLOGICAL.

repress, suppress, *v.* The words are contrasted here as used in psychiatric or psychoanalytic terminology.

When you *repress* a thought,

impulse, feeling, etc. that is unacceptable or painful, you are unaware that you are doing so—that is, the thought, impulse, or feeling is buried in your unconscious, and you will not permit it to surface so that you can become conscious of it.

When you *suppress* such a thought, impulse, or feeling, you do so deliberately—you know it is in your mind and you consciously push it out of awareness.

repulse, *v.* see REPEL, REPULSE.

repulsive, *adj.* See REPEL, REPULSE.

reproof, *n.* For plural, see NOUN, 6G1.

repugnant, *adj.*; **repugnance,** *n.* These words are used with prepositions as follows:
That is absolutely **repugnant** to *me.*
I feel great **repugnance** *for* (against, toward, *or* to) *such people.* (The prepositions are given in the order of frequency of use.)

residuum, *n.* For plural, see NOUN, 6Q.

resolution, resolve, *n.* Meaning *a decision or promise* (often to oneself) *as to future action* or *behavior,* **resolution** is the noun of choice: *New Year's* **resolutions.**

Resolve is *purposefulness, determination: a person of firm* **resolve.**

But *resolve* is the *verb* from

which the noun *resolution* derives: *resolved* to stop *smoking*.

(*Resolution* and *resolve* have other meanings not relevant to the two nouns that are here contrasted.)

In short, it is better style to say or write *make a resolution* (rather than *a resolve*) *to stop smoking*.

restaurateur, *n.* Oddly enough, the person who owns, operates, or manages a restaurant is a *restaurateur*—no *n* in the professional title.

restive, restless, *adj.* The words are often used interchangeably, but *restive* may also imply impatience under discipline or restraint; and therefore may mean *hard to control; balky.*

RESTRICTIVE CLAUSE, NONRESTRICTIVE CLAUSE

In grammatical terminology, a *restrictive clause,* usually starting with a form of *who* or with *that,* restricts the preceding noun or pronoun—i.e., defines the noun specifically. For example:

    1. The person *who indulges in overeating* will gain weight. (The italicized clause defines the *person* who will gain weight.)

    2. Herbivores are animals *that do not eat meat.* (The clause defines the *animals.*)

    3. The brother *whose car I am driving* left for Europe yesterday. (The clause identifies which *brother* I mean.)

Punctuation rule: A restrictive clause is not set off by a comma or commas.

Nonrestrictive clauses may start with a form of *who* or with *which;* they give additional, but nonessential, information and are, in a sense, parenthetical in nature. For example:

    1. My oldest brother, *whose car I am driving,* left for Europe yesterday. (The clause gives additional information—the brother has already been identified.)

    2. My obese friend, *whom you met last year,* has finally gone on a diet. (Additional information.)

    3. Ed McBain's novels, *which as it happens are written by Evan Hunter,* are all superbly crafted. (Additional information—the novels have already been identified.)

Punctuation rule: A nonrestrictive clause is set off by a comma or commas.

Who may introduce a **restrictive** or a **nonrestrictive clause**.

That introduces only a **restrictive clause**.

Which preferably introduces a **nonrestrictive clause**.

See also THAT, WHICH, WHO; WHOSE, OF WHICH.

---

retract, *v*. See RECANT, RETRACT.

retrogress, regress, *v*. Both verbs mean *move back or backward*, but **retrogress** involves backward motion to a less satisfactory, less complex, more primitive, or worse condition.

revenge, *n*. See VENGEANCE, REVENGE.

revenge, *v*. See AVENGE, REVENGE.

revengeful, *adj*. See VENGEFUL, REVENGEFUL.

revere, reverence, *v*. As verbs, the words are close synonyms; *reverence*, however, is best followed by an abstraction or thing, rather than a person, as a direct object; *reverence the high ethics of the medical profession*. On the other hand, one can *revere* a person, thing, or idea. *Reverence* is, of course, also the noun form of *revere*, and is not in very common use as a verb.

Reverend, the Reverend As a title of respect for a member of the clergy, strict usage requires *the* preceding *Reverend* when referring to the person—i.e., *The Reverend Smith is here*, not *Reverend Smith is here*. In addressing a person of the cloth (it will be noticed that I am using circumlocutions to avoid the term *clergyman*, for women also today belong to the clergy), follow *Reverend* with the person's name—i.e., *Thank you, Reverend Smith*, not *Thank you, Reverend*.

reverse, *adj, n*. See OBVERSE, REVERSE.

review, revue, *n*. The musical production is a *revue*; but the variant spelling, *review*, is occasionally used in this context.

revolt, *n*. See REBELLION, REVOLT, REVOLUTION.

revolution, *n*. See REBELLION, REVOLT, REVOLUTION; REVOLVE, ROTATE.

revolve, rotate, *v*. As here compared, in reference to spinning (i.e., turning round and round), the words are synonymous. However, by common consent, the earth *rotates* on its axis, but *revolves* around the sun. Nouns: *revolution, rotation*.

revue, *n*. See REVIEW, REVUE.

reward, *n, v*. See AWARD, REWARD.

rhinoceros, *n.* Plural is **rhinoceroses** or, especially in the wild or as objects of hunting, **rhinoceros**: *went hunting for rhinoceros.* See also NOUN, 6H.

rhyme, rime, *n., v.* **Rhyme** is the preferable spelling in reference to poetry or sounds. *Rime* (*n.*) is *hoarfrost; rime* (*v.*) means *cover with hoarfrost.*

rickets, *n. sing.* See MEASLES.

riffle, rifle, *v.* As here contrasted, you *riffle* (i.e., thumb through) the pages of a book; you *riffle* (i.e., shuffle) a deck of cards; you *rifle* (i.e., ransack, taking the contents of) a desk, safe, purse, etc.

right, rightly *Right* is used as both an adjective and an adverb: *the right* (adj.) *answer; did it right* (adv.).

Rightly (adv.) is used before participles: *was rightly called the foremost expert . . .; was rightly acknowledged to be the best player on the team.*

See also PARTICIPLE; WRONG, WRONGLY.

rime See RHYME, RIME.

ring, *v.* The past tense is *rang;* the participle is *rung.* The past tense *rung* is dialectal rather than standard English.

But when the verb means

encircle or *form a circle* the past tense and participle are **ringed**.

rise, arise, *v.* See ARISE, RISE.

rise, raise, *n.* See RAISE, RISE, *n.*

rise, raise, *v.* See RAISE, RISE, *v.*

rob, steal, *v.* When you *rob* a safe, you steal its contents; when you *rob* someone, you steal that person's possessions, money, etc.

In short, *to rob* is *to steal from,* or *to illegally remove the contents or possessions of* (a person, thing, or place); *to steal* (something or someone) is *to take the thing itself, or the person, away with you*—illegally, of course.

See also THIEVERY.

(the) Rockies, *n. pl.* See NOUN, F2.

rodeo, *n.* For plural, see NOUN, 6K.

rondeau, *n.* For plural, see NOUN, 6S.

roof, *n.* For plural, see NOUN, 6G1.

roommate, *n.* Write as a solid word.

rotate, *v.* See REVOLVE, ROTATE.

rotund, *adj.* See OROTUND, ROTUND.

ROUGH-

The following words are hyphenated:

> rough-and-ready *(adj.)*
> rough-and-tumble *(adj.)*
> rough-cut *(adj.)*
> rough-dry *(v.; also,* roughdry, *variant)*
> rough-hew *(v.; also,* roughhew, *variant)*
> rough-hewn *(adj.)*

These words are written solid:

> roughcast *(n. or v.)*
> roughhouse *(n. or v.; colloquial)*
> roughneck *(n.; colloquial)*
> roughrider *(n.)*
> roughshod *(adj. or adv.)*

---

round, around See ABOUT, AROUND, ROUND.

round, rounder, *adj.* See EQUAL, MORE EQUAL.

rumor, rumour The latter is the British spelling. See also -OR, -OUR.

rural, rustic, *adj.* Both words describe the countryside, farm areas, etc. as opposed to cities or urban centers.

Rustic has added meanings and connotations, however: *unfinished, rough-hewn,* as furniture, buildings, etc.; *not*

cultured or *sophisticated*—used derogatively; *artless, simple, naive*—applied to persons.

A *rustic (n.)* designates either a person who lives in a country area or a crude, unsophisticated person.

ruthful, ruthless, *adj.* *Ruthless* means *without ruth,* **ruth** being a rare or obsolete term for *pity, compassion,* etc.

So *ruthful* should mean just the opposite, and indeed it does, but *ruthful,* too, is a rare or obsolete word.

S

saber, sabre, *n.* See -ER, -RE.

sac, sack, *n.* The first word is a term in anatomy or botany, a noun for *a pouchlike part.* For other meanings, noun or verb, the spelling is *sack.*

saccharin, saccharine The noun for the sugar substitute is preferably spelled without the final *e*; *saccharine (n.)* is a variant spelling.

But the adjective *is* spelled *saccharine,* and means, technically, *pertaining to, containing,* etc. *sugar,* or is a disparaging term describing a voice, tone, attitude, person, story, etc. as *so sweet or honeyed as to turn one's stomach,* figuratively speaking.

sacrilegious, *adj.* See IMPIOUS, SACRILEGIOUS, IRRELIGIOUS, NONRELIGIOUS.

sadist, *n.* See MASOCHIST, SADIST.

safe Most words compounded with *safe* as the first element are written solid: *safeblower, safebreaker, safecracker, safeguard, safekeeping, safelight.*

But *safe-conduct (n.)* and *safe-deposit (adj.)* are hyphenated.

safety Compounds with *safety* as the initial element are written as separate words: *safety belt, safety pin, safety zone,* etc.

Safety-deposit (adj.) is hyphenated.

said, *adj.* Meaning *previously mentioned (the said defendant),* this use of *said* as an adjective is suitable to legal terminology only.

salary, wages, *n.* A *salary* is usually earned by a professional or office employee who is paid weekly, monthly, etc.

Wages are paid for hourly or daily labor, for piecework, etc. Note that *wages* is treated as a plural noun, even though the concept is singular. (In the early days of our language, the word *wages* was construed as a singular noun— *The wages of sin is death.* Occasionally, the singular form *wage* may occur *(what is the wage for this kind of work?),* but most of the time the plural is used *(what are the wages . . . ?).*

salon, saloon, *n.* *Salon* is the current word for any large, public reception room *(the main salon of the hotel);* a room for an exhibition of art;

217

a service shop *(beauty salon)*; etc.

Saloon was the word used in pre-Prohibition days for what we today call a *bar*; currently, it sometimes denotes a large public room, especially on a passenger ship.

salvo, *n.* The plural is **salvos** or the variant **salvoes.** see NOUN, 6L2.

sanatorium, sanitarium, *n.* The first spelling is chiefly British; *sanitarium* is the American term.

The plural of either word usually ends in *-iums*, also in the Latinized *-ia*.

See also NOUN, 6Q.

sanction, *n., v.* Here is a word that, according to use, may have two almost opposing meanings:

1. Noun—*support, approval, permission: gave his sanction for using . . .; do we have your sanction to use . . . ? Verb—support, approve of, permit,* etc.: *do you sanction his use of . . . ?*

2. Chiefly a plural noun—*a measure, or measures, such as boycott, banning of imports, exports, or investments,* etc. *to enforce demands, usually in international relations: called for sanctions against South Africa.*

sanguinary, sanguine, *adj.* Though both adjectives derive from the Latin word for *blood*, only *sanguinary* refers to blood. Thus, a *sanguinary* battle, encounter, etc. is one resulting in much bloodshed, many deaths, carnage, etc.; a *sanguinary* scene is one in which blood has been shed all over the place; and a *sanguinary* person is bloodthirsty.

Sanguine, on the other hand, is *cheerful, hopeful, optimistic.* This meaning derives from the medieval theory of physiology that the person in whom blood is the predominating "humor" is warm, passionate, self-confident, cheerful, etc., and also of healthy, ruddy complexion. (So, in current use, a *sanguine* complexion is ruddy and healthy.)

See also BLOODY, GORY.

sanitarium, *n.* See SANATO-RIUM, SANITARIUM.

sarcasm, *n.* See IRONY, SAR-CASM.

sarcophagus, *n.* For plural, see NOUN, 6P.

satirical, satiric, satyric, *adj.* *Satirical* or *satiric* refers to satire, *satyric* to a satyr, the minor deity of Greek mythology noted for lechery.

satyromania, satyriasis, *n.* See NYMPHOMANIA, SATYRO-MANIA, SATYRIASIS.

sauerbraten, sauerkraut, *n.* These are the correct spellings for the German-derived words.

saught See SEEK.

saving, savings Do not use *savings* as a singular noun: *the price represents a saving* (not *a savings*) *of over twelve dollars.*

However, *these prices represent savings of thousands of dollars.*

savor, savour The latter is the British spelling. See -OR, -OUR.

saw, *v.* Meaning *cut with a saw,* this verb has the past tense *sawed;* the participle is *sawed* or *sawn.*

scan, skim, *v.* In reference to reading, *to scan* is *to look over quickly or carelessly, merely glancing at words, phrases, or sentences; to skim* is *to cover material rapidly by picking out the main ideas or important parts.*

scarcely, *adv.* see HARDLY, SCARCELY, BARELY.

scarf, *n.* For plural, see NOUN, 6G1.

scepter, sceptre, *n.* The second form is the British spelling. See -ER, -RE.

sceptic, skeptic The first spelling is British; American usage prefers *skeptic, skeptical, skepticism.*

scherzo, *n.* The plural is *scherzos* or *scherzi*—the latter popular in musical circles. See NOUN, L4.

scion, *n.* See CION, SCION.

scissors, *n. pl.* Though sin-gular in concept (i.e., a cutting instrument), the word is preferably construed as a plural noun: *the scissors are in the top drawer.* However, *a pair of scissors is in the top drawer;* the subject is the singular word *pair. See also* PAIR.

scofflaw, *n.* See CRIMINAL, SCOFFLAW.

Scotchman, Scotsman, Scot, *n. Scotsman* is preferred by natives of Scotland. To avoid the appearance of sexism, you might call a male or female of Scottish ancestry a *Scot.* (*Scottish* is similarly preferred, as an adjective, to *Scotch.*) However the whisky is called *Scotch,* of course, and the type of soup is *Scotch broth.*

scrutinize, *v.;* **scrutiny,** *n.* Both the verb and the noun signify a very close, careful, and searching inspection, examination, looking, watching, reading, etc.; so phrases like *scrutinize closely (carefully)* or *a close (careful) scrutiny* are redundant. Omit the unnecessary adjective or adverb in these phrases.

sculp, sculpt, sculpture, *v.* See ENTHUSE.

seasonable, seasonal, *adj. Seasonable* describes that which is normal or suitable for the time of year: *the heavy rains are seasonable for April.*

Seasonal means *pertaining or relating to, descriptive of, or relying on a season or seasons: enjoys the seasonal changes; has certain seasonal characteristics.*

second, secondly See FIRST, FIRSTLY.

secretary-general, *n.* For plural, see NOUN, 6U.

see, *v.* Past tense is *saw;* participle is *seen.*

see where, see that In the sense of *understand, see that* is preferable in standard or formal usage: *I see that* (not *where*) *you have won your court case.*

seek, *v.* Past tense or participle is *sought,* not *saught.*

seem to of, seems to of See COULD HAVE, COULD OF.

self, *n.* The plural form is selves.

Most compounds with *self* as the first element are hyphenated: *self-denial, self-effacing, self-preservation,* etc. The adjective *selfsame* is written solid.

See also HIMSELF, HIS SELF, HISSELF; MYSELF; OURSELF, OURSELVES; NOUN, 6G.

self-deprecate, self-depreciate, *v.* See DEPRECATE, DEPRECIATE.

self-destruct, *v.* See ENTHUSE.

semantics, *n.* See -ICS; LINGUISTICS, PHILOLOGY, SEMANTICS.

semasiology, *n.* See LINGUISTICS, PHILOLOGY, SEMANTICS.

SEMI-, DEMI-, HEMI-, *prefix*

Semi- and *demi-* both derive from Latin and mean *half* or *partly. Hemi-* derives from Greek, *half.* So *hemi-* is prefixed to roots of Greek origin, *semi-* and *demi-* to roots of Latin origin.

Semi- is by far the most frequently used of the three prefixes, and, like *demi-* and *hemi-,* is written solid with its root; however, if the root starts with a capital letter or the letter *i,* the word is hyphenated: *semi-Iroquois, semi-Iranian; semi-isolated, semi-illuminated, semi-infinite.*

Comparatively few words use the prefix *demi-: demigod, demijohn, dimilune, demimondaine, demimonde, demitasse, demiurge, demivierge, demivolt.* (You will notice that many of the examples come from French, which originally was a dialect of Latin.)

Hemi- is often, but not exclusively, found in terms from the various arts and sciences: *hemialgia, hemicycle, hemiplegia, hemisphere, hemistich.*

In most other words, *semi-* is the prefix used, and this

prefix can be attached almost at will to a great many words: *semi*retired, *semi*engaged, *semi*automatic, *semi*metallic, etc.

semiannual, semimonthly, semiweekly See BIANNUAL, BIENNIAL.

senescent, senile, *adj.* *Senescent* means *growing old; aging,* with no negative or derogatory connotation. *Noun: senescence.*

Senile means *old and deteriorated, usually mentally,* and is sometimes used as a term of disparagement or contempt. *Noun: senility.*

Both adjectives generally are applied to people.

See also ELDERLY, OLD, AGED.

senior citizen See ELDERLY, OLD, AGED.

sensate, *adj.* See SENSORY, SENTIENT, SENSATE.

sense in, sense of When *sense* means *logic* or *point,* it is followed by the preposition *in: what's the sense in losing your temper?; there's no sense in trying to please him.*

Sense may also signify *meaning,* in which case it is followed by the preposition *of: can you explain the sense of that poem to me?*

SENSORY, SENTIENT, SENSATE, *adj.*

Sensory refers to the five senses, to perception through one or more of these senses, or to the transmission of such perception to the nervous system: *sensory organs; sensory delights;* etc.

Sentient means, simply *able to feel, perceive,* or *have emotions;* also, *conscious.* So humans and animals are *sentient;* rocks are *insentient.* (Some people say that plants are *sentient*—the truth or falsity of such a statement has not yet been proved.)

Sensate has two meanings: *capable of receiving stimulus through the senses*—i.e., able to perceive physical sensation (*sensate beings*); and *perceived through the senses* (*sensate phenomena*).

The negative *insentient* is simply the opposite of *sentient,* hence *unable to feel, perceive,* etc.

The negative *insensate* is: the opposite of *sensate*—hence, *incapable of perceiving or receiving sensation; inanimate* (*insensate* objects); *foolish, lacking in the power to reason;*

and, finally, by extension, *cold and insensitive; lacking feeling or consideration for others.*

See also INSENSIBLE, INSENSATE, UNCONSCIOUS.

---

sensual, sensuous, *adj.* Both words describe pleasures that stimulate the senses, i.e., sight, touch, taste, smell, and hearing, rather than the intellect, or refer to people who are keenly responsive to such pleasures.

If a distinction is to be made, *sensual* often refers to the pleasures of sex and is then partially synonymous with *erotic* or *carnal.*

One may respond *sensuously* to art, music, or nature. If art or music is called *sensual,* the implication is that it is sexually stimulating. If one responds *sensually,* one has been sexually aroused.

The noun form of *sensuous: sensuousness;* of *sensual: sensuality, sensualness,* or *sensualism.*

SENTENCE PATTERNS

In its basic framework, an English sentence will fall into one of five patterns.

In the explanations below, various grammatical terms and symbols will be used; such terms and symbols are discussed in their proper alphabetical positions in the book.

N is the symbol for *noun.* (See NOUN.) N_1 indicates the first noun in a sentence, N_2 the second noun, etc.

V is the symbol for *verb.* (See VERB.)

ADJ is the symbol for *adjective.* (See ADJECTIVE.)

ADV is the symbol for *adverb.* (See ADVERB.)

DET is the symbol for *determiner.* (See DETERMINER.)

P-GROUP is the symbol for a *preposition plus its object.*

OP is the symbol for *object of a preposition.* (See PREPOSITION, 1.)

For *auxiliary,* see VERB, 6.

1. Pattern One

    N_1 V N_2
    Dogs chase cats.

We can add other elements to this pattern—determiners, adjectives, auxiliaries, adverbs, P-GROUPS, etc., but we will still have the framework (N_1 V N_2) intact, just as brick-, stone- or stucco-facing, windows, doors, etc. do not alter the wood or steel framework of a building.

N_1 is the *subject*(S) of the verb; N_2 is the *direct object* (DO). (A *pronoun*, which is a substitute noun, can always take the place of either N_1 or N_2.)

So another shorthand way of indicating *Pattern One* is:

     S   V   DO
     Dogs chase cats.

In *Pattern One*, the verb is *transitive*, indicating that it is followed by a *direct object* (N_2). The symbol for *transitive verb* is VT.

So we can now be more specific in writing the symbols for *Pattern One*:

     N_1 VT N_2 *or:*
     S   VT   DO

2. Pattern Two

     N_1 V
     Men   flirt.
     N_1 V
     Children play.

Again, the basic pattern of each sentence above can be expanded.

     DET   ADJ N_1 ADV   V   <u> P-GROUP </u>
1. Some courageous men usually flirt with all women
        <u> P-GROUP </u>
of every shape or size.

     ADJ N_1 V   ADV   <u> P-GROUP </u>
2. Happy children play noisily with each other.

Note that neither the noun *women* of sentence 1 nor the pronoun *other* of sentence 2 is considered N_2. *Nouns or pronouns in P-GROUPS do not count in the basic framework of a sentence.*

Let us expand *Pattern Two* as follows:

     N_1 V   ? <u> P-GROUP </u>
     They swam *all day* in the lake.

How do we analyze *all day*? *Day* is a noun, certainly. With the determiner *all*, *all day* is a noun phrase. But *all day* answers the question *when?* and is therefore adverbial in function. Also, the noun phrase can be moved to another position in the sentence: *All day they swam in the lake.* So *all day* is called an *adverbial* (i.e., it functions in the sentence like an *adverb*). *Nouns as adverbials do not count in the basic framework of a sentence.* See ADVERB, 3, 4.

A verb in the pattern N_1 *V* is called an *intransitive verb* (VI). An *intransitive verb* (VI) is *not* followed by N_2 (or a *direct object* [DO]); a *transitive verb* (VT) *is* followed by a *direct object* (DO).

Pattern Two can also be written as:

    S VI

3. Pattern Three
Consider these two sentences:

    S   V   ?   P-GROUP

    1. Selma is a member of the jury.

    S   V   ?   P-GROUP

    2. George became a lieutenant in the Air Force.

Selma is N_1 or *subject of the verb* (S) in sentence 1. *George* is N_1 or *subject of the verb* (S) in sentence 2.

What about *member* and *lieutenant* in these sentences?

Selma and *member* refer to the same person in sentence 1.

George and *lieutenant* refer to the same person in sentence 2.

The verb *is* links the two nouns *Selma* and *member* in sentence 1. The verb *became* links the two nouns *George* and *lieutenant* in sentence 2. Since *member* and *lieutenant* merely repeat *Selma* (N_1) and *George* (N_1), *member* and *lieutenant* are also called N_1.

Pattern Three, then, is:

    N_1 V N_1

Since the second N_1 *completes* our information about the subject (S), we call it the *subject complement* (SC). (Note that *complement* is spelled with an *e* after the *l*, as in the verb *complete*.)

The verb in the pattern N_1 *V* N_1 is called a *linking verb* (VL). (In traditional grammar, such a verb is called a *copulative* [or *coupling*] verb, because it *couples* the *subject* [S] with the *subject complement* [SC].)

So we can also write *Pattern Three* as:

    S VL SC

(In traditional grammar, a *subject complement* [SC] is sometimes called a *predicate noun*.)

A *linking verb* in grammar is analogous to an equal sign

(=) in mathematics. *Selma = member; George = lieutenant.*

If a personal pronoun is the *subject* of a verb (S) it is in the *nominative case (I, he, she, we, they)*. What if a personal pronoun is the second N_1, or *subject complement* (SC) in a sentence? Then, in formal usage, it is also in the *nominative case.*

A *linking verb* (VL), we have noted, is a kind of grammatical *equal sign*. If a sentence starts *It is . . .* and we need to add a personal pronoun—for example, *I* or *me*—we realize that we have *Pattern Three* at work:

$$N_1 \text{ (S)VL } (=)N_1 \text{ (SC)}$$
It   is   (I, me)

The noun or pronoun before the verb—i.e., the *subject* (S)—is in the *nominative* (NOM) case. Since *is*, in the pattern
$$N_1 \text{ (SUBJ) } = N_1 \text{ (SC)}$$
above, is a linking verb (VL *or* =),It (NOM) = _____ (NOM). In short, NOM = NOM. The correct answer, then, is *I*, a *nominative* pronoun. In formal usage, we should say *It is I.* Many educated speakers find this usage a bit stuffy, and prefer *It is me.* Know the rule (NOM = NOM) and break it, if you wish to, in informal, colloquial usage. The problem will occur mainly when you use a personal pronoun after any form of the *verb* (not the *auxiliary*) *to be.*

See also PRONOUN, 8, 8A.

A test on the correct use of personal pronouns

The *nominative* personal pronouns are *I, he, she, we, they.* (*It* and *you* can be either *nominative* or *objective*—they do not change in form.)

The *objective* personal pronouns are *me, him, her, us,* and *them.*

A *nominative* personal pronoun is used as *subject* of the verb. A *nominative* personal pronoun is also used as *subject complement* (SC) after a linking verb (VL), especially the verb *to be.*

The *objective* personal pronoun is used as N_2 or DO or *after* a preposition, i.e. *object of a preposition* (OP).

Keep in mind that a *subject* (S), *direct object* (DO), or *object of a preposition* (OP) can be *compound*—i.e., two or more words combined with the connector *and* or *or.*

Check the correct pronoun required for *formal usage* in each sentence. Check, also, whether the pronoun you choose is the *subject* (S), *subject complement* (SC), *direct object* (DO), or *object of a preposition* (OP).

1. Let *(he, him)* who is without sin cast the first stone. *[S, SC, DO, OP]*
2 . *(She, Her)* and Stan have eloped. *[S, SC, DO, OP]*
3. Was it you or *(they, them)* who did that? *[S, SC, DO, OP]*
4. Is it *(I, me)* you are referring to? *[S, SC, DO, OP]*
5. *[Telephone dialogue]:* "I wish to speak to Roberta Smith." "This is *(she, her).*" *[S, SC, DO, OP]*
6. It wasn't *(I, me)* who called you. *[S, SC, DO, OP]*
7. Call my wife or *(I, me)* if you need help. *[S, SC, DO, OP]*
8. It will be either Zelda or *(I, me)* who will help you pack tomorrow. *[S, SC, DO, OP]*
9. It was Stan and *(I, me)* who robbed the bank. *[S, SC, DO, OP]*
10. Do you have any message for *(he, him)* or *(I, me)*? *[S, SC, DO, OP]*

KEY: 1. **him** *[DO]* 2. **She** *[S]*; 3. **they** *[SC]*; 4. **I** *[SC]*; 5. **she** *[SC]*; 6. **I** *[SC]*; 7. **me** *[DO]*; 8. **I** *[SC]*; 9. **I** *[SC]*; 10. **him, me** *[OP]*.

(For another test on the correct use of personal pronouns, see the test following PRONOUN, 8B.)

3A. Alternate Pattern Three

An *adjective* that follows a *linking verb* (VL) is also labeled *subject complement* (in traditional grammar, such an adjective is sometimes called a *predicate adjective*). The pattern is still:

S   VL   C

The alternate form of *Pattern Three* may also be written as:

S   VL   ADJ

The following verbs, among others, are *linking verbs* (VL) when they are followed by *adjectives* that refer, or are *linked*, to the subject (S) of the verb:

to be	to feel	to remain
to smell	to seem	to stay
to taste	to become	to turn
to look	to appear	to get
to sound	to act	to grow

These verbs are *linking verbs* (VL) only if they appear in one of the forms of *Pattern Three*:

$$N_1 \quad V \quad N_1$$
$$N_1 \quad V \quad ADJ$$

In the following examples, some of the verbs in the list above are used as linking verbs. Note that in each instance the verb is followed by an adjective that refers, or is linked, to the subject (N_1).

N_1 (S)	VL	ADJ (SC)
She	is	happy.
The food	smells	good.
You	look	tired.
It	sounds	weird.
He	seems	depressed.
We	stayed	calm.
The river	turned	muddy.
These trees	grow	tall.

4. Pattern Four

An example of *Pattern Four* is the sentence

$$N_1 \quad V \quad N_2 \quad N_3$$
Jean gave her husband an allowance.

We can rewrite the sentence as follows, without changing the meaning:

$$N_1(S) \quad V \qquad N_2 \text{ (DO)} \quad \underline{\text{P-GROUP}}$$
Jean gave an allowance to her husband.

In this revised form, N_3 becomes N_2, and N_2 is transferred to a P-GROUP.

In the original pattern, *Jean* (N_1) is the *subject* of the verb (S); *husband* (N_2) is the *indirect object* (IO); *allowance* (N_3) is the *direct object* (DO).

Pattern Four, then, is:

$$N_1 V \quad N_2 \quad N_3 \quad or:$$
$$S \quad VT \quad IO \quad DO$$

The test for an *indirect object* (IO) is that N_2 (N or PRON) can be placed at the end of the sentence in a P-GROUP. This P-GROUP will start with the preposition *to* or *for*.

Two more examples of Pattern Four:

$$N_1 \text{ (S)} \quad VT \quad DET \ N_2 \text{ (IO)} \quad DET \ N_3 \text{ (DO)}$$
She baked her friend a cake.

N_1 (S)   VT N_2 (IO) DET N_3 (DO)
We   offered   him   a   partnership.

Here is a list of some of the verbs that can occur in *Pattern Four*:

to give	to sew	to tell
to send	to fix	to make
to sell	to prepare	to bake
to write	to get	to ship
to take	to find	to offer
to cook	to buy	to mail
to bring		

When a personal pronoun is the *indirect object* (IO) of a verb, it is in the *objective* case (*me, him, her, us, them*). You have to be especially careful when such a pronoun is part of a compound *indirect object*—i.e., two pronouns, or noun and pronoun.

Check the correct personal pronoun in these sentences:

1. The college sent my husband and *(I, me)* an invitation to the commencement exercises.
2. They offered you and *(I, me)* a good deal.
3. We sent Ralph and *(she, her)* an anniversary gift.
4. Mrs. Marx has cooked you and *(he, him)* some lunch.

KEY: 1. **me**; 2. **me**; 3. **her**; 4. **him**.

5. **Pattern Five** *(two forms)*
Examine these two sentences:

1. We consider him a fool.
2. We consider him foolish.

In sentence 1: *We* is N_1 or *subject* (S); *consider* is a *transitive verb* (VT); and *him* is N_2 or *direct object* (DO). What about *fool* in sentence 1? *Fool*, obviously, refers to *him*—i.e., *he is* (or *we consider him to be*) a fool. So *fool* gives us more information about *him*, or *completes* our statement about *him*, the *direct object* (DO); *fool* is the *object complement* (OC). *Fool*, then, is also N_2.

In sentence 2: *We* is N_1 (S); *consider* is a VT; *him* is the DO; and *foolish* (ADJ) is also the *object complement* (OC).

So Pattern Five has two forms:

1. N_1 VT N_2 N_2
   She called me a hero.

2. N_1 VT N_2 ADJ
   She called me heroic.

These forms may be written, also, as follows:

1. S   VT   DO   OC
Tom called his friend an idiot.

2. S   VT   DO OC
Tom called his friend idiotic.

Here is a list of verbs commonly used in Pattern Five.

to consider	to call
to find	to name
to think	to nominate
to believe	to elect
to judge	to choose
to make	to designate
to appoint	

If a personal pronoun is the *direct object* (DO) in a *Pattern Five* sentence, the *objective case* of the pronoun is required. Be careful when a sentence contains a *compound direct object*—i.e., two pronouns or a noun and a pronoun.

Check the correct personal pronoun:

1. They called *(he and I, him and me)* crazy.
2. I consider *(you and she, you and her)* reckless.
3. The club will elect either *(you or he, you or him)* president.

KEY: 1. *him and me*; 2. *you and her*; 3. *you or him*.

6. There, Here, What, Where, When, Why, How Patterns
Many sentences in English start with one of the words in the section heading above, followed immediately by a *verb* (V) or an *auxiliary* (AUX). For example:

           VI   N$_1$ (S)   P-GROUP
1. There are two men in the corner.

        AUX N$_1$ (S) VT   N$_2$ (DO)
2. Where did   you find the money?

           VI   N$_1$ (S)
3. Here comes the judge.

        AUX N$_1$ (S)   VI
4. When are   you leaving?

        AUX N$_1$ (S) VT   N$_2$ (DO)
5. Why did   he stop the car?

        AUX N$_1$ (S) VI
6. How did   she react to you?

AUX N$_1$ (S)   VL   N$_1$ (SC)
7. When did Susan become an adult?

AUX N$_1$ (S)   VT   N$_2$ (DO)   N$_2$ (OC)
8. Why do you consider Max a victim?

AUX N$_1$ (S)   ADJ (SC)
9. Why is she so happy?

Sentences like these do not constitute a new pattern—they are simply rearrangements of the five basic patterns discussed earlier.

In interrogative sentences, the *verb* (V) or *auxiliary* (AUX) precedes the *subject* (S), as it does in *There, Here,* etc., *Patterns.*

AUX S   V
Is he leaving?

AUX S   V
Have you eaten?

V   S
Was he happy?

In such instances, N$_1$ (or *subject*) follows the *verb* (V) or the *auxiliary* (AUX).

See also ADJECTIVE; ADVERB; NOUN; PREPOSITION; PRONOUN; VERB.

---

sentient, *adj.* See SENSORY, SENTIENT, SENSATE.

sentimental, maudlin, mawkish, *adj.* *Sentimental* is the general term, and is usually neutral in connotation. The adjective may occasionally, however, be used disparagingly: *how can you read those stupid, **sentimental** novels!* *Sentimental* as a derogatory term implies excessive, foolish, or exaggerated tenderness of feelings.

Maudlin is derogatory, suggesting, tearful, overdone, or ridiculous *sentimentality,* sometimes from intoxication: *a **maudlin** drunk.* (The word derives from Mary Magdalene, who was often pictured with her eyes red from weeping.)

Mawkish is *sentimental to an excessive and nauseating degree*—this is the most strongly derogatory of the three adjectives.

septet, septette, *n.* The shorter spelling is more common.

sepulcher, sepulchre The latter spelling is British. See also -ER, -RE.

seraglio, *n.* The plural is *seraglios.* See NOUN, 6K.

seraph, *n.* The plural is *seraphs* or *seraphim.*

serf, *n.* For plural form, see NOUN, G1.

sergeant-at-arms, *n.* For plural, see NOUN, 6U.

series, *n.* *Series,* meaning *one* set, is singular. So if *series, singular,* is the subject, it is followed by the corresponding form of the verb: *A series of rainstorms was expected.*

The plural, however, is also spelled *series;* so, *several series of numbers were examined.*

serum, *n.* For plural, see NOUN, 6Q.

sestet, *n.* See SEXTET, SEXTETTE, SESTET.

set, sit, *v.* *Set* is regional or dialectical in an expression like *set a while and chat.*

However, a hen *sets* (or *sits*) on eggs; an object *sits* (not *sets*) on the table; you *sit* on a chair; you *sit* yourself down; you *sit* the child in the high-chair; you *set* the vase on your desk.

set, suit, suite, *n.* See SUITE, SUIT, SET.

sew, sow, *v.* *Sew* (i.e., use needle and thread) has these inflections: *past—sewed; participle—sewn* or *sewed.*

Sow (i.e., scatter, as seeds, etc.) has these inflections: *past—sowed; participle—sown* or *sowed.*

sewage, sewerage, *n.* Either noun is used for the waste material carried away by the sewers or sewage system; *sewage* is more commonly used in this sense.

Sewerage also designates the sewer system itself, or the fact of carrying waste materials away through sewers.

sexless, *adj.* see ASEXUAL, NONSEXUAL, SEXLESS.

sextet, sextette, sestet, *n.* A *sextet* (*sextette* is a variant spelling) is any group of six, but especially a group of six musicians or singers, or a musical composition written for six performers.

In music, *sestet* and *sextet* have the same meaning.

However, for a six-line poem or stanza, or the last six lines of a sonnet, the correct word is *sestet.*

shake one's head See NOD ONE'S HEAD, SHAKE ONE'S HEAD.

SHALL, WILL

The strict rule, currently more ignored than observed, is as follows:

With a subject in the *first person (I, we)*, use *shall* to denote simply futurity, *will* to indicate promise or determination: *we **shall** see you tomorrow; I **will** get revenge (and no one **shall** stop me!)*.

With a subject in the *second person (you)* or the *third person (she, he, it, they, someone,* etc.) use *will* for simple futurity, *shall* for determination or promise: *you **shall** eat your cereal (even if it kills you); he **will** be late for the meeting.*

(There are further subtle ramifications I won't bore you with.)

In current usage, as previously mentioned, this rule is rarely followed; *will* is by far the more frequently used auxiliary.

However, *shall* is universally used in two circumstances:

1. In questions asking for permission, instructions, information, etc.: ***shall** I mail the papers to your office, or wait for you to pick them up?; **shall** I go now or wait my turn; when **shall** we have lunch?*

2. In legal, military, or other authoritative language, to designate a command: *the defendant **shall**, within five days . . . ; the sergeant **shall** inspect . . . ; no one **shall** enter this park after midnight;* etc.

See also PERSON (GRAMMATICAL TERM); SHOULD, WOULD.

---

shambles, *n.* *Shambles*, despite the *-s* ending, is treated as a *singular: left the place in a shambles; the shambles was now complete.*

(*Shamble [n. sing.]* is the noun form of the *verb* shamble—i.e., walk in a shuffling gait—and is not related in meaning to the entry word.)

shan't This is the correct contraction for *shall not*; it is acceptable in standard English. See also CONTRACTIONS.

shave, *v.* The participle is *shaved or shaven.*

As a compound adjective with *clean, smooth,* etc. use *shaven: he was clean-shaven; a clean-shaven (smooth-shaven) face.*

she, her For rules on using the correct form of this personal pronoun, see PRONOUN, 8–8B; SENTENCE PATTERN, 3–5.

sheaf, *n.* The plural form of the *noun* is *sheaves*. The *verb* is *sheaf or sheave.*

See also NOUN, 6G.

shear, sheer *Shear (v.)* refers to cutting or clipping; also depriving, as of power, privilege, etc. *Shear (n.)* is *the act of cutting or what is cut off.*

To *sheer (v.)* is *to swerve*

or *cause to swerve*, as from a straight course. *Sheer (n.)* is such a swerve or deviation from course.

Sheer (adj.) is *thin; transparent; perpendicular; undiluted: sheer agony.*

shears, *n. pl.* Though a single implement, *shears,* like *scissors, pliers,* etc., is construed as a plural: *the shears are on the table.* (However: *a pair of shears is on the table;* the subject *pair* is singular.)

See also PAIR.

sheath, sheathe *Sheath* is a noun, the *th* pronounced as in *thing; sheathe* is a verb, the *th* pronounced as in *this.*

sheep, *n.* For plural, see NOUN, 6J.

sheepherder, shepherd, *n.* Either word refers to one who tends sheep; *shepherd* can also be used figuratively to mean *a minister, teacher,* etc. Feminine of *shepherd* is *shepherdess,* but English is becoming less and less gender-oriented; so a *shepherd* in either sense can be either a male or a female.

Shepherd (v.) means *act like a shepherd*—i.e., *guard, tend, lead, take care of,* etc.: *The teacher shepherded the class through the museum.*

sheer *n.* See SHEAR, SHEER.

shelf, *n.* The plural is *shelves.* The verb is *shelve.* See also NOUN, 6G.

shepherd, *n.* See SHEEP-HERDER, SHEPHERD.

shine, *v.* When the verb is intransitive, *shone* is the preferable past tense and participle: *the sun shone briefly; the sun hasn't shone all day; the table shone with a high gloss.*

When the verb is transitive, *shined* is the preferable past tense and participle: *we shined the doorknobs on the big front door; she has shined her shoes.* In the passive voice, use the participle *shined*: *the table top was shined to a high gloss.*

For *transitive* and *intransitive verbs,* see SENTENCE PATTERNS. For *passive voice,* see VERB, 9.

shingles, *n. sing.* See MEASLES.

ship, boat, *n.* See BOAT, SHIP, VESSEL.

shoe, *v.* Past tense is *shod,* or, especially for blacksmiths shoeing a horse, *shoed;* the participle is *shod, shoed,* or, infrequently, *shodden.*

shoplifting, *n.* See THIEVERY.

should, would In current American usage, *should,* not *would,* is chiefly found in three constructions:

1. as a synonym for *must* or *ought to,* though not quite so strong; *you should take better care of your health;*

2. after *if,* to show possibility: *if I should die before I wake; if the need should arise;*

3. when possibility is implied: *should I die before I wake; should the need arise.*

Otherwise, *would* is more generally used than *should* for expression of contingency, condition, etc.; *would* you like to go?; I *would* if I could; etc.

should of See COULD HAVE, COULD OF.

shovelful, *n.* For plural, see -FUL, -FULS.

show, *v.* The past tense is showed. The participle is either *shown* or *showed*.

sick, ill, *adj.* In American usage, the words are interchangeable to describe one who is in poor health—**ill** is not, despite rumors to the contrary, the more polite term. (In British usage, **sick** usually means *nauseated*.)

However, in American usage, **sick** may also mean *overcome by nausea*, especially in the phrase *sick to* (or *at*) *one's stomach*.

sideward, sidewards *Sideward* is both an *adjective* (*a sideward glance*) and an *adverb* (*moved sideward*). *Sidewards* is an alternate adverbial form. See also -WARD, -WARDS.

sideway, sideways, sidewise All three words can be used as either *adjectives* or *adverbs*.

simile, metaphor, *n.* A *simile* is a figure of speech in which, for rhetorical effect, dissimilar objects and/or people are compared. The word *like* or *as* occurs in a *simile*: she fought like a tigress; the sea raged like any angry god; as fast as a streak of lightning.

A **metaphor**, also a figure of speech, makes the comparison by stating that one is the other: *Nellie is a tigress when her children are threatened; the sea, that day, was an angry god*. *Adjective:* **metaphoric, metaphorical**.

simple, simplistic, *adj.* A *simplistic* explanation, solution, theory, etc. is oversimplified and unrealistic. (The word is often used disparagingly.) A variant form of *simplistic* is **simplist**; one who makes a habit of giving *simplistic* answers, solutions, explanations, etc. when problems, etc. are in reality complex, is a *simplist* and engages in *simplism*.

since *Since* is a *preposition* when it is followed by a noun or nominal to form a P-GROUP: *have been waiting since Christmas*.

Since is a *conjunction* when it introduces a clause: *since we're late anyway, let's stop rushing*.

Since is also an *adverb*, and then usually occurs as the last word of a sentence and is preceded by *ever*: *he started smoking at the age of twelve and has been smoking heavily ever since*.

See also AGO, SINCE; NOMINAL; PREPOSITION.

sing, *v.* The preferable past tense is **sang; sung**, as a past tense, is not incorrect but is infrequently used in standard English. The participle is *sung*.

singeing This is the -ING form of the verb *singe*—i.e., *scorch*—and is pronounced SINJ'-ing.

Singed (SINJD) is the past tense and the participle.

Similarly, the -ING form of the slang verb *binge* is *bingeing* (BINJ'-ing); past tense and participle are *binged* (BINJD).

The archaic verb *swinge*—i.e., beat or whip—has these inflections; *swingeing* (or *swinging*), and *swinged*; the g in each form is pronounced j.

See also CRINGE.

sink, *v.* *Sank* is preferable to *sunk* as the *past tense*; *sunk* is the form currently in use as the *participle: the ship has sunk; the ship was sunk*. When the participle is used as an adjective preceding a noun, *sunken* is the proper form: *sunken cheeks; sunken treasure;* etc.

sirup, syrup, *n.* The latter spelling is standard; *sirup* is a variant form.

sister-in-law, *n.* See IN-LAWS.

sit, set, *v.* See SET, SIT.

skeptic, skeptical. See SCEPTIC, SKEPTIC.

skim, *v.* See SCAN, SKIM.

slacks, *n.* Singular in concept (i.e., one garment), *slacks* is nevertheless, like *pants*, *trousers*, etc., construed as a plural: *those slacks look like the right size for you.* However: *that pair of slacks is the wrong color* (the subject now is the singular noun *pair*). See also PAIR.

slander, libel see LIBEL, SLANDER.

slaughter, *n.* see CARNAGE, SLAUGHTER.

slay, *v.* The *past tense* is *slew*; the *participle* is *slain*.

sled, sleigh, *n.* Though the terms are generally used interchangeably to designate a vehicle with runners for riding on snow or ice, *sleigh* often refers to a larger, horse-drawn, conveyance. Both words function also as verbs.

slew, *n.* An informal word for a large, but indeterminate number: *a slew of people* (*books*, etc.). Variant form is *slue*.

Slew (*n.*) is also a variant form of the noun *slough*, when the latter refers to despair, despondency, depression, etc.

See also MORASS, QUAGMIRE, SLOUGH; SLUE, SLEW.

slew, *v.* See SLAY; SLUE, SLEW.

slide, *v.* *Slid* is the past tense and the participle. *Slidden*, a variant form of the participle, is infrequently used.

slink, *v.* *Slunk* is both the *past tense* and the participle.

slough, *n.*, *v.* See MORASS, QUAGMIRE, SLOUGH.

slow, *adv.* Yes, *slow* may be, and in current educated usage, often is, used adverbially, especially in short sentences and following a verb: *go slow; walk slow; do it slow;* etc.

Of course, *slowly* is more formal in such instances and especially suitable to a careful literary style in written English.

slue, slew Referring to *twisting, veering, turning sideway,* etc., *slue* is the standard spelling for both the verb and the noun; *slew* is a variant spelling for the verb or noun. See also SLEW.

smite, *v.* Past tense is *smote;* preferable form of the participle is *smitten.*

smolder,   smoulder See SMOULDER.

smooth, *adj.*, *v.* The verb and adjective forms are spelled identically; *smoothe (v.)* is a misspelling, but the error is understandable, for the verbs *breathe, loathe, soothe, teethe,* etc. do end in *-the.*

smoothen, *v.* A correct, though less frequently used, verb form of the adjective *smooth.* See also, SMOOTH.

smother, suffocate, strangle, *v.* In the sense of *depriving,* or *being deprived, of air to breathe,* the three words are synonymous: *strangle,* however, has the additional specific meaning of *killing by means of a choke hold around the throat,* as with one's hands, a noose, cord, etc.

smoulder This is the British spelling of the word *smolder.* see also MOL-, MOUL-.

snail's pace See STONE'S THROW.

snitch, steal, *v.* See THIEVERY.

so . . . as, as . . . as See AS . . . AS, SO . . . AS

so-called, *adj.* Quotation marks around the term that *so-called* refers to are redundant: *a so-called "liberal"; the so-called "big five"*—omit the quotation marks in these and similar instances.

SOCIABLE, SOCIAL, *adj.*

Both words describe a person who is friendly, fond of companionship, etc., but *sociable* is the more commonly used adjective for such a person. *Sociable*, rather than *social*, characterizes an event, meeting, etc. in which there is a friendly exchange of conversation, in which food and/or drink is served, etc.: *spent a very sociable time together; enjoyed a sociable evening with his relatives.*

A *social* event, on the other hand, is one in which people gather to play, chat, be entertained, etc., not to work. (The distinction in this instance is fine, but does exist: one may attend a *social* gathering and find some *unsociable* people who delight in spoiling the fun.)

Social has other meanings all relating in some way to society, i.e., the way people live or function together.

See also UNSOCIABLE, UNSOCIAL.

---

sociopath, sociopathic See PSYCHOPATH, SOCIOPATH.

solarium, *n.* For plural, see NOUN, 6Q.

soliloquy, *n.* For plural, see NOUN, 6E.

Solon (solon), *n.* See LEGIS-LATOR, SOLON, (SOLON).

somber, sombre, *adj.* *Sombre* is the British spelling. See -ER, -RE.

some, somewhat *(plus, adj.)* *Somewhat* (i.e., rather; to some degree) is preferable to *some* as a qualifier of an adjective: *somewhat unhappy; somewhat annoyed.*

somebody, *pron.* See ANY-BODY.

somebody else's, somebody's else See ELSE.

someday, some day *Someday*, as a solid word, is an adverb; *some day* is the determiner *some* plus the noun *day*. If you mean *an indefinite time*, use the adverb: *someday we'll have to get together; let's have lunch someday.*

If you are referring to an

actual day, separate the words: *if you're free some day, call me; can you find some day when you are free for lunch?*

somehow, someway, *adv.* See SOMEWAY, SOMEWAYS, SOMEHOW.

someone, *pron.* See ANY-BODY.

someone else's, someone's else See ELSE.

someplace, some place Used adverbially to mean *somewhere*, *someplace* or *some place* is colloquial or informal; *somewhere* is the preferable word in formal speech or writing.

If you use *place* as a noun, *some place* is standard English: *can you find some place for all these books? stop at some place where we can park the car off the road.*

somersault, summersault, somerset, summerset *Somersault* is the preferable form; the other words are acceptable, but variant, spellings.

sometime, sometimes; some time, some times *Sometime (adv.)* designates an indefinite time: *I did it **sometime** yesterday; I will do it **sometime** tomorrow.*

Sometime may also be used as an *adjective* to mean *former; sporadic or occasional: a **sometime** teacher* (i.e., formerly a teacher); *love is a **sometime** thing* (i.e., sporadic); *a writer and **sometime** actor* (i.e., occasionally an actor).

Sometimes *(adv.)* means *occasionally; at various times: **sometimes** I'm happy, **sometimes** I'm sad; **sometimes** he comes home early.*

When you use *time* as a noun, write ***some time*** or ***some times*** as separate words: *can you find **some time** for my typing?; there are **some times** when I feel thoroughly confused.*

someway, someways, somehow, *adv.* Meaning *in some manner or other* (**someway,** *we'll raise the money*), **somehow** may be the preferable word in formal usage. (As in many other instances, authorities disagree.) See also: -WAY, -WAYS.

somewhat, some *(plus adj.)* See SOME, SOMEWHAT.

son-in-law, *n.* See IN-LAWS.

soon, presently, directly, *adv.* See PRESENTLY, DIRECTLY, SOON.

sophistry, casuistry, *n.* See CASUISTRY, SOPHISTRY.

soprano, *n.* For plural, see NOUN, 6L4.

sorceress, *n.* See NOUN, 2C.

sort, *n.* See KIND, KINDS.

sort of *(plus adjective)* see KIND OF.

sourbraten, sourkraut, *n.* See SAUERBRATEN, SAUERKRAUT.

South, south; Southern, southern Write these words with a capital *S* if *South* or *Southern* is part of the official name of a place or organization: *South America, South Bend, South Dakota, Southern Hemisphere, Southern Alps.* Write *South* (capital *S*) when designating the southern region of the earth or of a country, especially the U.S.: *she was born in the South.*

Otherwise, to show direction or location, write the words with a lowercase *s: rode south for two miles; lives in the southern part of the state.*

See also EAST, EAST, EASTERN, EASTERN; NORTH, NORTH, NORTHERN, NORTHERN; WEST, WEST, WESTERN, WESTERN.

southward, southwards See -WARD, -WARDS.

sow, sew, *v.* See SEW, SOW.

spaded, spayed In reference to sterilizing a female animal, the correct spelling of the past tense or participle of the verb *spay* is *spayed—spaded,* in this context, is a misusage. See also CASTRATE, GELD, ALTER, FIX, CAPONIZE, EMASCULATE, SPAY.

spay, *v.* See CASTRATE, GELD, ALTER, FIX, CAPONIZE, EMASCULATE, SPAY; SPADED, SPAYED.

spayed See SPADED, SPAY.

speak to, speak with Either preposition may be used to indicate a conversation; *speak to* while less logical, is more commonly used. Obviously, one *speaks to* a person or an audience that merely listens and does not respond. (The same comments apply to *talk to, talk with.*)

special, especial, *adj.* See ESPECIAL, SPECIAL, ESPECIALLY, SPECIALLY.

specially, especially, *adv.* See ESPECIAL, SPECIAL, ESPECIALLY, SPECIALLY.

specie, species, *n.* *Specie* is *not* the singular of *species* (i.e., category, kind, type, etc.), but means *coin* as distinguished from *paper money.*

Species, like *series,* is both the singular and the plural inflection of the noun: *a species that is now endangered; several species of animal life are to be found.* See also SERIES.

spectators, audience, *n.* See AUDIENCE, SPECTATORS.

specter, spectre, *n.* *Spectre* is the British spelling. See -ER, -RE.

spectrum, *n.* For plural, see NOUN, 6Q.

speculum, *n.* For plural, see NOUN, 6Q.

speed, *v.* *Sped* is the preferable, and more commonly used, past tense and participle; *speeded* is also correct.

spill, *v.* *Spilled* is the more frequently used past tense and participle; *spilt* is also correct and is equally acceptable: *Never cry over spilt milk.*

spin, *v.* *Spun* is the past tense and participle. *Span* is the archaic past tense.

spinster, *n.* See OLD MAID, SPINSTER.

spit, *v.* *Spit* is the past tense and participle for the verb meaning *expel from the mouth.* (*Spat* for these inflections is more British than American.) For the verb meaning *put on a spit*—i.e, a slender, pointed stick or rod, as for broiling meat or fish, etc. —the past tense and participle are *spitted.*

splitting the infinitive An infinitive consists of two words: *to* and the uninflected form of a verb—e.g., *to see, to understand, to grasp,* etc.

In a **split infinitive,** an adverb "splits" *to* from the verb—e.g., *to finally see; to quickly understand; to thoroughly grasp;* etc.

An ancient rule of English grammar (dating, in fact from the nineteenth century) forbids the split infinitive. Reputable writers (including Benjamin Franklin, Washington Irving, John Greenleaf Whittier, Nathaniel Hawthorne, Theodore Roosevelt, Woodrow Wilson, and Herbert Spencer, among many others) have split an infinitive whenever they felt that style or meaning was served by doing so.

It is, in short, pedantic to deliberately go out of your way to avoid the split infinitive.

spoonful For plural see -FUL, -FULS.

spring, *v.* The past tense is either *sprang* or *sprung;* the participle is *sprung.*

square, squarer, *adj.* See EQUAL, MORE EQUAL.

stadium, auditorium, *n.* See AUDITORIUM, STADIUM.

staff, *n.* For plural, see NOUN, 6G1.

stalactite, stalagmite, *n.* The *stalactite* hangs *down* from the room of a cave or cavern; the *stalagmite* projects *upward* from the floor. How to remember which is which if you're not into speleology (the science or exploration of caves)? Alphabetically, *down* precedes *up,* and *stalactite* precedes *stalagmite.*

stammer, stutter, *v.* In reference to human speech, these verbs are generally used interchangeably. However, if a distinction is to be made, *to stammer* is *to speak with involuntary pauses, breaks, or repetitions of words that impede the normal flow of lan-*guage; *to stutter* is *to repeat, painfully, syllables or initial consonant sounds in an effort to complete a word.*

If such a distinction is made, it is not redundant to say *he stammered and stuttered.*

stanch, staunch The *verb* (*stop the flow,* etc.) is preferably spelled *stanch; staunch* is a variant, but popular, spelling.

The *adjective* (*firm, steady, loyal,* etc.) is preferably spelled *staunch; stanch* is a variant spelling.

Staunch is pronounced STÖNCH or STANCH.

starboard, port, *n.* See PORT, STARBOARD.

stationary, stationery *Stationary* (adj.) is *not movable, fixed in position,* etc.

stationary (n.) is an object or thing that is *stationary* (adj.).

Stationery is a *noun* only, and designates paper, writing materials, etc., or a store that stocks such goods. (*Stationer's* or *stationery store* is more commonly used for the latter.)

How to remember which spelling is which? Think of the *-er* ending of *paper,* and the *-ery* ending of *stationery.*

statistics, *n.* See -ICS.

status, *n.* For plural, see NOUN, 6P.

staunch See STANCH, STAUNCH.

stave, *v.* Past tense and participle are *staved* or *stove.* When the participle functions as an *adjective,* **stove** is the form generally used: *wore a stove-in hat.*

steal, rob, *v.* See ROB, STEAL; THIEVERY.

step, half see HALF, STEP.

sterile, barren, infertile, impotent, *adj.* In reference to childbirth and sexual intercourse:

A female is *sterile, barren,* or *infertile* if she is incapable of becoming pregnant.

A male is *sterile* if his semen cannot impregnate a female. He is *impotent* if he is unable to have, or to sustain, an erection during the sexual act, and thus cannot penetrate the female.

stern, bow, *n.* see BOW, STERN.

stevedore, *n.* see LONGSHOREMAN, STEVEDORE.

stigma, *n.* **Stigmata** is the more commonly used plural, especially in medicine, botany, and religion. **Stigmas** is also correct.

stiletto, *n.* For plural, see NOUN, 6L2.

still life, *n.* The plural form is *still lifes* for this term in art. See also NOUN, 6G.

stimulus, *n.* For plural, see NOUN, 6P.

sting, *v.* **Stung** is both the past tense and the participle.

stink, *v.* The past tense is *stank* or *stunk.* The participle is *stunk.*

stone's throw, *n.* Standard English for *a short distance.* Remember to use the apostrophe in *stone's,* as also in *snail's pace, day's pay,* etc.

story, storey, *n.* Meaning *a level or floor in a building,* *story* is the American spelling, *storey* the British form. The plural of *story* is, of course, *stories* (*four stories in that house*), of *storey,* *storeys.*

See also MONEYED, MONIED, MONEYS, MONIES.

stove, *v.* see STAVE.

strait, *n.,* **straiten,** *v.* **straitjacket,** *n.* or *v.* **strait-laced,** *adj.* Note that these words are *not* spelled *straight*—they all derive from the Middle English *streit,* meaning *narrow* or *tight.* (However *straight jacket* is a variant spelling of *straitjacket.*)

So a narrow water passage is a *strait;* you may find yourself in *straitened* circumstances; etc.

strangle, *v.* See SMOTHER, SUFFOCATE, STRANGLE.

strap, strop, *n.* A thin band of leather or other material is a *strap;* such a band used for sharpening a straight razor is a *strop.* You *strop* (*v.*) a razor to sharpen it.

Nevertheless, since words in English have the delightful habit of being the same while they are different, and vice versa (*loosen* and *un-loosen*, for example), a razor *strop* may also be called a *strap*, and you can *strap* a razor in order to sharpen it.

stratagem, strategy, *n.* A *stratagem* is any scheme, trick, ploy, planned deception, etc.

Strategy is the system, plan, or method of using *stratagems*. *Strategy* need not involve deception, and may simply designate any scheme, plan, or method for accomplishing something, usually something difficult to accomplish.

(Note the difference in spelling following the second *t* of each word.)

Both *stratagem* and *strategy* also have the meanings explained above in reference to military operations or the conduct of a war.

stratum, *n.* For plural, see NOUN, 6Q.

strew, *v.* Past tense is *strewed*. Participle is *strewn* or *strewed*.

stricken, *participle* See STRIKE.

stride, *v.* Past tense is *strode*; participle is *stridden*.

strike, *v.* The past tense is *struck*; the participle is also *struck*, except in the following contexts, in which *stricken* is preferable and more commonly used:
    1. *Your name will be*

stricken from the list; the remark was **stricken** *from the record;* etc. (i.e., removed).

    2. *Was* **stricken** *with a fatal disease,* (pneumonia, remorse, guilt, fear, pangs of conscience); etc. *conscience-stricken; a stricken person;* etc. (i.e., afflicted, as with a disease, something unpleasant, etc.)

    3. *Stricken soldiers* (i.e., wounded by projectiles, etc.). Either **struck** or **stricken** may be used in the following contexts:
    1. *We have* **struck** (**stricken**) *out in new directions.*
    2. *Stricken* (**struck**) *by a venomous snake.*

string, *v.* *Strung* is the correct past tense and participle.

strop, *n., v.* See STRAP, STROP.

strive, *v.* The past tense is *strove*; the participle is either *striven* or *strived*.

study on *(something)* This is at best a dialectical or regional usage. Omit **on**.

stupefy, *v.* see LIQUEFY, RAREFY, PUTREFY, STUPEFY, TORREFY.

stutter, stammer, *v.* See STAMMER, STUTTER.

subconscious, subliminal, unconscious, *adj.* As here compared (in the sense of *unavailable to the conscious mind*), **subconscious** is rarely used in psychiatry or psychoanalysis—the preferred term in these fields is *unconscious*, which may also be used as a noun (i.e., the *unconscious*).

When you call feelings, fears, ideas, etc. *subconscious*, you may be implying that they are just below consciousness and may possibly become available, by some means, to the conscious mind.

Subliminal, as a term in psychology, usually describes stimuli that one is not aware of: *a subliminal message was flashed on the screen: "Buy popcorn!"*

(In nontechnical language, however, the three words are often used interchangeably.)

subcutaneous, *adj.* See IN-TRAMUSCULAR, INTRAVENOUS, SUBCUTANTEOUS,INTRADERMAL.

subject *(grammatical term)* In Structural Grammar, the term *subject* designates Noun 1 (N_1)—or the pronoun that substitutes for Noun 1—in a clause or sentence. To understand subjects, see SENTENCE PATTERNS.

subject complement See SENTENCE PATTERNS, 3, 3A.

SUBJECT, VERB AGREEMENT

1. Forms of the verb that agree with a subject: In Structural Grammar, a verb has two inflections in the present tense—the S-FORM and the NON-S FORM. The S-FORM adds the S-inflection to the verb; the NON-S FORM does not. For example:

VERB	S-FORM	NON-S FORM
to go	goes	go
to eat	eats	eat
to kiss	kisses	kiss
to speak	speaks	speak
to have	has	have
to be	is	are

The verb *to be*, and only the verb *to be*, has an S-FORM and a NON-S FORM in the past tense: *was* (S-FORM); *were* (NON-S FORM).

The problem of subject, verb agreement occurs *only in the present tense*—except for the verb *to be*, in which instance the verb agrees with the subject *in the past tense also.*

(The verbs *to be* and *to have*, and occasionally certain other verbs, function as *auxiliaries*. To understand auxiliaries, see VERB, 6.)

2. Rule for subject, verb agreement: The rule for subject, verb agreement is very simple: *a singular subject is followed by* the *S-FORM* of a verb or auxiliary; a plural subject is followed by the *NON-S FORM* of the verb or auxiliary. (*Mnemonic:* Singular—S-FORM; Plural—(plain) NON-S FORM.

In the first four sentences below, note that a *singular subject* is followed by the S-FORM of the verb or auxiliary:

> He laughs.
> She *is* laughing.
> He was laughing.
> She has laughed.

In the next four sentences, note that a *plural subject* is followed by the NON-S FORM of the verb or auxiliary:

> We *laugh*.
> They *are* laughing.
> We *were* laughing.
> They *have* laughed.

(In traditional grammar, the rule for agreement states that a singular subject takes a singular verb, a plural subject takes a plural verb. This rule can be confusing, since so-called singular verbs end in an -*s* inflection, and so-called plural verbs do not end in -*s*. In Structural Grammar, only nouns and pronouns are singular or plural.)

3. Compound subject (connector: and): When there is a *compound subject* (i.e., two or more nouns or pronouns, or a combination of noun(s) and pronoun(s)), the connector of the subjects (or *conjunction*) is usually *and*, *or* or *nor*.

Let us tackle, first, compound subjects connnected by *and*. The rule: a compound subject connected by *and* is considered *plural* (but note the exceptions below). Examples:

> He and I *are* ready.
> You and she *have* eaten all the leftovers.
> John and Mary *walk* to school together.
> She and her husband *were* playing tennis.
> A man and a woman *were* waiting to see you.

Exception 1: If *and* connects two nouns referring to the same person, the compound subject is considered *singular*. Examples:

> Her husband and best friend *is* Sam. (*Husband* and *friend* are the same person.)
> His wife and severest critic *is* Betty (*wife* and *critic* are the same person.)

Exception 2: If *and* connects two nouns that refer to a

single entity, the compound noun is considered singular. Examples:

> Ham and eggs *makes* a tasty dish. (*But*: The ham and the eggs *are* both in the refrigerator.)
>
> Meat and potatoes *was* his favorite dinner. (*But*: Beef and pork *are* excellent sources of protein.)

4. Compound subject (connector: or or nor): When a compound subject is connected by *or* or *nor*, the verb agrees with the closer (or closest) subject. Examples:

> A doctor or *nurse is* always available. (*Nurse* is closer to the verb *is.*)
>
> His uncle or his *cousins are* always home. (*Cousins* is the nearer subject.)
>
> *Are* your *fingers* or your shoulder still painful? (*Fingers* is closer to the verb.)
>
> *Is* your *shoulder* or your fingers still painful? (*Shoulder* is the nearer subject.)
>
> *Has she* or her secretaries left yet? (*She* is closer to the auxiliary *has.*)
>
> Neither Pam nor *Evelyn was* ready. (*Evelyn* is closer.)

(For further examples of subject, verb agreement when the connector *or* or *nor* is used, see EITHER . . . OR, NEITHER . . . NOR, ONE OR TWO; OR.)

5. Subjects followed by P-GROUPS: When a subject is separated from its verb by a P-GROUP (prepositional phrase), *ignore the noun or pronoun in the P-GROUP.* Examples:

> The *cat*, with its litter of kittens, *has* finally been sold. (Subject is *cat; with its litter of kittens* is a compound P-GROUP.)
>
> *Paula*, as well as all her relatives, *is* very wealthy. (Subject is *Paula; as well as all her relatives* is a P-GROUP.)
>
> *Ray*, together with his sisters, *is* sitting for a family portrait. (*Together with his sisters* is a P-GROUP.)
>
> *Neither* of us *is* ready. (*Neither* is a singular pronoun meaning *neither one; of us* is a P-GROUP.)
>
> *Is either* of my answers correct? (*Either*, like *neither*, is a singular pronoun; *of my answers* is a P-GROUP.)
>
> The *buyer* of all these books *wants* to pay for them with a credit card. (*Of all these books* is a P-GROUP.)
>
> Your record *collection* plus all your rare books *has* just been sold at auction. (*Plus* is a preposition.)

Boatload after boatload of supplies *has* been arriving all week. (The subject is the italicized *boatload; after boatload* is a P-GROUP; *of supplies* is a second P-GROUP.)

No one but the Americans *has* been able to accomplish such a feat. (When *but* means *except*, it is a preposition; so *but the Americans* is a P-GROUP.)

A new *round* of drinks *has* just been ordered. (*Of drinks* is a P-GROUP.)

See also EITHER OF, NEITHER OF; LOT; NONE; NOUN, 1; NUMBER; ONE IN, ONE OUT OF; ONE OF THOSE WHO . . . ; PLUS; PREPOSITION.

6. Subjects in There, Where, etc. sentence patterns: In a sentence starting with *There, Where, Here, What, When, Why,* or *How* (often a question), the subject may *follow* the verb or auxiliary. See SENTENCE PATTERNS, 6.

Examples:

              S   S
There *are* your brother and sister now.

              S   S
Where *were* your brother and sister going?

           S
Here *is* the box of plums I promised you.

           S
When *is* either of your parents returning?

           S   S
How *is* a doctor or lawyer affected by the new law?

           S
Why *is* each of you doing the same work?

(If a sentence starts with *There is more than one* (*way, method, problem*, etc.), the -S FORM of the verb is correct, even though *more* sounds like a plural subject; *There is more than one way to skin a cat.*

7. Fractions as subject: When the subject is a plural fraction (*two-thirds, three-fourths,* etc.), the form of the verb to use depends on whether such fraction represents a *single entity or proportion*, on the one hand; or, on the other hand, *a number of individuals or items*. For example:

Two-thirds of the population of that country *is* illiterate. (i.e., a certain proportion)

Two-thirds of my friends *are* very wealthy. (i.e., a number of individuals)

Three-fourths of this book *doesn't* make sense. (i.e., a proportion)

Three-fourths of the pages *are* torn. (i.e., a number of pages)

See also NOUN, 1.

8. Plural nouns that are singular in meaning: When a plural noun, usually one showing amount, quantity, or measurement, refers unquestionably to a *single entity*, such a noun is construed as a singular and takes the S-FORM of the verb or auxiliary. Examples:

Five thousand *dollars* a month *is* a good salary. (i.e., one specific amount)

Thirty-five *cents is* too much for that bar of candy. (i.e., a specific amount)

Six *yards was* more than she needed for her dress. (i.e., one piece of material)

Ten *bushels* of fruit per tree *is* phenomenal! (i.e., a specific quantity)

Three *pounds* of meat *is* more than enough to feed six people. (i.e., one piece, or one amount)

9. All that ..., what ...: When these or similar words introduce a clause, and the clause itself is the subject of the verb, strict usage requires that the clause be construed as singular *even if the subject complement following the verb is a plural noun*. (A *subject complement* is a noun or pronoun following any form of the verb *to be* or any other *linking verb*; see SENTENCE PATTERNS, 3, 3A.)

For example:

All that I need *is* five days more.
What I want *is* ten more workers.

In each instance above, the clause (*all that I need; what I want*) is the *subject; days* and *workers* are *subject complements*. However, in colloquial usage or informal writing, a plural *subject complement* often tempts a speaker or writer to use *to be* in the NON-S form (i.e., in the sentences above, *are*).

See also LOT; NUMBER; NOUN, 1.

A test on subject, verb agreement
Check the correct form of the verb in each sentence:

1. Carol and Jean *(is, are)* in the next room.
2. Neither Carol nor Jean *(has, have)* arrived.
3. *(Was, Were)* your grandfather or your parents at the party?
4. A carload of steel bars *(is, are)* expected tomorrow.
5. Your work as well as your attitude *(needs, need)* improvement.
6. Neither of these books *(is, are)* overdue.
7. Everyone but John and Sally *(is, are)* ready.
8. Here *(is, are)* the documents you requested.
9. Two-thirds of the work *(is, are)* still unfinished.
10. Three cups of milk *(is, are)* all the recipe calls for.
11. All that I need now *(is, are)* five more volunteers.
12. What he wants *(is, are)* five more volunteers.
13. Neither he nor I *(is, are, am)* very happy about this.
14. There *(was, were)* a couch and a coffee table in the corner of the room.
15. The supervisor or one of her assistants *(is, are)* always available if you need help.

KEY (the number in parentheses after each answer refers to the section in previous pages that contains the applicable rule): 1. **are** (3); 2. **has** (4); 3. **was** (4); 4. **is** (5); 5. **needs** (5); 6. **is** (5); 7. **is** (5); 8. **are** (6); 9. **is** (7); 10. **is** (8); 11. **is** (9); 12. **is** (9); 13. **am** (4); 14. **were** (8, 3); 15. **is** (4, 5).

---

subjective, objective, *adj.*
See OBJECTIVE, SUBJECTIVE.

SUBJUNCTIVE

This grammatical term refers to the form of a verb in certain constructions. For example:

> I suggest he *wait* until I call him.
> We insist that he *report* to work on time.
> It is essential that she *arrive* early.

You will notice that the subjunctive is the NON-S FORM of a verb following a singular subject. (See SUBJECT, VERB AGREEMENT.)

Problems may occur with the past tense of *to be* as a verb or auxiliary after *as if, if, if only,* and *wish.* (*If* I was/were; *as if he* was/were; *she wishes she* was/were; etc.) For full explanations and rules See AS IF ... WAS, AS IF ... WERE; IF ... WAS, IF ... WERE; WISH ... WAS, WISH ... WERE.

---

subliminal, *adj.* See SUB-CONSCIOUS, SUBLIMINAL, UN-CONSCIOUS.

subpoena, summons, *n.* In reference to legal matters:

A *subpoena* (variant spelling: *subpena*) requires that one appear in court, before a grand jury, etc., in order to give testimony.

A *summons* generally requires one to appear in court as a defendant in a suit; it may also refer to a legal paper demanding one's presence in court as a prospective juror or as a witness.

Note that *summons*, despite the *-s* ending, is a *singular noun: a summons was issued.*

subtile, subtle, *adj.* The two words are synonymous, but *subtile* is rare in current usage.

succuba, *n.* See **incubus, succubus.** For plural, see NOUN, 6M1.

succubus, *n.* See incubus, succubus. For plural, see NOUN, 6P.

such as *(plus pronoun)* In this construction a form of the verb *to be* is understood after the pronoun, so the *nominative case* of the personal pronoun is required: *a person such as he (is) would not ... ; people such as they (are) never ...*

You may, of course, substi-tute the preposition *like* for *such as*, provided you do not use the verb *to be* after the pronoun. After the preposition *like*, the *objective case* of the pronoun is used: *a person like him would not ... ; people like them never. ...* See also AS/LIKE, AS IF/LIKE; THAN, CONJ. (PLUS A PERSONAL PRONOUN).

suffocate, *v.* See SMOTHER, SUFFOCATE, STRANGLE.

suite, suit, set, *n.* In reference to connected rooms or pieces of matched furniture, *suite* is the correct word: *rented a suite at the hotel; bought a new suite of furniture for the den.* (In reference to rooms, *suite* is pronounced SWEET; in reference to furniture, preferably SWEET, but also, SOOT.)

Suit is not used for rooms or furniture—it refers to clothing, playing cards, and various other objects that form a related group.

Set is the general term for any group of related things or people: *chess set; set of tools; set of furniture; the jet set;* etc. (However, it is rarely, if ever, used for two or more connected rooms.)

summersault, summerset See SOMERSAULT, SUMMER-SAULT, SOMERSET, SUMMERSET.

summons, *n.*   See SUBPOENA, SUMMONS.

SUPER-, SUPRA-, *prefix*

Both prefixes mean *over, above, beyond, greater than,* etc. *Super-* is the more extensively used prefix: *supra-* is found chiefly in:

supraglottal	supranational
supralapsarian	supraorbital
supraliminal	suprarenal
supramolecular	

With other roots, *super-* is the correct prefix. Note that words with the prefix *super-* and *supra-* are written solid, not hyphenated.

---

superior to, superior than The correct word following *superior* is *to,* not *than: the new model has superior safety features to* (not *than*) *those found on earlier models; she is far superior in ability to her classmates.*

supine, *adj.*   See PRONE, SUPINE, PROSTRATE.

supplement, *n.*   See COMPLEMENT, COMPLIMENT, SUPPLEMENT.

suppose, *v.*   See FIGURE, SUPPOSE.

supposed to, suppose to In constructions like *he was supposed to finish by Wednesday, supposed,* not *suppose,* is the correct spelling. In speech, the two words do, of course, sound identical, so the misspelling is not surprising.

supra-, *prefix* See SUPER-, SUPRA-.

suppress, repress, *v.*   See REPRESS, SUPPRESS.

sure, surely *qualifier* In careful speech or writing, *sure* is unacceptable as a qualifier: i.e., *he was sure happy about that. He was surely happy* is preferable; or qualifiers like *certainly, very, extremely,* etc. may be substituted for *sure* in such constructions. See also QUALIFIER.

surgeon general, *n.*   For plural, see NOUN, 6U.

surprised at, surprised by One can be *surprised* (i.e., astonished, etc.) either *at* or *by* what one sees. But a burglar is *surprised by* the police (i.e., caught unawares, caught by surprise).

You feel or express *sur-*

prise at someone or something.

suspicion, suspect, *v.* *Suspicion* as a verb (i.e., *I suspicion that he . . .*) is at best a dialectical usage, not acceptable in standard English. The correct verb is *suspect*.

swell, *v.* The past tense is *swelled;* the participle is either *swelled* or *swollen*. After a form of *to be,* the participle functions as an adjective, and *swollen* is the preferred form: *his ankle was swollen*. As an adjective preceding its noun, *swollen* is used (*a swollen ankle*), unless one is speaking figuratively in reference to conceit, in which instance *swelled* is the adjective: *he has a swelled head, a swelled sense of importance,* etc.

swim, *v.* Past tense is *swam;* participle is *swum*.

swing, *v.* *Swung* is the past tense and the participle.

swinge, *v.* See SINGEING.

swipe, steal, *v.* See THIEVERY.

syllabus, curriculum, *n.* See CURRICULUM, SYLLABUS.

sympathize, emphathize, *v.* See EMPATHIZE, SYMPATHIZE.

sympathy, pity, *n.* See PITY, SYMPATHY.

symposium, *n.* For plural, see NOUN, 6Q.

synagog, *n.* See -OGUE, -OG.

synopsis, *n.* For plural, see NOUN, 6N.

synthesis, *n.* For plural, see NOUN, 6N.

syrup, *n.* See SIRUP, SYRUP.

T

tableau, *n.* For plural, see NOUN, 6S.

tablespoonful, *n.* For plural; see -FUL, -FULS.

taboo, tabu *Taboo* is the preferred spelling, *tabu* a variant.

tactics, *n.* See -ICS.

take, bring, *v.* See BRING, TAKE, FETCH.

talk, to, talk with See SPEAK TO, SPEAK WITH.

talus, *n.* For plural, see NOUN, 6P.

tautological, *adj.* See WORDY, VERBOSE, PROLIX, PLEONASTIC, REDUNDANT, TAUTOLOGICAL.

tax- *prefix Taxpayer* and *taxpaying* (*n.* or *adj.*) are solid words. *Tax-exempt* (*adj.*) and *tax-free* (*adj.*) are hyphenated.

T-bar, *n.* *T-bar* is hyphenated, as are also *T-shirt* and *T-strap*; *T square* is written as two separate words.

tear, *v.* Past tense is *tore*; the participle is *torn*.

However, *tear* (*v.*), pronounced TEER, may also mean *to shed tears, as in weeping*, in which case the past tense and participle are *teared*.

teaspoonful, *n.* For plural, see -FUL, -FULS.

technic, technique, *n.* The two words are identical in meaning; the latter is far more common in current usage. *Technic* may be pronounced TEK'-nik or tek-NEEK'.

teen-age, teenage, *adj.* The hyphenated spelling is preferable. The noun *teen-ager* and the adjective *teen-aged* are written only as hyphenated words.

telecast, televise, *v.* These verbs are interchangeable. Some people use *televise* with the added meaning of *tape* (a program) *for later broadcasting*. The past tense and participle of *telecast* are preferably *telecast*. *Telecast* is also a noun.

telephone, *n.*, *v.* See PHONE, TELEPHONE.

televise, *v.* See TELECAST, TELEVISE.

temblor, tremblor, *n.* Only the first spelling is acceptable. The misspelling is understandable, since a very minor earthquake may be called a *tremor*, and *tremble* does mean *to shake*.

temerity, timidity, *n.* These

252

nouns are almost direct ant-onyms: *temerity* is *reckless-ness, rash boldness*, while *timidity* has as one of its meanings *a feeling of fear in the face of possible danger*. The adjective form of *temerity* is *temerarious*.

See also TIMID, TIMOROUS.

temperant, temperate, *adj.* It is one of the many quirks of the English language that *temperance* is one of the noun forms of *temperate* (the other is *temperateness*), but *tem-perant* is a nonword.

tempo, *n.* For plural, see NOUN, 6L4.

tenacious, pertinacious, *adj.* See PERTINACIOUS, TENACIOUS.

tendency, *n.* **(to, toward)** Generally, *tendency* is fol-lowed by *to* when the next word is a *verb* (*tendency to exaggerate*), by *toward* when the next word is a *noun* (*ten-dency toward* exaggeration).

terminal, terminus, *n.* In the sense of *either end* (or *a station at either end*) *of a transportation line*, the words are interchangeable. *Termi-nal*, however, is the more commonly used word. (For

the plural of *terminus*, see NOUN, 6P.)

terrapin, tortoise, turtle, *n.* A *terrapin* is a freshwater *turtle* found in North America. A *tortoise* is a land *turtle*. *Turtle* is the general term used for the species, although, strictly, a *turtle* is a sea reptile.

terrify, terrorize, *v.* Although these words may be used in-terchangeably in the sense of *filling with terror*, *terrorize* most often signifies *to use violence, or threats of vio-lence, in order to instill great fear, sometimes for political purposes: marauding gangs terrorized the neighborhood.* Nouns: *terrorist, terrorism.*

terror, horror, *n.* *Terror* is intense, paralyzing fear; hor-ror is shock and fear com-bined with disgust or loathing.

terrorize, *v.* TERRIFY, TER-RORIZE.

testator, *n.* A *testator* (i.e., one who has signed, or left, a legal will) may be either a male or female. However, if it is necessary to stress the gender of such a person, the feminine form is *testatrix*, the plural of which is *testatrices*.

THAN, conj. (plus a personal pronoun)

When a personal pronoun follows *than*, the case of the pronoun is governed by an *omitted*, but *understood, verb, auxiliary*, or *preposition*. In the following examples, the omitted verb, auxiliary, or preposition appears in parenthe-ses. (Note that the case of the pronoun is often determined by the meaning of the sentence.)

You are taller than *he* (is.).
She is shrewder than *I* (am).
You enjoyed the play more than *I* (did).
I'd rather speak to you than (to) *him*.
I spend more time with Paul than *she* (does).
I spend more time with Paul than (with) *her*.
You visit me more often than *he* (does).
You visit me more often than (you visit) *him*.

The same rule applies to the correlative conjuctions *as . . . as*.

Examples:

You're not as tall as *I* (am).
You spend as much money on me as *she* (does).
You spend as much money on me as (on) *her*.
Do you love me as much as *he* (does)?
Do you love me as much as (you love) *him*?

See also PRONOUN, 8; SUCH AS; THAN WHOM.

---

than, when, *conj.* See HARDLY, SCARELY, BARELY; SOONER . . . THAN, NO SOONER . . . WHEN.

than any, than any other/than anyone, than anyone else Consider the logic of the sentence *Your brother is taller than any member of your family.* The implication is that your brother is *not* a member of your family—a contradiction in terms.

The sentence, to be strictly logical, should read: *Your brother is taller **than any other** member of your family.*

Similarly: *Your brother is taller than anyone in your family* is preferably revised to: *Your brother is taller **than anyone else** in the family.*

than whom Despite, and contradictory to, the rule explained under the entry for *than, conj.*, the objective **whom** always follows **than:** *than whom no one is more difficult to get along with; the captain, **than whom** no one is more knowledgeable about navigation.*

THAT, WHICH, WHO

That may refer to people, things, ideas, etc.: *the person **that** you were waiting for is here now; the information **that** has come to light is more important; the book **that** was published in 1986.*

That, as a relative pronoun, introduces only a *restrictive clause*. (See RESTRICTIVE CLAUSE, NONRESTRICTIVE CLAUSE.)

Which refers to things, ideas, etc., or, occasionally, to a collective group of persons: *these special facts,* **which** *cannot be ignored, are . . . ; the senior class,* **which** *is now in the auditorium, is rehearsing.*

Which, as a relative pronoun, preferably introduces a nonrestrictive clause.

Who (or *whom*) refers to persons only: *the man* **who** *came to dinner; the woman* **whom** *I met in Paris.*

Who may introduce either a *restrictive* or *nonrestrictive* clause.

See also WHO, WHOM; WHOSE, OF WHICH.

---

theater, theatre, *n.*   *Theatre* is the variant spelling. See also -ER, -RE.

theft, *n.*   See THIEVERY.

their, there, they're   *Their* is a determiner: *their book.* (See DETERMINER.)

There is either an *adverb* or the opening word of a *there* sentence (see SENTENCE PATTERNS, 6): *Is he* ***there***; ***there*** *was once a . . .*

They're is a contraction for *they are: They're here now.* (See CONTRACTIONS.)

theirs, their's   An apostrophe is never used in the possessive inflection of personal pronouns. Correct form: *theirs.* See also PRONOUN, 8.

theirself, theirselves, themself, themselves   The first *three* forms are erroneous or illiterate substitutes for *themselves.*

Do not use *themselves* as a substitute for *they. Incorrect structure: Themselves and all their rowdy friends were* evicted *from the restaurant.*

theism, monotheism, polytheism, pantheism, deism, *n.* *Theism* accepts the concept of God or of godliness—so the term includes *monotheism* (belief in a single, supreme God) and *polytheism* (belief in a whole constellation of gods, as by the ancient Greeks or Romans).

Pantheism has two different meanings. The term can designate the doctrine that God is a combination of all the phenomena of nature; it can also, though less commonly, refer to the acceptance and worship of all gods.

Deism usually refers to the seventeenth- and eighteenth-century doctrine that God did indeed create the universe but no longer is involved in its operation.

them, they   For the correct pronoun to use, see PRONOUN, 8–8B.

themself, themselves   See

THEIRSELF, THEIRSELVES, THEM-SELF, THEMSELVES.

therapist, *n.* See PSYCHIA-TRIST, PSYCHOANALYST, PSY-CHOLOGIST, PSYCHOTHERAPIST, COUNSELOR, ALIENIST.

there See THEIR, THERE, THEY'RE.

there *(plus a verb)* See SEN-TENCE PATTERN, 6; SUBJECT, VERB AGREEMENT, 6.

there is more than one See SUBJECT, VERB AGREEMENT, 6.

therefor, therefore The first word is now archaic, except in legal terminology, and means *for it, for this,* or *for that.*

For the punctuation used

when *therefore* introduces a clause, see HOWEVER.

these kind, these sort, these type See KIND, KINDS.

thesis, *n.* For plural, see NOUN, 6N.

thespian, *n.* This word is generally used for *actor* or *actress* only if there is a deliberate intent to sound humorous, elegant, or pretentious.

As an adjective, however, it means *pertaining to drama* or *dramatic performance.*

they, them For the correct pronoun to use, *see* PRONOUN, 8–8B.

they're See THEIR, THERE, THEY'RE.

THIEVERY, n.

Thievery is the general, all-inclusive term for *stealing.* There are various kinds of thievery, many of them defined by law or state or city legal codes.

Burglary involves breaking into a house or other building to commit theft. (*Burglar,* n.; *burglarize,* v.; *burglarious,* adj.)

Defalcation is the misuse or theft of funds entrusted to one. (*Defalcator,* n.; *defalcate,* v.)

Embezzlement is the stealing of the funds of another that have been left in one's care. (*Embezzler,* n.; *embezzle,* v.)

Kleptomania is a morbid, irresistable, and usually habitual urge to steal someone's money or possessions, not out of economic necessity but for the (perhaps unconscious) thrill that such thievery provides. (*Kleptomaniac,* n.; *kleptomaniacal,* adj.)

Larceny, a legal term, is a general word for the theft of another's money or property. (*Larcenist, larcener,* n.; *larcenous,* adj.)

Pilferage is the stealing of small amounts of money or of objects of little value. (*Pilferer,* n.; *pilfer,* v.)

Robbery, as legally defined, is the theft of someone's money or property while the owner is present, and usually through force or intimidation, as by threatening with a knife, gun, etc. (*Robber*, n.; *rob*, v.)

Shoplifting is the stealthy theft of an object or objects from a store during shopping hours. (*Shoplifter*, n.; *shoplift*, v.)

In addition to the verbs in parentheses in the entries above, there are also *filch*, synonymous with *pilfer*; *purloin*, a literary term meaning *steal another's possession or possessions for one's own use, often illegal or nefarious (purloined letters (documents, etc.);* and the slang verbs *lift*, *pinch*, *snitch*, and *swipe*, all synonymous with *filch* or *pilfer*.

See also ROB, STEAL.

---

third, thirdly See FIRST, FIRSTLY.

tho Informal spelling of *though*. See also ALTHOUGH, THOUGH, ALTHO, ALBEIT; -OUGH, -O, -U.

thoro, thorough See -OUGH, -O, -U.

thorofare, thoroughfare, n. See -OUGH, -O, -U.

those kind, those sort, those type See KIND, KINDS.

though See ALTHOUGH, THOUGH, ALTHO, ALBEIT; THO.

thrive, v. Past tense is *thrived* or *throve*. Participle is *thrived* or *thriven*.

throw, v. Past tense is *threw*. Participle is *thrown*.

thruway, n. See -OUGH, -O, -U.

thus, *conj.* For the punctuation used when this conjunction introduces a clause, see HOWEVER.

thus, thusly *Thus* itself is an adverb; to add *-ly* to the adverb is totally unnecessary, and indeed creates a nonword. (*Thusly* is sometimes used deliberately for the sake of humor or pretentiousness.)

tidbit, titbit, n. The second word is a variant form.

tight-, *prefix* Adjective compounds are hyphenated: *tight-belted*, *tight-fitting*, *tight-lipped*. But *tightfisted* (*adj.*) is written solid.

Noun compounds are written solid: *tightrope*, *tightwad*, *tightwire*.

tight, *suffix* Adjective compounds are written solid: *airtight*, *raintight*, *skintight*, *watertight*, etc.

till, until, til (*conj.* or *prep.*) The first two words are interchangeable. *Til* is a nonword or a misspelling.

time-, *prefix* Adjective compounds are generally hyphenated: *time-honored*, *time-tested*, etc. However, the adjectives *time*saving, *time*serving, and *time*worn are written solid.

time, *suffix* Compounds are written solid whether *adjectives* or *nouns*: *bedtime, dinnertime, mealtime, suppertime, wartime,* etc.

timid, timorous, *adj.* While these adjectives may be used interchangeably, there is a fine distinction worth observing.

Timid stresses shyness, extreme caution, lack of self-confidence, and/or a shrinking back when there is any perception of danger or loss.

Timorous implies feelings of uneasiness, worry or fear.

Both adjectives describe actions, reactions, attitudes, etc. as well as persons.

timidity, temerity, *n.* See TEMERITY, TIMIDITY.

timpano, tympano, *n.* The second spelling is a variant form. Since a kettledrum is generally played in sets, the plural *timpani* (or *tympani*) is more often encountered than the singular *timpano* (or *tympano*). See also NOUN, 6L4.

timorous, *adj.* See TIMID, TIMOROUS.

tinge, *v.* The -ING form is preferably spelled *tingeing,* but *tinging* is also correct. Either way, the -ING form is pronounced TINJ'-ing.

tinker's damn, tinker's dam Tinkers were itinerant menders of metal household uten-sils; they were famous, in days gone by, for their salty language. Hence, *tinker's damn* is historically the more accurate spelling. However, people sensitive to curse words left the final *n* off *damn*. Today, both spellings are used, though the first is preferable.

tiro, *n.* See TYRO, TIRO.

titbit, *n.* See TIDBIT, TITBIT.

title, honorific, *n.* See HONORIFIC, TITLE.

to, too, two *To* is the preposition (*to the house*) or the sign of the infinitive (*to go; to see*), and in casual speech is often pronounced tǝ. See also PREPOSITION.

Too means *also* (*he, too, is here*) or is a qualifier before an adjective or adverb (*he is too slow; she whirled too quickly*). *Too* is clearly pronounced TOO. See QUALIFIER.

Two, of course, is the numeral.

tocsin, toxin, *n.* Though these words have identical pronunciations, a *tocsin* is a warning bell or any warning sound; a *toxin* is a kind of poison.

today, tomorrow, tonight These solid forms are the current spellings; formerly, the hyphenated words (*to-day,* etc.) were also popular.

toga, *n.* The plural is *togas* or *togae* (TO'-jee). See also NOUN, 6M.

together with, *prep.* See AS

WELL AS; PREPOSITION; PRO-
NOUN, 8, 8B; SUBJECT, VERB
AGREEMENT, 5.

toilet, toilette, *n.* Either
word may refer to the process of dressing, putting on
makeup, etc. (chiefly in reference to a woman), but
toilette (twah-LET') is the
more commonly used form
for this meaning.

tolerant, tolerance, toleration
The preferable preposition following any of these words is
of; for and *toward* may also
be used (*tolerant* of *weak-
ness*). In medical parlance, you
have a *tolerance* for certain
drugs, medications, etc.

tomato, *n.* For plural, see
NOUN, 6L1.

tomorrow, to-morrow See
TODAY, TOMORROW, TONIGHT.

tongs, *n.* Though designating *one* tool, this noun is
construed as a plural: *the
tongs are on the shelf.* On
the other hand, *a pair of tongs
is required.*
    See also PAIR.

tonight, to-night See TODAY,
TOMORROW, TONIGHT.

too See TO, TOO, TWO.

tooth-, *prefix* Compounds
are generally written solid:
*tooth*ache,   *tooth*brush,
*tooth*paste,   *tooth*pick.
Tooth powder is written as
two separate words.

toothed, *suffix* Adjective
compounds are hyphenated:
even-**toothed**, sharp-**toothed**,
snaggle-**toothed**, etc.

top-, *prefix* Adjective compounds are usually hyphenated: *top*-drawer, *top*-flight,
top-heavy, *top*-level, *top*-
notch, *top*-secret.
    These *adjectives* are writ-
ten solid: *top*less, *top*lofty,
*top*most.

top, *suffix* Compounds are
generally solid words: *flattop,
hilltop, housetop,* etc.

tornado, *n.* For plural, see
NOUN, 6L2.

torpedo, *n.* For plural, *see*
NOUN 6L1.

torrefy, *v.* See LIQUEFY,
RAREFY, PUTREFY, STUPEFY,
TORREFY.

tortoise, *n.* See TERRAPIN,
TORTOISE, TURTLE.

**tortuous, torturous, torture-
some,** *adj.* *Tortuous* is *wind-
ing, full of twists and turns,*
and may refer literally to the
course of a road, river, etc.
Figuratively, the adjective may
describe an argument, logic,
or reasoning; in this sense, it
is a synonym of *devious* or
*tricky. Nouns: tortuousness,
tortuosity.*
    Torturous, or its rarely used
variant *torturesome,* refers,
of course, to *torture,* n. (i.e.,
extreme pain).
    To *torture (v.)* is, of course,
to *inflict extreme pain;* it may
also mean *to distort or twist*
(language, meaning, etc.):
tortured prose; a **tortured** sen-

tence; to *torture* the language.

tossup, toss up *Tossup* is a noun. *Toss up* is the *verb toss* plus the word *up*.

tote, tot, *v.* *Tote* is informal or colloquial for *carry*, *haul*, etc.; (tote up is informal or colloquial for *add up* or *total (v.).*) Tot up is a British colloquialism equivalent to the American *tote up*.

touchdown, touch down *Touchdown* is the *noun*; *touch down* is the *verb touch* plus the word *down*.

touch-up, touch up *Touch-up* is the *noun*; *touch up* is the *verb touch* plus the word *up*.

toward, towards See -WARD, -WARDS.

toxin, tocsin, *n.* See TOCSIN, TOXIN.

transient, transitory, *adj.* Both adjectives describe that which lasts or stays a while and then leaves or moves on. People—*transient guests* (*visitors*, etc.)—as well as phenomena can be *transient*.

Transitory characterizes events, phenomena, etc. that are by nature impermanent and that one therefore expects to move on, fade away, or end: *transitory fads*; *transitory* clouds (*sunspots*, etc.).

transitive verbs See SENTENCE PATTERNS, 1, 4, 5.

transparent, translucent, **opaque,** *adj.* *Transparent* describes that which can be seen through, literally or figuratively: *transparent glass*; *transparent motives*; *transparent falsehoods*. Noun: *transparency*.

A *translucent* object (such as etched or stained glass) admits light, but not clear vision.

Opaque objects, shades, drapes, etc. admit neither light nor vision. *Opaque* may also be used figuratively to describe reasoning, explanations, etc. that do not admit of comprehension; hence, in such instances, *opaque* is a synonym of *obscure* or *incomprehensible*. A person with an *opaque* mind is slow in comprehension or learning. *Nouns: opaqueness, opacity*.

transpire, *v.* Though widely used as a synonym of *come to pass, happen,* or *occur* (*it transpired that . . . ; certain results will transpire if . . .*), many authorities frown on such usage. Aside from its application in chemistry and biology, *transpire* has the nontechnical meaning of *become known*: *it transpired that the true villain was . . .* (i.e., it became known that the true villain was . . .).

transsexual, transvestite, *n.* A *transsexual* has undergone certain medical and/or surgical procedures to change his/her sex; or, less commonly, identifies more closely with the opposite sex than with her/his own. *Noun; transsexualism*.

A *transvestite* gets a sexual kick from dressing in the clothing, especially the intimate garments, of the opposite sex. For reasons not completely known, more men than women are *transvestites*. *Nouns; transvestism, transvestitism*.

travelogue, travelog, *n*. See -OGUE, -OG.

tread, *v*. Past tense is *trod*. The participle is either *trodden* or *trod*, but only *trodden* is used in a compound adjective: *downtrodden masses; well-trodden paths*.

treat of, treat with In the sense of *dealing with a subject or topic; treat (v.)* is preferably followed by the preposition *of: the paper treated of the effects of carcinogenic emissions*. However, *with* is also acceptable in this context.

treble, triple As an adjective or verb, the words are interchangeable. *Triple* is the more commonly used term.

tremblor, temblor, *n*. See TEMBLOR, TREMBLOR.

triad, *n*. See TRIO, TRIAD, TRINITY, TRIUMVIRATE.

triannual, triennial, triennium The current word is *triennial*, which, as an adjective, means *occurring every three years* or *lasting for three years;*

as a noun, a *triennial* is an event, celebration, etc. that occurs every three years.

Triannual, which once meant *three times a year*, is an obsolete word.

A *triennium (n.)* is a three-year period; plural is *trienniums* or *triennia*. See also NOUN, 6Q.

tributary, tributory The only correct form is *tributary*, whether *noun* or *adjective*.

triennial, triennium See TRIANNUAL, TRIENNIAL, TRIENNIUM.

trinity, *n*. See TRIO, TRIAD, TRINITY, TRIUMVIRATE.

trio, triad, trinity, triumvirate, *n*. A *trio* is a *related* group of three (usually persons, but also things). *Trio* also designates either a musical composition for three performers or the performers of such a composition. *Plural: trios*.

A *triad* is *any* group of three persons, things, or ideas. When a discussion group breaks into units of three, each such unit may be called a *triad*.

Trinity implies a *union* of three (things, people, or ideas).

A *triumvirate* may be any group of three people who are usually together, but more often designates a group of three persons associated in some position of authority or power, as in the government, an institution, a corporation, etc.

These words are *singular collective nouns*: *the trio was ready*; *the triad was in animated discussion*; *there is a trinity*; *the triumvirate was feared*.

See also NOUN, 1, 6L.

triple See TREBLE, TRIPLE.

triumphal, triumphant, *adj.* *Triumphal* means *pertaining to* or *celebrating a triumph*: *triumphal march*.

Triumphant describes a person elated or exulting over a triumph, or an action or attitude showing such elation or exultation: *triumphant smile*; *return of the triumphant hero*.

troche, trochee, *n.* A *troche* is a medicinal lozenge; a *trochee* is a certain kind of metrical foot in poetry. Both words are pronounced TRŌ′-kee.

troop, troupe, *n.* A *troop* is any group of people, things, or animals; a *troupe* is a company of actors, performers, etc.

trooper, trouper, *n.* A *trooper* is a cavalry soldier, a mounted police officer, or a member of the police force of a state.

A *trouper* is a member of a *troupe*, i.e., an acting or performing group; a veteran actor; or, in colloquial usage, a dependable hard-working member of a group.

troupe, *n.* See TROOP, TROUPE.

trousers, n. pl. Though a single garment, *trousers* is construed as a *plural* noun: *his trousers were torn*. On the other hand, *this pair of trousers is size 36*. (*Trousers* incidentally, is *not* a more formal word than *pants*).

The singular form, *trouser*, is used in *trouser leg*, *trouser cuff*, etc.

See also PAIR, PANTS.

trousseau, *n.* For plural, see NOUN, 6S.

true fact See FACT, ACTUAL FACT, TRUE FACT.

trustee, trusty, *n.* A *trustee* is a person, bank, etc. officially entrusted with the management of funds or property; also, a member of the governing board of an institution. A *trusty*, in a prison, is a convict granted special privileges or duties.

try and *(plus verb)* As a substitute for *try to* (*try and make me . . .*), this usage is acceptable only on an informal or colloquial level.

tryout, try out As a solid word, *tryout* is a *noun*; separated, *try* is a *verb* followed by the word *out*.

tsar, *n.* See CZAR, TSAR, TZAR.

tsarina, *n.* See CZARINA, TSARINA, TZARINA.

T-shirt, T square, T-strap See T-BAR.

tumefy, *v.* One of the few

verbs ending in *-efy* rather
than *-ify*. See also LIQUEFY,
RAREFY, PUTREFY, STUPEFY,
TORREFY.

TUMESCENT, TUMID, TURGID, TURBID, *adj.*

Tumescent describes a bodily part or organ that is starting
to swell, or that is in the process of becoming *tumid*. (Yet,
contradictorily, a *tumescence (n.)* is either a partial or full-
blown swelling.)

Tumid is *swollen*. When applied to a language, *tumid*
characterizes prose, sentences, style or verbiage that is in-
flated, pompous, or grandiloquent. *Nouns: tumidity, tumidness.*

Turgid is a close synonym of *tumid* and, like *tumid*, may
be used both literally and figuratively. Applied literally to a
bodily part, or to any living cells or tissue, *turgid* usually
suggests normal or healthy distention, while *tumid* often
implies abnormal or morbid bloating. *Nouns: turgidness,
turgidity, turgor.*

Turbid, on the other hand, means *muddy, cloudy, roiled,
dense,* or *confused* and this word, too, is used both literally
and figuratively. *Nouns: turbidness, turbidity.*

---

tumid, *adj.* See TUMESCENT,
TUMID, TURGID, TURBID.

turbid, *adj.* See TUMESCENT,
TUMID, TURGID, TURBID.

turf, *n.* For plural, see NOUN,
6G1.

turgid, *adj.* See TUMESCENT,
TUMID, TURGID, TURBID.

turntable, *n.* See PHONO-
GRAPH, GRAMOPHONE, RECORD
PLAYER, TURNTABLE, VICTROLA.

turtle, *n.* See TERRAPIN, TOR-
TOISE, TURTLE.

twaddle, twattle *Twaddle* is
the preferable spelling; *twattle*
is a variant.

twain, *n.* See DUO, DUET,
DUAD, DYAD.

twattle See TWADDLE,
TWATTLE.

twice-, *prefix* *Adjective* compounds preceding a noun are
hyphenated: *twice-told tales;
a twice-blessed life; a twice-
removed cousin.*

twinge, *v.* The -ING form
is *twinging*, pronounced
TWINJ'-ing. See also SINGEING.

two, *prefix* *Adjective* compounds are generally hyphenated: *two-cycle, two-edged,
two-faced, two-fisted, two-*

handed, *two-legged, two-piece, two-way*, etc.

Two-by-four, referring to lumber, is hyphenated as either a *noun* or *adjective*.

Twofold and *twopenny* are written as solid adjectives.

two, to, too See TO, TOO, TWO.

twosome, *n.* See DUO, DUET, DUAD, DYAD.

tympano, *n.* See TIMPANO, TYMPANO.

tympanum, *n.* For plural, see NOUN, 6Q.

type-, *prefix* Compounds are generally written solid: *typecast, typescript, typeset, typewrite, typewriter, typewriting.*

type, *n.* See KIND, KINDS.

type of See KIND, KINDS, KIND OF.

typhus, typhous Typhus is a *noun,* a shortened form of *typhus fever,* the disease. *Typhous* is an *adjective* referring to the disease.

tyro, tiro, *n.* The first form is the preferable spelling. For plural, see NOUN, 6L3.

tzar, *n.* see CZAR, TSAR, TZAR.

tzarina, *n.* See CZARINA, TSARINA, TZARINA.

U

-U See -OUGH, -O, -U.

U-boat Most compounds starting with a capital letter as the first element are hyphenated. But *T square, A one, V sign* are written separate.

UFO, U.F.O. The commoner spelling is without the periods. For plural, see NOUN, 6T.

uglify, *v.* Acceptable but awkward. Preferable usages: *make, render,* or *cause to be ugly.*

ultimatum, *n.* For plural, see NOUN, 6Q.

ultra- *prefix* Compound words are written solid unless the root starts with the letter *a* or a capital letter: *ultra*conservative, *ultra*modern: *ultra*-atomic, *ultra*-American, *ultra*-British.

umpire, referee, *n.* In reference to competitive team sports, the person who makes the rulings is an *umpire* in baseball or cricket, a *referee* in boxing.

un-, *prefix* Words with this prefix are written solid, unless the root starts with a capital letter; *un*-American, for example.

unabridged, unexpurgated, *adj.* An *unabridged* edition of a work is complete—it has not been cut, condensed, or shortened.

An *unexpurgated* copy, edition, etc. is one from which material considered indelicate, offensive, or, occasionally, erroneous, has not been removed.

See also CENSOR, BOWDLERIZE, EXPURGATE.

unavoidable, *adj.* See INEVITABLE, INELUCTABLE, UNAVOIDABLE.

unaware, unawares *Unaware* is the *adjective: she was unaware of the peril. Unawares* (also, less commonly, *unaware*) is the *adverb: caught him unawares (unaware).*

unaware, unconscious, *adj.* See conscious, aware, *adj.*

unbeknownst, unbeknown Either word is acceptable in standard usage as a participle, especially at the start of a sentence: *unbeknownst (unbeknown) to the committee members, the witness had* . . . See also PARTICIPLE.

uncalled-for, *adj.* Hyphenated when the adjective pre-

265

cedes a noun: *uncalled-for insult.*

unconscious, *adj.* See CONSCIOUS, AWARE; INSENSIBLE, INSENSATE, UNCONSCIOUS; SUBCONSCIOUS, SUBLIMINAL, UNCONSCIOUS.

under-, *prefix* All compounds are written solid, even if the root starts with *r*: *underrate, underripe, underrun.*

underhand, underhanded *Underhand* is used both as an *adjective* and an *adverb*: *underhand* pitch, *underhand* activities (adj.); *threw the ball underhand* (adv.).

Underhanded is only an *adjective*: *What an underhanded thing to do!* The adverbial derivative of *underhanded* is *underhandedly*; the noun is *underhandedness.*

underlay, underlie, *v.* Both verbs are *transitive*, but with different meanings:

Underlay: *to place (something) under some other thing; to cover the bottom surface of: underlay the rug with felt.* The past tense and participle are both *underlaid*. An *underlay (n.)* is something covered by, or under, something else.

Underlie: *to lie under or be the basis or motive for: what underlies her accusation?; the felt underlies the rug.* The past tense of *underlie* is *underlay*; the participle is *underlain*: *a desire for revenge underlay her actions;*

a need for financial security has underlain all her hard work.

See also LIE, LAY; OVERLIE, OVERLAY; PARTICIPLE. For transitive and intransitive verbs, see SENTENCE PATTERNS, 1–5.

underpants, *n.* Though a single garment, *underpants* is construed as a *plural* noun: *the underpants were freshly ironed.* On the other hand, *a new pair of underpants is on the top shelf.* See also PAIR, *n.*

understand, *v.* See APPRECIATE, UNDERSTAND; APPREHEND, COMPREHEND.

underway, underweigh See WAY, WEIGH.

undoubtedly, *adv.* See DOUBTLESS, NO DOUBT.

uneatable, *adj.* See INEDIBLE, UNEATABLE.

unequivocable, unequivocal, *adj.* See AMBIGUOUS, EQUIVOCAL, EQUIVOCABLE.

unexceptional, unexceptionable, *adj.* See EXCEPTIONAL, EXCEPTIONABLE.

unexpurgated, *adj.* See UNABRIDGED, UNEXPURGATED.

unhealthy, unhealthful, *adj.* See HEALTHY, HEALTHFUL.

unheard-of, unhoped-for Hyphenate these words when they are used as *adjectives* preceding nouns: *unheard-of insults; unhoped-for results.*

uninterested, disinterested, *adj.* See DISINTERESTED, UNINTERESTED.

unique, *adj.* Strictly, unique means *alone of its kind; having no equal.* It is considered unacceptable in formal English to use this word as a synonym of *unusual, rare,* or *extraordinary.* See also EQUAL, MORE EQUAL.

unless, without, *conj.* It is unacceptable, even in informal English, to use *without* as a conjunction in place of *unless.* Incorrect: *You can't cross the bridge without you pay the toll.*

unless and until, unless or until Authorities object, and with good reason, to this legalistic gobbledygook in a construction such as *he won't be released unless and until* (or *unless or until*) *he pays the fine.* Use either conjunction, not both in tandem.

unlooked-for, *adj.* Hyphenate when this compound is an *adjective* preceding a noun: *an unlooked-for consequence.*

unloose, unloosen, *v.* See LOOSE, LOOSEN, LOSE.

unmentionable, *adj.* See INDESCRIBABLE, INEFFABLE, UNSPEAKABLE, UNMENTIONABLE.

unmoral, *adj.* See AMORAL, NONMORAL, UNMORAL, IMMORAL.

unprincipled, *adj.* See PRINCIPAL, PRINCIPLE.

unravel, *v.* See RAVEL, UNRAVEL.

unrepairable, irreparable, *adj.* See REPAIRABLE, REPARABLE.

unsanitary, *adj.* See INSANITARY, UNSANITARY.

unsatisfied, *adj.* See DISSATISFIED, UNSATISFIED.

unsociable, unsocial, *adj.* Characterizing a person who does not enjoy, or who avoids, the company of others, the adjectives are interchangeable.

However, a party, an event, a gathering, etc., can be *unsociable,* but not *unsocial.* If you are talking about an event, meeting, etc. at which there will be no socializing, use the adjective *nonsocial.*

See also ANTISOCIAL, ASOCIAL, UNSOCIAL, UNSOCIABLE, NONSOCIAL; SOCIABLE, SOCIAL.

unsolvable *adj.* See INSOLUBLE, INSOLVABLE, UNSOLVABLE.

unspeakable, *adj.* See INDESCRIBABLE, INEFFABLE, UNSPEAKABLE, UNMENTIONABLE.

unsufferable, *adj.* See INSUFFERABLE, UNSUFFERABLE.

unsupportable, insupportable, *adj.* See INSUPPORTABLE, UNSUPPORTABLE.

until See TILL, UNTIL, TIL.

up-, *prefix* Words starting with the prefix **up-** are generally written solid whether adjective, noun, or verb: *upbeat, upcoming, update, uphill,* etc.

The following words, however, are hyphenated: *up-and-coming* (adj.), *up-and-down* (adj.), *up-bow* (n.), *up-to-date* (adj.). The slang term is written in any of three ways: *up-tight*, *uptight*, *up tight*.

-up, *suffix* Most nouns ending with the suffix **-up** are written solid: *breakup*, *blowup*, *windup*, etc.

The following nouns are hyphenated: *cover-up*, *line-up*, *make-up*, *tie-up*, *write-up*.

up, *v.* Meaning *to raise*, as in *he upped the price*, *up* (v.) is acceptable only on a colloquial or informal level.

In a construction like *he up (upped) and did it*, such use of *up* (v.) is slang.

up to one, up to two, up to three, *etc.* The form of the verb that follows this phrase depends on whether you mean a single concept or a number of individual items, objects, or persons. Thus:

Up to one yard *is* enough.
Up to five feet *is* enough.
Up to seven people *are* expected.

upon See ON, UPON, UP ON, ON TO, ONTO.

upward (upwards) of In correct usage, a phrase like *upward (upwards) of five hundred people were expected* means *more than five hundred people. Upward (upwards) of* should not be used to mean *nearly* or *approx-*

imately. See also -WARD, -WARDS.

us, we See PRONOUN, 8–8B; WE, US.

usage, use, *n. Usage* is preferably restricted to these meanings: *Custom, habit: it was the usage of some primitive tribes to . . . ; Treatment: resented the ill-usage he received; manner of using words*, etc. *in a language: in formal usage, this word . . .*

Although in some instances, *usage* and *use* are interchangeable, *use* preferably should signify the act, fact, or instance of using, employing, utilizing, etc.: *the use of narcotics was strictly prohibited.*

used to, use to In normal speech patterns, the *d* of **used to** is silent and the *s* is hissed. In writing, however, **used to** is the correct spelling, except after *did*: *did he use to; she didn't use to.* On the other hand: *he used to run; they were not used to such treatment.*

useless, more useless See HOPELESS, MORE HOPELESS.

usen't to Incorrect substitution for *did not use to* or *used not to.* See also USED TO, USE TO.

uterus, *n.* For plural, see NOUN, 6P.

uvula, *n.* For plural, see NOUN, 6M.

uxorial, uxorious, *adj.* *Uxorial* characterizes the actions, duties, attitudes, etc. that relate to, or are befitting of, a *wife*.

Uxorious, on the other hand, describes a *husband* or his actions, attitudes, etc. that show excessive indulgence or submissiveness to, or worship of, his wife.

V

vacate, *v.* See EVACUATE, VACATE.

vaccinate, *v.* See INOCULATE, VACCINATE.

vacillation, *n.* See OSCILLATION, VACILLATION.

vacuum, *n.* For plural, see NOUN, 6Q.

vagina, *n.* For plural, see NOUN, 6M.

vain, vane, vein *Vain* (adj.) means *conceited, futile,* etc. It is used as a noun in the phrase *in vain.*

Vane (n.) is an indicator (*weather vane*) or the flat part of a feather.

Vein (n.) is a blood vessel; rib of an insect's body or of a leaf; crack in a rock; or quality, strain, state of mind, etc. (*in a serious vein*). *Vein* may also function as a verb with meanings analogous to those of the noun. The adjective form of *vein* is *venous.*

All three words that head the entry are pronounced identically.

vale, veil, *n.* *Vale* is the poetic word for *valley.*

A *veil* is a covering of some sort. The verb *to veil* is to cover, conceal, etc.

valley, *n.* See VALE, VEIL; for plural, see NOUN, 6F.

valor, valour, *n.* See -OR, -OUR.

valuable, invaluable, *adj.* Though the prefix *in-* often makes a word negative (*competent, incompetent,,* etc.), *invaluable* means *extremely valuable; valuable beyond measurement.* (In this instance, the prefix *in-* is an *intensifier.*) See also FLAMMABLE, INFLAMMABLE, NONFLAMMABLE.

vane, *n.* See VAIN, VANE, VEIN.

vapor, vapour, *n.* See -OR, –OUR.

varied, variegated, *adj.* Though the two words are synonymous in many senses, *variegated* especially means *marked or characterized by different colors or streaks.*

variety (of) See NOUN, 1.

veil See VALE, VEIL.

vein See VAIN, VANE, VEIN.

velour, velours, velure, *n.* Three different, equally acceptable, spellings of the same word (i.e., the velvety fabric), all pronounced və-LOOR'.

venal, venial, *adj.* *Venal—*

open to bribery or corruption: *venal* politicians. *Noun:* **venality**.

Venial—excusable: **venial** errors, sins. *Noun:* **veniality**.

vengeance, revenge, *n.* These nouns are more or less interchangeable in everyday use. *Vengeance* is perhaps the more literary word, and only *revenge* can also be used as a verb. See also AVENGE, REVENGE.

vengeful, revengeful, *adj.* These adjectives, like the words in the preceding entry, are interchangeable. See also AVENGE, REVENGE; VENGEANCE, REVENGE.

venial, *adj.* See VENAL, VENIAL.

venturous, venturesome, *adj.* These adjectives are interchangeable; both may apply either to persons who are bold, daring, and/or willing to take risks, or to situations or circumstances that are risky. See also ADVENTUROUS, ADVENTURESOME.

VERB

1. **Tense:** Of the four parts of speech, only a verb has a present and past tense.

present	past
go, goes	went
eat, eats	ate
bake, bakes	baked
work, works	worked

Most English verbs are regular—i.e., like *bake, work* and many others, they have past tenses ending in *-ed*. (In Structural Grammar, the past tense of a verb is also called the *-ED FORM*.)

2. **Verb pattern:** A verb will fit into the blank (or *slot*) of:

$$V$$
LET US _____.

So [LET US _____] is called the *verb pattern*.

3. **Verb inflections:** *a.* A verb has five *inflections* (i.e., different forms). The *infinitive* of a verb is a noninflected form and is preceded by *to: to go, to begin*. (In Structural Grammar, *to* preceding a verb to form an *infinitive* is called *the sign of the infinitive*.)

b. The *present tense* has two inflections: the S-FORM (*goes, begins*) and the NON-S FORM (*go, begin*). A singular subject takes the S-FORM, a plural subject the NON-S FORM, of a verb. (See SUBJECT, VERB AGREEMENT.)

c. The *past tense* has only a single inflection, except for the verb *to be* (see item 4, below.).

d. The fourth inflection (called the *present participle* in traditional grammar) is the -ING FORM: *going, beginning.*

e. The fifth inflection (called the *past participle* in traditional grammar) is the *participle,* or PART. (Because so many participles end in -*en* (*taken, given, driven,* etc.), this inflection is also called the -EN FORM.) The *participle* is the form of a verb that normally follows the auxiliary (AUX) *has, have* or *had:* (*has*) *gone,* (*have*) *done,* (*had*)*spoken.*

The five inflections of a verb are illustrated in the following chart.

INF.	PRESENT TENSE 1 -S FORM	2 NON-S FORM	3 PAST TENSE (-ED FORM)	4 -ING FORM	5 PARTICIPLE (-EN FORM)
1. to go	goes	go	went	going	gone
2. to begin	begins	begin	began	beginning	begun
3. to swim	swims	swim	swam	swimming	swum
4. to bite	bites	bite	bit	biting	bitten
5. to grow	grows	grow	grew	growing	grown

4. **To be:** *To be* has *eight* inflections.

In the *present tense,* there are three inflections: *am, is, are.* In the *past tense,* two: *was, were.* (*To be* is the only verb with an S-FORM and a NON-S FORM in the *past tense.*) The -ING FORM is *being,* the participle is *been,* and *be* follows certain auxiliaries (*will be, can be,* etc.).

5. **Verb suffixes:** Many verbs have common endings or suffixes. For example:

    a. **-ize:** *realize, sympathize,* etc.
    b. **-ify:** *clarify, simplify,* etc.
    c. **-ate:** *create, relate,* etc.
    d. **-en:** *listen, lengthen, enlighten,* etc.
    e. **-er:** *suffer, offer, prefer,* etc.

6. **Auxiliaries (AUX):** *a.* Certain *auxiliaries* (also called *helping verbs* in traditional grammar) have a present and past tense but no other inflections of a true verb. These auxiliaries do not fit into the verb pattern. Examples:

can, could	shall, should
may, might	will, would
must, had to	

b. An AUX is followed by an expressed or understood verb: *can go, could run, may stay, might leave*, etc.; *yes, I will (go, run,* etc.).

c. Any inflections of the verbs *to be* and *to have* are auxiliaries if combined with another verb: *I am going; he was working; they have seen; has he left?*

d. Certain other verbs, or verbs plus prepositions or adverbs, function as auxiliaries when they are followed by other verbs. Examples:

be about to (go)	had better (leave)
dare (stop)	keep (working)
dare to (remain)	keep on (running)
gets (going)	likes to (dance)
get to (go)	needs to (return)
go on (playing)	ought to (love)
had to (pay)	would rather (offer)

7. **Verb phrase:** A verb phrase consists of one or more *auxiliaries* plus the *verb: may speak; should have gone; might have been seen; are about to start.*

8. **Transitive, intransitive, linking verbs:** See SENTENCE PATTERNS.

9. **Passive, active voice:** A verb is in the *passive voice* when the subject is followed by a form of *to be* acting as an AUX plus the participle (PART) of the verb. Examples:

      S   BE   PART
The cat has been found.

      S   BE   PART
My wallet might have been stolen.

  S BE PART
He was seen.

A verb in any other structure is in the *active voice.*

verb, subject agreement See SUBJECT, VERB AGREEMENT.

verbal, oral, *adj.* A *verbal* agreement, contract, etc. is, strictly speaking, one that has been put into words, whether spoken or written. However, *verbal* in such a construction is so often used to mean *spoken, rather than written,* that it is certainly futile, and perhaps even pedantic, to fight the trend.

If you mean *spoken, rather than written,* **oral** will avoid any chance of ambiguity. (One is reminded of the classic remark attributed to Sam Goldwyn, "A verbal contract is not worth the paper it's written on.")

verbose, *adj.* See WORDY, VERBOSE, PROLIX, PLEONASTIC, REDUNDANT, TAUTOLOGICAL.

vertebra, *n.* For plural, see NOUN, 6M.

vertex, *n.* For plural, see NOUN, 6O.

VERY, VERY MUCH *(plus participle)*

In the passive voice (*see* VERB, 9), **very much** (or **very greatly**), rather than *very;*, preferably precedes the participle. Examples:

> This has not been *very much used* by its original owner.
> He was *very much implicated* in the crime.
> We were *very much delayed* by heavy traffic.
> She was *very much liked* by her classmates.

However, if the participle can also be used as an adjective preceding a noun, **very** is acceptable even in formal writing. Examples:

> I am *very interested.* (i.e., an *interested* look)
> She was *very worried.* (i.e., a *worried* frown)
> This will be *very simplified.* (i.e., a *simplified* explanation)

---

vessel, boat, ship, *n.* See BOAT, SHIP, VESSEL.

veterinarian,   veterinary Either word may be used as a *noun* designating the doctor who treats animals, but *veterinarian* is more frequently used. Only **veterinary** is the *adjective* form: *veterinary medicine.*

veto, *n.* For plural, see NOUN, 6L1.

viaticum, *n.* For plural, see NOUN, 6Q.

vice-, *prefix in titles* The modern trend is to omit hyphens in titles starting with *vice-* (*vice* chancellor, *vice* consul, *vice* president, etc.)

Vice regent is written either as two words or as a solid word (*viceregent*), and *vicegerent* is written as a solid word only.

vice, vise, *n.* The words are pronounced identically, but the device that clamps something between its jaws is spelled *vise*.

vicious circle, vicious cycle The correct term is *vicious circle*.

Victrola, *n.* See PHONOGRAPH, GRAMOPHONE, RECORD PLAYER, TURNTABLE, VICTROLA.

vie, *v.* You *vie with* someone *for* something.

vigor, vigour, *n.* See -OR, -OUR.

villainy, villainry, *n.* There certainly should be a word like *villainry*, meaning, perhaps, *a group of villains?* After all, there is *weaponry, cannonry, infantry, jewelry,* etc. But *villainry* is a nonword, and *villainy* is the only noun form for a villainous act, behavior, etc.

violoncello, *n.* For plural, see NOUN, 6L4. See also CELLO, 'CELLO, VIOLONCELLO.

virago, *n.* For plural, see NOUN, 6L2.

viral, virulent, *adj.* Viral: pertaining to, caused by, etc. *a virus.*

virulent: poisonous, highly infectious, spiteful, etc.

virtually, *adv.* See NOMINALLY, PRACTICALLY, VIRTUALLY, LITERALLY, FIGURATIVELY.

virtuoso, *n.* For plural, see NOUN, 6L4.

virulent, viral, *adj.* See VIRAL, VIRULENT.

virus, *n.* The plural is *viruses.*

vis-à-vis Written just this way, with hyphens and the French accent mark. Pronounced VEE'-zə-VEE'.

viscid, viscoid, viscose, vicous, *adj. Viscid, viscose,* and *viscous* are interchangeable in the sense of *thick and sticky, cohesive,* etc. *Viscoid* is *somewhat viscid, viscose, or viscous.*

vise, vice, *n.* See VICE, VISE.

visit, visit with, *v.* The preposition may, but need not, be used before a noun designating a person: *visited her uncle; visited with her uncle. Visit with* may imply a meeting to sit and chat, rather than a stay of any length.

vita, *n.* This Latin word, like its longer form, *curriculum vitae,* is a résumé of one's professional career. *Vita* may also mean any biography or autobiography. The plural of *vita* is *vitae;* the plural of *curriculum vitae* is *curricula vitae*.

See also NOUN, 6M1.

viviparous, oviparous, ovoviviparous, *adj.* *Viviparous* creatures, like most mammals, give birth to live young.

Oviparous creatures (birds, reptiles, insects, etc.) lay eggs that hatch outside the mothers' bodies.

Certain species of fish, reptiles, or snails give birth by means of eggs that hatch within the mothers' bodies; the young are then born live. Such creatures are *ovoviviparous*.

vixen, *n.* This is a female fox. It is also, of course, an affectionate term applied to a mischievous human female. See also NOUN, 2D.

voice (*active or passive*)—This grammatical term is explained under VERB, 9.

volcano, *n.* For plural, see NOUN, 6L2.

voracious, omnivorous, *adj.* As these words are contrasted in reference to reading, learning, etc.:

Voracious readers or learners are greedy, gluttonous, insatiable in the way they figuratively devour reading or learning.

Omnivorous readers or learners eagerly read or learn everything available to them.

The two adjectives are similar in implication, with only the fine distinction explained above.

V-shaped, *adj.* Always written hyphenated. See also T-BAR; U-BOAT.

V sign, *n.* Written without a hyphen.

W

wabble, wobble, *v.* *Wobble* is the preferable spelling, *wabble* a variant.

wages, *n.* See SALARY, WAGES.

waif, *n.* For plural, see NOUN, 6G.

wail, wale, whale, *n.* A *wail* is a cry of grief, pain, etc.

A *wale* is a ridge in cloth or a raised streak on the skin caused by a blow. A *wale* on the skin is also called a *weal,* *wheal,* or *welt.*

Whale is the sea mammal.

wait, wait on, *v.* See AWAIT, WAIT, WAIT ON.

waive, wave, waver, *v.* To *waive* is to give up, not insist on, or postpone (rights, privileges, etc.): *waived her right to a jury trial.* Noun: *waiver.*

To *wave* is to engage in physical movement: *wave the flag; wave goodbye; wave one's hair; the trees waved in the wind.* Noun: *wave.*

To *waver* has a number of different meanings: *flutter; fluctuate (the stock market wavered); falter (her voice wavered); be unsteady or totter in one's walk; tremble or quiver; swing back and forth in indecision*—i.e., be unable to make up one's mind (*wavered between going and staying).* Noun: *waver.*

WAKE, AWAKE, AWAKEN, WAKEN, v.

The past tense of *wake* is preferably *woke.* The participle is *waked* or, in British usage, sometimes also *woke* or *woken.*

The past tense of *awake* is preferably *awoke; awaked* is also acceptable, though less commonly used. The participle is *awaked.* In British usage, the participle is sometimes *awoke* or *awoken.*

Awaken and *waken* have regular forms for the past tense and participle: *awakened, wakened.*

All four verbs may be used either *transitively* or *intransitively* (for *transitive* and *intransitive,* see SENTENCE PATTERNS, 1, 2): *The child wakes up (awakes, awakens,* or *wakens); we wake (awake, awaken,* or *waken) the child.*

However, *awake* is more commonly *intransitive (the child*

277

awakes); *waken* is usually *transitive (do not waken the child)*.

In the *passive voice* (for passive voice, *see* VERB, 9), the participles *awakened* and *wakened* are generally used: *she was awakened (wakened) at noon by the ringing of her alarm clock.*

---

wale, *n.* See WAIL, WALE, WHALE.

wane, wax, *v.* As here contrasted, to **wane** is to decrease *gradually*, to **wax** is to increase *gradually*.

want, *n.* A **want** is, of course, something one desires.

But the noun is also used as a synonym of *lack*: *for want of any alternatives, we will . . . ; enraged at the want of respect due him . . .*

Want may also mean *impoverished circumstances: lived in want all his life.*

WANT, WISH, *v.*

Both verbs mean *desire*; **want**, however, is preferable to **wish** when a direct object follows: *Do you want some sugar in your coffee?*

Only **wish** may be used when both an *indirect* and *direct object* follow (see SENTENCE PATTERNS, 4); *We wish you good luck.*

Only **wish** is followed by a clause: *We wish that he would leave. Not: We want that he should leave.*

Wish is often followed by the preposition *for: We were wishing for a break in the hot weather.*

When **want** is followed by *for*, it means *lack; be without. We don't want for transportation*—i.e., we have transportation; we are not lacking in transportation. (With this meaning, **want** is often used in a negative construction.)

They want for you to do the work is an incorrect usage if the meaning is they **want** (or **wish**) *you to do the work.*

Otherwise, the verbs are largely interchangeable: *We want (wish) to go; we want (wish) him to leave;* etc.

See also: WISH . . . WAS, WISH . . . WERE.

-ward, -wards *Adverbs* indicating direction or time are preferably used without the final *s*: **afterward, backward, downward, eastward, forward, frontward, homeward, north-**

ward, sideward, southward, westward, upward: *looked backward, forward,* etc.

(However, the words are also acceptable with an *-s* ending.)

As *adjectives,* the words are used without the *s: a backward* movement, *a downward* glance; *an upward* change; *westward* migration, etc.

The preposition is preferably written *toward* rather than *towards,* though, again, *towards* is acceptable: *walked toward* the door.

See also: UPWARD (UPWARDS) OF; -WAY, -WAYS.

ware, wear *suffix* Nouns designating utensils or other items end in *-ware: chinaware, giftware, hardware, silverware.* Also, *software* (for a computer).

Clothing items end in *-wear: footwear, neckwear, sportswear, underwear.*

warlock, *n.* See WITCH.

warranty, guarantee, *n.* In commercial transactions, *warranty* and *guarantee* are often used synonymously. To strain for a fine distinction, a *warranty* is an assurance by the seller that the merchandise or property is, will be, or will work as promised; a *guarantee* is a statement that an automobile, appliance, etc. will be repaired or replaced if it is defective.

A *guarantee* usually has a specified time limit.

The *verb* from *warranty* is *warrant; guarantee* is a *verb* as well as a noun.

was, were (*following* **if**) See IF ... WAS, IF ... WERE; see also AS IF ... WAS, AS IF ... WERE; IF ONLY ... WAS, IF ONLY ... WERE; WISH ... WAS, WISH ... WERE.

wash (*prefix in noun compounds*) Noun compounds are generally solid words: *washbowl, washcloth, washday,* etc.

washed-, *adj.* *Washed*-out and *washed*-up are hyphenated adjectives.

waste-, (*prefix in adjective compounds*) Adjectives are hyphenated: *waste-producing, waste-saving,* etc.

waste-, (*prefix in noun compounds*) *Wastebasket* and *wasteland* are solid words. *Wastepaper* is preferably solid, but may also be written as *waste paper.* (But in *wastepaper basket,* only the solid form is correct.)

Otherwise, noun compounds with *waste* as the first element are separate words: *waste can, waste collector, waste pipe.*

watch (*in noun compounds*) Noun compounds with *watch* as the first element are generally solid words: *watchcase, watchdog,* etc.

The following are written as separate words: *watch cap, watch dial, watch fire, watch* night, **watch** pocket, **watch** repair.

water *(in adjective compounds)* Adjectives with **water** as the first element are generally hyphenated: **water**-cooled, **water**-resistant, **water**-soaked, etc. But **water**proof, **water**tight, and **water**worn are solid words.

water *(in verb compounds)* Verb compounds with **water** as the first element are generally hyphenated: **water**-ski, **water**-soak, **water**-wave. *Waterproof (v.)* is a solid word.

watercraft, *n.* See CRAFT.

wave, *v.* See WAIVE, WAVE, WAVER.

waver, *v.* See WAIVE, WAVE, WAVER.

wax, *v.* See WANE, WAX.

way, ways When signifying distance, the preferable word is *way*, not *ways: we have a way* (not *ways*) *to go; a long way* (not *ways*) *from the terminal; only a short way* (not *ways*) *from here.*

-way, -ways As *adverbs,* *anyway* and *someway* are preferable to *anyways* and *someways*. See also SIDEWAY, SIDEWAYS, SIDEWISE; -WARD, -WARDS.

way, weigh A vessel is *underway* (or *under way*), not *under weigh*, when it is no longer anchored or moored.
    However, one *weighs* (i.e., pulls up) the anchor so that

the vessel can get *underway*; and the anchor, once pulled up, is *aweigh* (anchors *aweigh!*).

we, us When *we* or *us* is used to refer to one person, it is either the editorial *we, us* (i.e, an editorial writer indicating the opinion or position of the newspaper, magazine, etc.) or the *royal we, us* (i.e., a king queen, etc. speaking or writing.) See also OURSELF, OURSELVES; PRONOUN, 8–8B.

weak *(in adjective compounds)* When **weak** is the first element in an *adjective* compound, hyphenate the word: **weak**-eyed, **weak**-kneed, **weak**-minded. *Weakhearted,* however, is a solid word.

weal, *n.* See WAIL, WALE, WHALE.

wear, *v.* Past tense: **wore.** Participle: **worn.**

weather *(in adjective compounds)* *Weather*-beaten, *weather*-bound, *weather*-tight, and *weather*-wise are hyphenated adjectives.
    The adjectives *weatherproof* and *weatherworn* are written solid.

weather, whether *Weather* is a *noun* or *verb* (bad *weather; weather* the storm). *Whether* is a conjunction (I don't know *whether* she will . . .).

weave, *v.* The past tense is *wove*; the participle is *woven*. These are the inflections of the verb that refers to *looming fabric*.

The verb *weave* also means *move in and out or from side to side*, in which case both the past tense and the participle are preferably *weaved*: *she weaved the car from lane to lane; the car weaved through the traffic*.

wed, *v.* Past tense: *wed*. Participle: *wed* or *wedded*. In the figurative sense, the participle *wedded* is more frequently used: *she was wedded to her career*.

week Compounds with *week* as the first element are preferably written solid; *weekday*, *weekend*, *weekender*, *weekends*.

weep, *v.* Past tense and participle: *wept*.

weigh, way See WAY, WEIGH.

welch, *v.* See WELSH, WELCH.

WELL, *adv. (in compounds)*

Well plus a participle *preceding a noun* is a hyphenated word: *a well-known judge, a well-prepared lawyer, a well-done steak*.

If *well* is used in the sense of *greatly, properly*, etc., and the compound with the participle does not precede the noun, the two words are generally separate: *well known for her philanthropy; the judge was well known; the lawyer was well prepared; that was well done*.

Compounds with *well* as the first element that are *distinctly adjectives* (generally such compounds precede the noun) are hyphenated: *well-advised, well-appointed, well-balanced, well-behaved, well-bred, well-content, well-off, well-to-do*, etc.

*Well*born may be written solid or hyphenated.

The noun *well-being* is hyphenated; the noun *well*spring is written solid.

The adverb *well-nigh* is hyphenated.

See also ILL-.

---

well, good See GOOD, WELL.

welsh, welch, *v.* The first spelling of this slang verb is preferable.

Welsh rabbit, Welsh rarebit Though both terms are correct, *Welsh rabbit* is preferable as it is closer to its original derivation.

welt, *n.* See WAIL, WALE, WHALE.

west, West, Western, western

When capitalized, the *West* refers to the Western Hemisphere, the western part of the U.S., or the U.S. and its non-Communist allies in Europe and the Americas. *West* has a capital *W* if the word is part of the official name of a region: *West Africa, West Berlin, West Germany*. Otherwise, *west* is written with a lowercase *w*: *go west, headed west, west of town*.

Western is written with a capital *W* if the word is part of the official name of a region: *Western Australia, Western Church, Western Hemisphere, Western Reserve*, etc. Otherwise, a lowercase *w* is used: *western part of town; in a western direction*.

See also EAST, EAST, EASTERN, EASTERN; NORTH, NORTH, NORTHERN, NORTHERN; SOUTH, SOUTH, SOUTHERN, SOUTHERN.

wet nurse, *n.* **wet-nurse,** *v.* The *noun* is written as two words; the *verb* is a hyphenated word.

whale, *n.* See WAIL, WALE, WHALE.

wharf, *n.* See PIER, DOCK, MARINA, QUAY, WHARF; for plural, see NOUN, 6G1.

what ... is, what ... are See SUBJECT, VERB AGREEMENT, 9.

whatever, whatsoever/whenever, whensoever *Whatsoever* and *whensoever* are more emphatic than *whatever* and *whenever*.

wheal, *n.* See WAIL, WALE, WHALE.

when, than See HARDLY, SCARCELY, BARELY; NO SOONER ... THAN, NO SOONER ... WHEN.

when, where (is when, is where) It is unacceptable usage to define or explain a term with a *when* or *where* clause. Incorrect: *Happiness is when you have more money than you need.* Correct: *Happiness is having more. . . .* Incorrect: *A gridlock is where traffic is so heavy that no vehicle can move.* Correct: *A gridlock is a situation in which traffic. . . .*

whence, from whence See FROM WHENCE, WHENCE.

whensoever See WHATEVER, WHATSOEVER, WHENEVER, WHENSOEVER.

where (*plus* **at** or **to**)—I know where the place is at; where is she going to?; Where is it at? These and similar usages are nonstandard. Omit *to* or *at* in such constructions.

where, wheres Adverbs preferably end in *where* rather than *wheres*: *anywhere, elsewhere, everywhere, nowhere, somewhere*. The adverbs *anywheres, elsewheres*, etc. are nonstandard English.

whereabouts, *n. Whereabouts* may be construed as either a singular or plural noun: *the thief's whereabouts was* (or *were*) *unknown*.

whereat, whereby, whereof, whereon, whereunto These are archaic words, some of which are still found in legal language.

wherever See EVERYPLACE, EVERY PLACE.

whether, if, *conj.* See IF, WHETHER.

whether,   weather See WEATHER, WHETHER.

which, that See THAT, WHICH, WHO.

while, *conj.* Strictly, this conjunction, should indicate time: *while you set the table, I'll get the food ready.*

However, *while* is fully acceptable as a synonym of *although* or *but*: *while he is not rich, he certainly is not poor; some people spend money recklessly, while others are more interested in economizing.*

while, whilst *Whilst* is chiefly a British, poetic, or dialectal word.

whiskey, whisky, *n.* The American and Irish alcoholic beverage is spelled *whiskey* (*plural: whiskeys*); the Scotch and Canadian liquor is spelled *whisky* (*plural: whiskies*).

See also NOUN, 6E, 6F.

who *(in restrictive clauses)* See RESTRICTIVE CLAUSE, NON-RESTRICTIVE CLAUSE.

WHO *(plus verb)*

In constructions like the following, *who* takes the same form of the verb as its *antecedent*—i.e., the word that immediately precedes it. The italicized noun or pronoun in each sentence below is the antecedent of *who.* The italicized verb or auxiliary is the form governed by the *antecedent.*

It is *I* who *am* your only true friend.

It is *he (she)* who *is* responsible.

It is *you (we, they)* who *are* responsible.

She is one of those *people* who *are* always willing to help.

He is one of those *men* who always *spend* more than they earn.

It is *they* who *have* taken all the credit.

It is *you* who *have* left us stranded.

See also ONE OF THOSE . . . WHO; VERB, 3.

---

who, that, which See THAT, WHICH, WHO.

WHO, WHOM

1. **Who** is the *nominative* case, **whom** the *objective* case of this relative pronoun. (For the rules governing the use of nominative and objective pronouns, see PRONOUN, 8–8B; SENTENCE PATTERNS, 1, 3, 4, 5.)

2. In everyday, informal speech, **whom** is seldom used except directly after a preposition *(to whom are you referring?)*. Such a structure, however, is quite formal—most people would say **who** *are you referring to?* The objective **whom** is otherwise required only in formal writing or business correspondence. See also PREPOSITION; PREPOSITION ENDING A SENTENCE.

3. Often the relative pronoun **whom** can be, and is, omitted: *(Is this the man you saw?* instead of *Is this the man* **whom** *you saw?)* See also THAT, WHICH, WHO.

4. The relative pronoun in many sentences is separated from its governing verb or preposition. If you do not wish to take the trouble to decide whether **who** or **whom** is the *subject, direct object, indirect object,* or *subject complement* in a sentence, you can use a simple, foolproof, method for determining whether **who** or **whom** is correct in a sentence in formal writing.

Take, for example, the problem *(Who, Whom) shall I say is calling?* Follow these steps:

    a. Start reading *after* the point at which a choice is to be made. In the example given, start with *shall I say . . .*

    b. Insert either *he* or *him* in the sentence wherever it fits and makes sense—i.e., *shall I say he is calling?* Since *he* fits, **who** is the correct choice. (*He* and **who** are both *nominative pronouns.*)

Consider this problem: *(Who, Whom) are you visiting?* You start reading after the **who, whom**: *are you visiting him?* Since *him* fits, the correct choice is **whom**. (*Him* and **whom** are both *objective pronouns.*)

When the reference is feminine, fit *she* or *her* into the sentence. If *she* fits, **who** is correct; if *her* sounds right, **whom** is the correct choice. (Note that *he, she,* and **who** end in vowels; *him, her,* and **whom** end in *consonants* [*m, r, m*]; also *him* and **whom** end in the letter *m.*)

In the example, *Is this the woman (who, whom) you believe has been calling me?* start with *you: you believe she has been calling me.* Hence, **who.**

Bear in mind that any pronoun following the *linking verb to be* is in the *nominative* case—i.e., *it is he; was it she?; this is he (she).* (For *nominative pronouns* after *to be,* see PRONOUN, 8, 8A; SENTENCE PATTERNS, 3.)

A test on *who, whom*

To decide which pronoun is correct in formal writing, start reading after **who, whom** and insert *he (she)* or *him (her)* wherever the personal pronoun fits and makes sense. If *he (she)* fits, select **who;** if *him (her)* fits, choose **whom.**

1. *(Who, Whom)* do you wish to speak to?
2. *(Who, Whom)* are you expecting?
3. Is this the person *(who, whom)* you claim held up the bank?
4. Is this the person *(who, whom)* you saw holding up the bank?
5. *(Who, Whom)* is it at the door?
6. *(Who, Whom)* did you think it was?
7. Anyone *(who, whom)* you find at the desk can help you.
8. Anyone *(who, whom)* is at the desk can help you.
9. *(Who, Whom)* will you choose as the next contestant?
10. *(Who, Whom)* do you suspect of taking your money?
11. This is the fugitive *(who, whom)* the police say escaped from San Quentin.
12. *(Who, Whom)* shall I say wishes to talk to her?

KEY: 1. **whom** (do you wish to speak to *him?*); 2. **whom** (are you expecting *him?*); 3. **who** (you claim *he* held up the bank); 4. **whom** (you saw *him* holding up the bank?); 5. **who** (it is *he* at the door); 6. **who** (did you think it was *he?*); 7. **whom** (you find *him* at the desk); 8. **who** (*he* is at the desk); 9. **whom** (you will choose *him*); 10. **whom** (do you suspect *him?*); 11. **who** (the police say *he* escaped); 12. **who** (shall I say *he* wishes to. . . . ?).

5. **Whoever, whomever:** The same rules apply to **whoever** and **whomever** that govern **who** and **whom**—i.e., **whoever** is *nominative,* **whomever** is *objective.* Follow the same method for determining whether to use **whoever** or **whomever** in writing that you used for **who** or **whom.** (**Whoever** means *anyone who;* **whomever** means *anyone whom.* So: *talk to*

whoever is waiting; means *talk to anyone who is waiting;
ask **whomever** you see* means *ask anyone whom you see.*]

A test on *whoever, whomever*

1. Give this to *(whoever, whomever)* is at the desk.
2. Stop *(whoever, whomever)* tries to come in.
3. We will sell the house to *(whoever, whomever)* is the highest bidder.
4. Choose *(whoever, whomever)* you prefer.
5. Talk to *(whoever, whomever)* you find at the desk.
6. Tell *(whoever, whomever)* is waiting to come in.
7. She gave help to *(whoever, whomever)* needed it.
8. Ask *(whoever, whomever)* is on the line to call back later.

KEY: 1. *whoever* (*he* is at the desk); 2. *whoever* (*he* tries to come in); 3. *whoever* (*he* is the highest bidder); 4. *whomever* (you prefer *him*); 5. *whomever* (you find *him*); 6. *whoever* (*he* is waiting); 7. *whoever* (*he* needed it); 8. *whoever* (*he* is on the line).

6. **Whosoever, whomsoever:** These words, used chiefly for emphasis or in legal terminology, follow the rules for **who** and **whom**.

7. For an infrequent use of **whom** as object complement after the infinitive *to be*, see INFINITIVE, SUBJECT OF.

---

who else's, whose else See ELSE.

whoever, whomever See WHO, WHOM, 5.

whole-, *prefix Adjective* compounds are generally hyphenated, especially preceding a noun: *whole-souled, whole-wheat.* The slang term *whole-hog* (*adj.* or *adv.*) is also hyphenated.
　Wholehearted (*adj.*) is written solid.

whose, of which *Whose* may refer to a thing or abstraction—the word need not be re-stricted to a person or persons: *an idea whose time has come.*
　Smoothness of style should govern your decision. Thus, *the book of which the cover is torn* is awkward compared to *the book whose cover is torn.* Which of the following sounds better to you: *it is a plan whose merits are obvious; it is a plan of which the merits are obvious?*
　Make your choice accordingly.

whose, who's *Whose* is the possessive inflection of the relative pronoun *who*: *Whose money did you steal?*

Who's is a contraction of *who is*; *who's there?* See also CONTRACTIONS.

whosoever, whomsoever See WHO, WHOM, 6.

wide-, *prefix* Adjective compounds, especially preceding a noun, are hyphenated: *wide-angle, wide-awake, wide-eyed, wide-open; wide-eyed wonder.*

The adjective *widespread,* however, is written solid.

-wide, *suffix* Adjective or adverb compounds are written solid: *countrywide, statewide, worldwide,* etc.

widow, widower, *n.* *Widow* designates a woman whose husband has died and and (usually) who has not remarried; *widower* refers to a man whose wife has died and who (usually) has not remarried. *Widow* may be used as a verb, chiefly in the participle inflection. (see PARTICIPLE): *widowed early in her marriage. Widowered,* referring to the male, is not standard usage; substitute *became* (or *was made*) *a widower.*

wife, *n.* Noun compounds are written solid: *fishwife, housewife.* For plural, see NOUN, 6G.

wild-, *prefix* Adjective compounds especially preceding a noun, are hyphenated: *wild-eye, wild-goose (chase), wild-spirited.*

will, shall See SHALL, WILL.

win, *v.* The past tense or participle is *won.* You *win* a game or contest, but *win over,* or defeat, an opponent.

wind-, *prefix* Adjective compounds are generally hyphenated: *wind-borne, wind-driven, wind-swept.*

Windblown may be written solid or hyphenated (*wind-blown*).

Windproof and *windtight* are written solid.

window, *n.* Noun compounds with *window* as the first element are generally separate words: *window box, window seat, window shade,* etc.

These noun compounds are written solid: *windowpane, windowsill.*

Window-shopper is hyphenated, as are the verbs *window-dress* and *window-shop.*

windup, wind up Write *windup* (n.) as a solid word. Write *wind* (v.) plus the adverbial *up* as two words.

wine-, *prefix* The *adjectives wine-colored, wine-growing,* and *wine-red* are hyphenated.

The *nouns winebibber, winebibbing, wineglass, winegrower, winegrowing, Winesap* (the apple), *wineshop,* and *wineskin* are solid nouns.

Other noun compounds are written as separate words: *wine cellar, wine press,* etc.

wintry, wintery, *adj.* Despite the adjective *summery,* **wintry** is the only correct spelling for the adjective form of the noun *winter.*

-wise, *suffix* Attaching this suffix to a noun (*costwise, colorwise, dangerwise, weatherwise*) to mean *in regard to, in reference to,* etc. is frowned upon by some authorities, perhaps because such constructions are overused, especially in commercial and advertising parlance.

The suffix is established usage when it indicates direction or manner: *clockwise, counterclockwise, lengthwise, sidewise,* etc.

wish, want, *v.* See WANT, WISH.

wish ... was, wish ... were The correct formal usage after *wish* is *were: I wish I were* rich; she *wishes she were* taller; does he *wish he were* going?

See also AS IF ... WAS, AS IF ... WERE; IF ONLY ... WAS, IF ONLY ... WERE; IF ... WAS, IF ... WERE.

witch, *n.* The masculine forms are **warlock** and **wizard.**

See also NOUN, 2C.

with *(prep.)* Use the *objective* personal pronoun and the *objective* relative pronoun *(whom)* after a preposition: *with John and me; with you and her; with us and them; with whom he was working.*

With introduces a P-GROUP (or prepositional phrase)—it is not *grammatically* equivalent to *and,* though in many instances there is a *logical* equivalence. The noun in the P-GROUP is *not* part of the subject and therefore does not govern the verb or auxiliary. Note these examples: *Paula,* **with** *all her relatives,* **is** *waiting for you;* the queen, **with** *her entire staff,* **has** *just entered the hotel.*

See also PREPOSITION, 8; PRONOUN 8B; SUBJECT, VERB AGREEMENT, 5.

with regard (regards) to See REGARD, REGARDS.

within, *adv.* See WITHOUT.

without, *adv.* As contrasted to the adverb *within* (i.e., *inside*), **without** *(adv.)* may mean *outside: the car is waiting* **without.** However, such use of *without* as an adverb, though correct, is infrequent and somewhat unidiomatic. The adverb *within* has a greater frequency of usage: *seated* **within,** *waiting for me, were five clients.* **Within,** like *without,* occurs most often as a preposition: *within the house;* **without** *his friends.*

without, *prep.* Followed by objective pronouns (*me, him, her, us, them, whom*). See also WITH.

without *(plus clause)* See UNLESS, WITHOUT.

without, unless See UNLESS, WITHOUT.

without doubt See DOUBT-
LESS, NO DOUBT.

**without regard (regards)
to** See REGARD, REGARDS.

wizard, *n.* See WITCH.

wobble, *v.* See WABBLE,
WOBBLE.

woebegone, wobegone, *adj.*
The preferable spelling is
woebegone.

woeful, woful, *adj.* *Woful* is
the archaic spelling.

womanish, womanly, *adj.*
As these words are currently
used, *womanish* describes undesirable female characteristics, especially if found in a
male; this adjective is generally derogatory. *Womanly*
characterizes the natural attributes of a woman, and is
applied only to females. The
adjective is either neutral or
complimentary. See also
MANLY, MANNISH. *adj.*

wont, won't *Wont* (pronounced WUNT, WŌNT, or
WAHNT) as a noun means

custom, habit, or *practice,* and
is usually followed by the
preposition *to*: *it was his* **wont**
to rise early on Sundays.

Wont is also a participle
used in the passive voice and
is then followed by an infinitive: *she was* **wont** *to work
hard at anything she did.*

Won't is the contraction of
will not, and is pronounced
WŌNT.

See also CONTRACTIONS;
PARTICIPLE; VERB, 9.

wooden-, *prefix Adjective*
compounds are generally hyphenated: *wooden-faced,*
*wooden-legged. Woodenhead-
ed (adj.),* however, is written
solid.

woods, *n.* Meaning *a for-
est,* **woods** is usually construed as a plural: *the* **woods**
*were alive with the chatter
of birds.*

However, **woods** may be
preceded by *a,* and is then
treated as a singular: *there
was a* **woods** *behind the property; a house built in a* **woods.**

WORDY, VERBOSE, PROLIX, PLEONASTIC, REDUNDANT, TAUTOLOGICAL, *adj.*

These adjectives are more or less synonymous, with an
occasional distinction.

Wordy is the general term describing the use of more
words than necessary to communicate an idea. In implication, this adjective is usually derogatory. *Noun:* **wordiness.**

Verbose indicates excessive **wordiness** that is boring,
repetitious, high-flown, long-winded, or pretentious. *Verbose*
may describe a person or a style of speaking or writing.
Nouns: **verbosity, verboseness.**

Prolix characterizes speech or writing that tediously goes on and on about trivial or unimportant details. *Noun:* **prolixity.**

Pleonastic, redundant, and **tautological** are interchangeable synonyms describing the unnecessary use of an additional word or additional words that simply repeat one another without adding information. The nouns **pleonasm, redundancy,** and **tautology** may signify either the use of such unnecessary words or a specific instance of such use. *Free gift; natal birthplace; refer back; recur again; repeat again; essential necessities*—these are examples of **pleonasms, redundancies,** or **tautologies. Pleonastic** and **tautological** (and their noun forms) are somewhat more literary in flavor than **redundant** and **redundancy.**

See also REPETITIOUS, REPETITIVE.

---

work-, *prefix* Adjective compounds are hyphenated: **work**-*weary,* **work**-*worn.* However, **work**aday *(adj.)* is written solid.

Noun compounds are generally solid words: **work**day, **work**horse, **work**man, etc. But **work**-*up (n.)* is hyphenated, except in (medical) **work**up, in which case the word is written solid.

-work, *suffix* Noun compounds are written solid: *foot***work,** *home***work,** *house***work,** etc.

work, *v.* The past tense and participle are **work**ed. However, in expressions like *What hath God* **wrought***?,* **wrought** *havoc,* **wrought** *great damage,* or **wrought** *a miracle,* and also in the terms **wrought** *iron, over***wrought** *(adj.),* and **wrought**-*up (adj.),* **wrought** is the past tense or participle of choice. See also PARTICIPLE; WREAK.

-worker, *suffix* Words with this suffix are written solid: *field***worker,** *metal***worker,** *steel***worker,** etc.

working-class, working class Hyphenated as an adjective *(***working-class** *people),* written separately as a noun *(belongs to the* **working class***).*

world-, worldly-, *prefix* Adjective compounds are hyphenated: **world**-*shaking,* **world**-*shattering,* **world**-*weary,* **worldly**-*wise.* But **world**wide *(adj.* or *adv.)* is a solid word.

worm, worm's, *prefix* Adjective compounds are hyphenated: **worm**-*eaten,* **worm**-*riddled,* **worm's**-*eye (view).*

-worn, *suffix* Adjective compounds are generally solid: *care***worn,** *shop***worn,** *time***worn,** *toil***worn.**

worse, worst, *adj.* These are the comparative and superlative forms, respectively, of *bad* or *ill*. *Worser* is nonstandard or illiterate for the comparative. (*Incorrect: the worser of the two.*)

worse, worst, *(of two)* In comparing *two,* use **worse** *(the* **worse** *of the two choices);* in comparing *three* or more, use **worst** *(the* **worst** *of five possibilities).* See also COMPARISON.

worse-, worst-, *prefix* *Adjective* compounds preceding the noun are hyphenated: **worse- (worst-)** *governed,* **worse- (worst-)** *timed,* **worse- (worst-)** *used,* etc.

worsen, *v.* Standard English meaning *to become* or *make worse.*

worst, *v.* **Worst** *(v.)* means, oddly enough, *get the better of; defeat.* **Worsted** is the past tense and participle. Still more oddly, **worst** *(v.)* and **best** *(v.)* have identical meanings. **Best** is the verb more frequently used.

worthless, more worthless See HOPELESS, MORE HOPELESS.

worthwhile, *adj.* Written as a solid word, except, obviously, in constructions like **worth** *my while;* **worth** *your while;* etc.

-worthy, *suffix* *Adjective* compounds are written solid: *noteworthy, seaworthy,* etc.

would, should See SHOULD, WOULD.

would have liked to have *(gone, done, seen,* etc.) Too many *haves* in this construction. Revise to *would have liked to* (*go, do, see,* etc.) or *would like to have* (*gone, done, seen,* etc.).

would of, would have See COULD HAVE, COULD OF.

would rather—See HAD RATHER, WOULD RATHER.

-woven, *suffix* *Adjective* compounds are hyphenated: *hand-woven, loose-woven, tight-woven,* etc.

wrack, rack See RACK, WRACK.

wreak, *v. Past tense and participle:* **wreaked. Wrought** is an alternate past tense or participle of the verb **work.** See also WORK.

wreath, wreathe The first word is a *noun,* the *th* pronounced as in *thing (a* **wreath** *of holly).* **Wreathe,** the *th* pronounced as in *this,* is the verb: *will* **wreathe** *her in silk and satin.*

wring, *v.* **Wrung** is the past tense and participle.

wring, ring, *v.* Meaning *encircle,* **ring** is the correct verb. *Past tense and participle:* **ringed.**

writ, *v.* This is an archaic past tense or participle of **write** *(v.).*

write, *v.* Past tense is **wrote;** participle is **written.**

write-in, write-off, write-up,
n. These nouns are hy-
phenated.

wrong, *adj., adv.;* **wrongly,**
adv. **Wrong** is correctly used
as both an adjective and an
adverb: *the* **wrong** (adj). *answer; did it* **wrong** (adv.).

The adverb **wrongly** is preferably used before a participial
adjective; *a* **wrongly** *arranged
pattern; a* **wrongly** *understood word; a* **wrongly** *inter-
preted remark.*

wrought   See WORK; WREAK.

X, Y, Z

x ray, x-ray, X ray, X-ray, *n.* To denote the type of photograph, the *X* is usually capitalized, but may also be written as a lowercase letter. The *noun* may be written as separate words, but the *adjective* and *verb* are hyphenated. *Exray* or *ex-ray* is a misspelling. See also U-BOAT.

Xmas, *n.* Informal shortened form of *Christmas*, not acceptable in serious writing.

yclept, y-clept, *participle* Archaic word (spelled solid or hyphenated) for *called, named,* or *known as,* used today only for humorous effect.

ye Archaic word meaning *the* (as in *ye olde tea shoppe*) and used for humorous or eye-catching effect. In such usage, the word is pronounced identically with the word *the. Ye* is also the archaic or Biblical *you.*

year *(in compounds)* Write *yearbook* (n.), *yesteryear* (poetic), and *yearlong* (adj.) solid. To indicate age or other time periods, hyphenate: *two-year* subscription; *ten-year-old* Scotch; *a five-year-old child; a four-year-old* (n.).

yes, *n.* The plural is **yeses.**

yodel, yodle, *v.* The preferable spelling is *yodel;* other forms are preferably spelled *yodels, yodeled, yodeling.* The nouns are preferably spelled *yodeler, yodeling.*

yoga, yogi The discipline, type of exercise, meditation, etc., is *yoga.* A practitioner of *yoga* is a *yogi* (plural: *yogis*) or a *yogin.*

yogurt, *n.* This is the preferable spelling. *Yoghurt* and *yoghourt* are variant spellings, not commonly used.

yoke, yolk, *n.* The yellow of an egg is spelled *yolk.*

you and I, you and me See PRONOUN, 8–8B.

you-all, *pron.* Southern regionalism for *you* in reference to more than one person.

your, you're *Your* is possessive (*your money*); *you're* is a contraction of *you are* (*you're a strange person*). See also CONTRACTIONS.

your's, yours The possessive personal pronoun is never spelled with an apostrophe: *hers, ours, yours, theirs, its;* not *her's, our's, your's, their's, it's.*

293

See also PRONOUN 8.

Yugoslavia, Jugoslavia, *n.* *Yugoslavia* is now the preferred spelling.

-yze   See PARALYZE, ANALYZE, PSYCHOANALYZE.

zenith, nadir, *n.* These are terms from astronomy. In figurative usage, the *zenith* is the *highest* point, the *nadir* the *lowest* point of something (career, success, accomplishment, etc.) See also APOGEE, PERIGEE.

zero, aught, ought, naught, nought, *n.* In the sense of the numerical figure (0), these words are indentical in meaning and are interchangeable. (*Zero* is the most commonly used term.) The plural of *zero* is *zeros* or *zeroes.*

See also NOUN, PLURAL, 12B.

zoom, *v. (up, down)* In reference to motion, *zoom* is preferably used for ascent rather than descent. *Zoom* up, then, is more logical than *zoom* down.

NORMAN LEWIS has written a great many well-known and popular books on improving language skills, including *How to Read Better and Faster, 30 Days to a More Powerful Vocabulary* (with Wilfred Funk), and *Instant Word Power* and *30 Days to Better English* (both available in Signet editions). He taught for many years at the City College of New York and at New York University. He is now Professor of English at Rio Hondo College, in Whittier, California.